Praise for *Confidential*

"Be it from the clinical investigator or the attorney or the factory worker, unintentional information leaks are flowing like a flood. Written in a revealing and provocative manner, *Confidential* is must-reading for those who should be guarding shareholders' information assets."

—Lewis W. Lehr, former chairman of the board
and chief executive officer, 3M

"*Confidential* brings into the private sector the most misunderstood, and consequently, underused facet of government intelligence—the human source. In a thoroughly enjoyable fashion, John Nolan educates the reader on how to access and use this critical intelligence resource, for both competitive advantage and security."

—Jan P. Herring, former director of business intelligence, Motorola

"*Confidential* is a must-read for anyone wanting to conduct and utilize competitive intelligence the right way. Nolan concisely captures the elicitation techniques executives can use to ethically and legally capture competitive information to prevail in the hypercompetitive marketplace."

—Ava Harth Youngblood, president,
Society of Competitive Intelligence Professionals

"Remarkably thorough, engagingly written, and above all, useful the day one starts to read it, *Confidential* describes ethical and legal procedures and thought processes that, with some practice, yield greater confidence in decisions that must be made 'ahead of the curve.' The increased return on investment in opportunities taken, trade secrets kept, and market advantage gained make *Confidential* worth its weight in consultants' invoices."

—George A. Dennis, director of competitor intelligence, Bellcore

"John Nolan is the Sherlock Holmes of the new millennium. This is absolutely the best book I have ever read on competitive information elicitation."

—Geary Soska, director of business intelligence, Goodyear

"Intellectual property is the fuel of economic growth in our global economy. How to effectively safeguard intellectual capital is one of the most daunting tasks facing companies in today's cyber-based world. John Nolan provides an effective road map for establishing competitive intelligence collection programs within legal and ethical boundaries, while providing defensive measures to help counter competitive intelligence collection on your own company!"

—Lynn Mattice, corporate director of security,
Boston Scientific Corporation

"A 'must read' for the executive who is losing market share because of a lack of competitive intelligence. The intelligence tools and techniques necessary to compete and thrive in today's business climate are laid out in a clear and practical way. This witty and serious book is a 'tour de force' of the competitive intelligence world that many business executives do not understand."

—Milton (Mick) Moritz, former president,
American Society for Industrial Security

"Excellent . . . Nolan skillfully weaves into commercial practice many of the proven techniques from the world of government intelligence, and does so in a language that is easy to understand. *Confidential* is the best handbook on competitive intelligence I've seen in more than twelve years in business intelligence."

—James A. Williams, former director of
the Defense Intelligence Agency

"An easily understood and highly readable field manual that guides professionals in mastering the art of intelligence collecting."

—Tom Parker, principal, business intelligence, NIPSCO

Confidential

Uncover Your Competitors' Top
Business Secrets Legally and
Quickly—and Protect Your Own

John Nolan

HarperBusiness
A Division of HarperCollins*Publishers*

HarperCollins books may be purchased for educational, business, or sales promotional use. For information please write: Special Markets Department, HarperCollins Publishers, Inc., 10 East 53rd Street, New York, NY 10022.

FIRST EDITION

Designed by William Ruoto

Library of Congress Cataloging-in-Publication Data

Nolan, John
    Confidential : Uncover your competitors' top business secrets legally and quickly—
and protect your own / John Nolan.
      1st ed.
      p. cm.
      Includes index.
      ISBN: 0-06-661984-X
      1. Business intelligence. 2. Trade secrets. 3. Competition.
I. Title.
HD38.7.N65 1999
658.4'7—dc21   99-26034

---

99 00 01 02 03 ❖/RRD 10 9 8 7 6 5 4 3 2 1

To Helen, the childe bride of my youth and companion for the eternities
and to our greatest treasures:
Alexis, John, Maggie, and Josh

CONTENTS

Appendices

ACKNOWLEDGMENTS

At the risk of sounding like a night at the Academy Awards, there are large numbers of people whose contributions to this book have been enormous. There's simply no way that I could ever name all those who have helped me to learn our trade, our craft. And, there are others whose lives have been so exemplary and provocative that I couldn't help but learn from them. It's to them that I hope to repay that great debt by gathering their teachings, thoughts, and suggestions of a professional lifetime into things useful for those who come after us.

In particular, I'm grateful to terrific mentors such as the late Andrew V. (Jake) Jacobs and Albert J. Bari who taught the really human dimension of Human Intelligence operations; to John Alexander, *agent provocateur* who really does believe in serendipity; to Ralph Blum, a great agent because he's first and foremost a great writer; to Laureen Connelly Rowland, Princess Leia of EditorLand and her irrepressible editorial assistant and quintessential HarperBusiness Babe, Jodi Anderson; to Bill DeGenaro, my partner and friend at The Centre for Operational Business Intelligence; and to David Sindel and James Fountain at Phoenix Consulting Group, who are more like my brothers than the great business partners they are; and to Joy Hart Arnold, my daily adult supervision disguised as an administrative assistant.

And most of all, to the most important part of any of us. Family. To Miss Kitty, who as my Mom taught me The Art of the Possible; to Helen, that childe bride of lo these many years, who still tries to teach me The Art of the Practical; to our daughters Alexis and Maggie who've taught me The Art of Perseverance; to our sons, John and Josh, who've taught me more about courage from their experiences in lands foreign and far away than I ever learned on any battlefield of my own; and to our grand-daughters, Michaila and Cassidy, who've taught us the Promise of the Future.

What Do Intelligence Professionals and Sharks Have in Common?

After a career in the government intelligence community as a case officer involved in clandestine operations and now after more than a decade in what is called Business Intelligence, I think I can say with some authority that I know the answers to the question in the title to this preface.

This title wasn't chosen lightly. It certainly wasn't just a shameless play on the popularity of other business books with references to sharks in their titles. Instead, it was chosen specifically because the shark has a variety of characteristics that can be found in the way Business Intelligence collectors apply their craft: characteristics that apply whether they are of the legal and ethical variety—called competitive intelligence—or of the illegal industrial and economic-espionage variety. Here are some of those characteristics.

- *Sharks do not have bones but instead have soft and hard cartilage—* which provides them, as well as intelligence professionals, with the speed and flexibility to attack their targets and prevail.

- *Sharks, with their dark top sides and their light undersides, are perfectly camouflaged for a predator whose success depends on stealth—* which provides them, and intelligence professionals, with various means of covering and concealing their actions from their targets until it's too late.

- *Adult sharks may go through as many as twenty thousand teeth in ten years—*like the intelligence professional, who may go through a similarly staggering number of individual sources in the quest for information.

- *Sharks, if they bite a human, usually bite once and then leave—*like business intelligence professionals, who don't use up a source through frequent and repetitive contacts, knowing that overuse will cause the source to become suspicious and dry up.

- *Sharks are so attracted to the color of international orange in emergency equipment that researchers call it "yum-yum yellow"*—just as intelligence professionals follow the color green as they track the flow of money in commerce, knowing that wherever money changes hands, it leaves an exploitable trail of information.

- *Sharks will eat almost anything, including license plates, tree stumps, beer cans, and reindeer; they can even eat diseased fish without getting sick themselves*—like intelligence professionals, who collect and consume prodigious amounts of information before digesting it properly in the analytical process and disposing of the detritus as a natural function.

- *Sharks have to swim almost constantly in order to get oxygen from the water*—like the professionals who rely on the cyclical and continuous intelligence process to constantly collect information and put it to the best possible use, and without which they would die.

- *Sharks we encounter today are almost the same as the sharks that lived a hundred million years ago*—just as the second oldest profession has experienced little fundamental change in the past three thousand years.

- *Sharks have another sense in addition to touch, smell, vision, hearing, and taste—a sense that allows them to detect the weak electrical field that all animals give off*—just as intelligence professionals are using more and more electronic aids to winnow down through all the available information and focus on their precise target.

But this is not to say that there aren't certain defenses that can be used against shark attacks. Those defenses—what we call counterintelligence as opposed to security—take into account certain shark weaknesses. Here are some of those weaknesses:

- *Sharks sometimes confuse surfers paddling on the surface with sea lions, and that's the reason that so many surfers are attacked*—like intelligence professionals, who can sometimes be distracted, confused, or sent off in the wrong direction.

- *Sharks are also called the "swimming nose" because almost a third of their brain is devoted to their sense of smell*—like some intelligence professionals, who use only a limited number of skill sets and talents and can thereby be defeated by relatively simple means.

In the intelligence world, collection and protection are not mutually exclusive, as many people think. In fact, in the world of sophisticated international intelligence operations, the two functions are typically integrated and complementary.

More and more businesses are finding out how important it is to both collect and protect information in a rapidly changing world. They're learning how and when to move with speed and flexibility, when and how to defend themselves in an increasingly aggressive environment. They're learning how to prevail in the business world at the dawn of the new millennium.

And, a word or two about perspectives.

First, an article of faith in my old world of clan ops was that being a case officer was a lot like being a professional football player—you have to be big enough to play and dumb enough to think it's important. That was a way of trying to keep yourself from the trap of thinking everything you did was Oh So Important or Oh So Secret. Certainly, much of what we did—and do in Business Intelligence—is quite important and quite sensitive. But you don't have to get so carried away that you lose sight of what you're supposed to be doing and for what purpose.

Second, some people will read this book and come away— especially after reading some of the more malignant ways that companies collect information about their rivals—saying that just by describing intelligence operations to this extent for use in business is simply wrong: either illegal, immoral, bad business, or at least fattening. Not so. The people who'll be inclined to do the things that others may find problematic already know how to do them—and are doing them to people who are disarmed and defenseless by their own lack of understanding.

And third, some of the most effective users of some of the principles and techniques presented in this book—particularly the elicitation techniques—are among those in the so-called helping professions such as counseling, social work, and ministering who have clearly noble purposes.

This book is all about tools and techniques. Tools and techniques that'll allow you and your firm to develop the information that leads to competitive advantage and success in the marketplace. Tools and techniques that will also allow you to anticipate what your rivals may be doing to and against you in time to protect yourself. Tools and techniques that you can apply quickly and effectively with your own company's resources, without having to rely on high-speed, low-drag consultants except in special cases and situations.

I learned how to use an ax when I was young and still prefer chopping my own firewood over just buying a cord or two a year. I'm grateful that no one outlawed axes just because Lizzie Borden tried to give them a bad name. You, too, will be grateful that no one has yet outlawed the use of the intelligence tools and techniques you'll need to compete and thrive in today's business world.

All History Is Merely Prologue on the Business Battlefield

It's July 1942. Your name is Dwight David Eisenhower and you've just received your assignment. "Ready Allied forces for a landing on the European mainland no later than the Summer of 1944."

You had good grades on the tactical and strategic sandtables at Command and General Staff College, but you've never led men into combat. Strategic thinking has always been your strong suit. You also know that you haven't got a clue about what you're really up against. You know that no matter how well formulated a strategy is, it can't be developed in an information vacuum. You learned early on in your career that the intelligence professionals have a saying that sums it all up: *Text without context is pretext.* Your next call is to your intelligence chief, who had been a marketing research executive for a large manufacturing firm before the war.

Tell me everything I'll need to know so that we can prevail in an invasion of France and the Low Countries. Get back to me in six months.

Six months later he's back. He's got pictures and charts and graphs. He has hydrology studies that show how fast and how slow the rivers run, where they run, and how deep they are. He has all the forested areas cataloged by deciduous and nondeciduous and can hypothesize about how impenetrable they might be. He has a good description of the many different languages that are found in the countries, along with the more common dialects within those languages. He has historical studies that set the stage for the present conflict, routes taken by previous warring armies, and the successes and failures of belligerent nations. He can also tell you that the Germans are led by a fellow named Adolf Hitler, that he has a pretty good army, navy, and air force at his disposal, and that he's taken over the continent.

While your intelligence chief has obviously put in a lot of effort and provided you a lot of information, he has reaffirmed your opinion of bureaucrats: What they tell you is almost always true—and rarely what you need to know.

So, you fire him.

You call in another colonel, only this one has been an intelligence officer for his entire career. He's served as an operational officer for years in backwaters and international capitals. You give him the same instructions: "Tell me everything I'll need to know so that we can prevail in an invasion of France and the Low Countries. Get back to me in six months."

Instead of the expected "Yes sir, yes sir, three bags full," the intelligence officer pulls up a chair. He starts asking *you* questions—and the longer he's there, the sharper and more illuminating his questions become. He begins to develop specific kinds of questions that need answers—mostly about the military forces arrayed against the Allies. By the time he leaves, you understand that you don't have to waste everyone's time trying to know everything in the world. You now know what you really need to know:

- How large is Hitler's army, his navy, his air force?
- What kind of equipment do they have, and how good is it compared with ours?
- What kind of training have they had? What kind of combat experience have they had and how did they perform?
- Who are the important strategists and leaders? What have they done on the battlefield, in the classroom, or in war games in the past?
- Where are the forces stationed and in what numbers? At what stages of readiness for combat? How is their morale?
- What new weapons systems are under development and when will they be fielded? Where will they be encountered?
- What are the personality and psychological profiles of Hitler and his principal advisers and how do they relate to their management of military operations?
- What are the weaknesses that we can exploit? How and where?
- What are the strengths we have to overcome? And how can we do that? Or, are there others that we should go around?

After interviewing you about what you really need, the colonel tells you what you can expect and when you can expect it. He knows what your real and specific needs are. He also tells you that this is just the first of many sessions you will have with him.

One month later he's back with his first reports. Each ensuing month produces another, more detailed, more definitive, more useable set of reports. And, as so often happens in the intelligence business, each report in turn raises more important, more focused questions. These questions are then sent to intelligence collectors in the field so that they can find the answers.

It also becomes pretty clear to you that some of the sources and the methods used in getting the basic information need to be protected. At the same time, your own preparations and operations have to be protected, too. Obviously, Hitler's very active intelligence services are conducting their own operations against you. You've already seen that the military police, with a completely different approach, are not in a position to do much about catching spies.

You tell your intelligence chief to get together with our counterintelligence guys. "Put together a coordinated program to ensure that we get all we need while denying Hitler what he wants. And do it now. *The idea is to prevail.*"

This World War II scenario can serve as an accurate metaphor for what's happening in companies across America today. In companies large, medium, and small, strategic leaders get their marching orders from the board, from their stockholders, and from other stakeholders. *Prevail in the marketplace.* They buy into the John D. Rockefeller philosophy:

The next best thing to knowing all about your own business is to know all about the other fellow's business.

Today's business leaders know they can't succeed in a vacuum. And they know they have to learn everything they can about their competition while protecting themselves. The growth of Business Intelligence, in all its associated forms and variations, is a testament to the value that's being placed on knowing what the competition is doing, when they're doing it, how they're doing it, and how well. Today's leaders also know that at the same time they have to protect themselves. That's what this book is about—helping companies prevail in the war zone of the marketplace.

But before we fast-forward into tomorrow's marketplace, I'd like to set the stage with a personal stop in the middle of the 1960s. It'll be the first of many case vignettes you'll read throughout this book, and perhaps it'll serve as a bridge between military and business applications of the intelligence process. It'll also show how naturally some of this happens in business each day, and how, with a little more forethought, the intelligence game can be played with real business payoffs.

Swimming Lessons

Fresh out of school in 1965, little did I know that the experiences of that first year in the business world would set the stage for a book on competitive intelligence over thirty years later. The term, and the concepts associated with the intelligence process itself, were as foreign to me then as they may be to you today, although the literature has certainly increased over the last decade. The concept of *countermeasures* to competitive intelligence, as well its evil twin cousins industrial espionage and economic espionage, was even further from my mind.

I started as a salesman for a small New Jersey company that sold a variety of office machines, ranging from electric typewriters to what would now be considered very primitive data-writing equipment. A very competitive marketplace those days, although almost all of the products have since gone the way of the buggy whip.

One of the best products we carried was the German-made Olympia typewriter, specifically the Olympia SGE–40, a direct competitor to the IBMs of that day. It was a superior product in virtually every respect except marketing. It was cheaper and had a better and longer warranty, features that secretaries loved immensely, and a very loyal following once you got one into the hands of the person who was ultimately going to use it.

But because there was practically no marketing budget, much of my life was spent in the pits of cold calling. Since I was a new guy, cold calling wasn't something that I did in between visits to established accounts; it was my lifeblood. Nobody ever called to say "Could you bring out a typewriter and dazzle me with it so much that I'll have no choice but buy it from you?"

On the other hand, I knew that the big guys with the deep pockets had all the business they could handle. Every once in a while I would happen upon someone who needed some equipment and who would be willing to at least hear me out. The usual result was that on those occasions when we'd have a product-comparison shoot-out, we'd win—again on price, quality, service, et cetera. Yet getting a customer in our crosshairs was a terribly difficult thing, since most didn't know we existed. But they certainly knew who IBM was.

One morning I was sitting in a coffee shop after leaving three or four companies in one large office building—with no success. With zero interest from people who mostly said, "We're buying IBM—have been and will continue to. Thanks for stopping by, young man, but don't waste your time on me."

I clearly recall that I wasn't in the best of moods. That got even worse shortly after I sat down. Within minutes, a car pulled into the parking lot of the one-story, storefront-type office building across the street. The driver who got out was none other than one of the IBM salesmen I'd encountered at a customer shoot-out a month or so before. He was just coming in to work and it was well after 10 A.M.—and I'd already had three or four abortive sales calls. What a bad deal!

He walked in the front door, and I could see him walk up to the receptionist, pick up his messages, drop his briefcase on his desk in this bullpenlike office arrangement, and put his feet up. He started to make calls from the messages in his hand. I knew that he was talking to people who had called *him* to buy typewriters. He was making appointments with people I didn't even know existed. He was shooting fish in a barrel and I was having trouble finding a hook! When I saw one of the support people come around the side of the building and start loading typewriters into my rival's station wagon, that was the final straw.

In a brief moment of clarity, I realized that he would be going to see the people he was making appointments with and I was going to be crying in my coffee cup if I didn't do something. I left the coffee shop and went to my car.

When he came out and drove off, I followed him. To his first appointment, then his second, and so on—sitting in the car in the parking lot while he went in to drop off a machine.

The next day, I started calling on the ten places that he'd visited the day before. I started off by telling them that I knew they were in the market for a typewriter or two and just asked if I could demo one for the typing pool. At the end, I would ask them to allow me to leave one of my machines for a direct apples-to-apples comparison. That week, I sold twelve machines from that first day's surveillance. That probably didn't make much of a ripple in the IBM guy's life, but it certainly boosted my morale. Over the course of the next few months, I dedicated one or two—and sometimes three—days a week to following him to companies in the area and returning to make sales calls of my own on the intervening days.

The payoffs were fast becoming wonderful. I must admit that a certain hubris began to settle in. Sometimes, instead of just waiting outside the location for him to go on to his next call, I'd wait until he cleared the receptionist and then I'd go in after him. Then, when he was in talking to the purchasing manager's secretary, I'd be in the lobby, chatting up the receptionist about the company's interest in buying typewriters. When the IBM guy was in talking with the purchasing manager, I'd be chatting up his secretary. When the manager came back to his office after the IBM guy had dropped off the machine with the ultimate user and had left the building with Elvis, I'd be waiting for the purchasing manager with true and certain knowledge that he was in a buying position. Once in a while, the scene played out with the IBM guy and me bumping into each other. He started giving me less pleasant looks as he saw me more frequently—and eventually associated those "chance encounters" with lost sales for IBM.

It was then that I learned that there is some danger in using the intelligence you have gathered without covering how you got it and what you did with it once you got it. Essentially, I had learned about intelligence collection and analysis without ever calling it that; but I had never thought about what I learned in later years was called *counter*intelligence. I know now, from the perspective of over thirty years in this business of intelligence, that I should've protected the fact that I was essentially "reading his mail" and using the derived intelligence to his disadvantage.

The long and short of it was that I got to be very successful in identifying who was buying what. More importantly, I was closing far more sales than I ever had thought I could with our limited resources for advertising and marketing.

Two Careers—One Ocean

It probably seems obvious now that when I was approached sometime later to enter the intelligence community, it was quite natural to accept the recruitment pitch. That I stayed in that line of work for the next twenty-two years—in almost an equal mix of intelligence-collection and counterintelligence assignments in Asia, Europe, and the United States—should not come as much of a surprise either. On the basis of those twenty-two years, and the decade that followed in the Business Intelligence world, I can look back on that experience in the office-products business with a different perspective.

If we'd used an organized way to chase after all the IBM guys and had planned things the right way, this process could have gone on for a long time. Many others could have been able to use it along other product lines as well.

There are a couple of other points that this anecdote demonstrates:

- Intelligence doesn't have to come through expensive or sophisticated processes.
- Intelligence pays large dividends.
- Intelligence collection doesn't necessarily involve scads of people.
- Small companies can collect it and use it just as well as large companies.
- And finally, once you've got it, protect it just like you'd protect anything else that helped you increase sales and profits.

It makes little difference whether you're reading this book as a corporate leader, a marketing executive, a strategic planner, a security director, or any number of other positions in industry. No matter whether you rely on prominent business strategists from the best B schools or whether you find Sun-tzu or Mao Tse-tung, von Clausewitz or Rommel, Eisenhower or Schwartzkopf more to your liking. The relationship between business success and the application of the intelligence process on the battlefield of business is clear.

If, however, the relationship isn't clear, consider a few questions.

Is your primary *competitor* using the intelligence to his advantage and to your disadvantage? Maybe a better question would be, how would you know if he was using it? You would look for certain indicators, such as those that my colleague Bill DeGenaro uses to answer the question: If your competitor is growing faster, is more profitable, is more innovative—even if some of his actions seem to be irrational or counterintuitive—the likelihood is high that a good intelligence operation is serving his decision-making process.

Does your competitor seem able to more closely and effectively anticipate legislative and regulatory changes, technology shifts, and customer/market shifts? Again and again these are characteristics of the companies that serve as benchmarks for users of the Business Intelligence process.

Does your competitor seem to be able to counter your new products rapidly—or even consistently anticipate them? Has your competitor been able to preempt your new products or strategic thrusts? Has he been able to attack your high-margin products and territories, attack you where you are the most vulnerable? Has he been able to identify the stars in your company who are working on your next-generation product lines and recruit them away from you at just the wrong time?

Now, irrespective of the answers to the previous questions, flip them over: Have you been able to do any of these things against your competitor? If the answers to the first set of questions are yes and the answer to the second set is no, then you've picked up the right book.

In this book, I'll provide a considerable number of case histories to illustrate how CI professionals operate. In large part, these cases are drawn from Phoenix Consulting Group's Commercial Services Practice, which provides direct competitive intelligence-consulting services to client firms—client firms that range from the *Fortune* 50 to the *Inc.* 500. To a certain extent, they are also drawn from comments, suggestions, and experiences that attendees in my various workshops and professional development programs have shared with me. I'm especially grateful to our students and fellow faculty at The Centre for Operational Business Intelligence in Sarasota, Florida, for the kinds of experiences they've shared—and the insights they've provided—during our training programs.

And based on the numerous *counter*measures projects we have undertaken over the years, I'll be using the same kind of case histories to show how companies can not only protect themselves from the techniques of CI professionals but also help guard against those who choose such illegal courses as industrial espionage, economic espionage, trade-secrets theft, and misappropriation of intellectual property.

There's a final lesson that comes from various presentations and it may have some relevance to you as you start this book. It has to do with the ways in which the mere term "intelligence" is viewed by a variety of groups ranging from MBA students to business executives and everywhere in between. This lesson provides some interesting insights about semantics and business.

This book is filled with case examples, and I use quite a few in presentations as well. Some of these presentations are given rather bland B-school sorts of titles that don't include the word "intelligence;" in others, the word "intelligence" appears as a central focus of the talk. Usually I'll start off with an example or two, such as the case of Johnson Controls and Honeywell in chapter 14 and BLACK KNIGHT in chapter 17.

I ask those who hear these and other cases without reference to intelligence operations of any sort, if the activities are either (a) good, sound, legitimate, and aggressive business practices that take advantage of everything they can to win for their shareholders, or (b) unethical, immoral, or close to illegal. The overwhelming majority of the respondents choose answer (a), along with words such as "clever" and "imaginative," and "good, smart business practices." Yet, when I present these case examples in connection with corporate intelligence operations, the answer is often (b), with perhaps some qualifications. You've already seen that for an intelligence officer, nothing exists without context. This is clearly one of those cases. But, we're not talking about situational ethics here, we're talking about perceptions and biases and prejudices—the lot. It almost seems that as soon as you put the pieces together with intelligence operations, they become unsavory, which of course really does mean distasteful. Now why would that be? Particularly when the issue is one of protection of operations, processes, or sources of information.

So, may I ask that you consider suspending any pre-judgments or biases against the word "intelligence" and what it might mean to you based on popular misconceptions bred by James Bond wannabes? Thank you.

Part I

Eliciting the Information You Want and Need

If people listened to themselves more often, they would talk a lot less.

—**Courtois' Rule**

For over thirty years, I've been collecting information for intelligence consumers—both federal as well as commercial. For the past ten years, I've run a company that specializes in collecting hard-to-find information that can be turned into competitive intelligence and then to competitive advantage. For much of that time, we've also provided courses in intelligence skills and techniques to business professionals who work for most of the largest—and many of the medium-sized—companies in the world.

How do we do this? We do it legally and ethically. We don't steal information, bribe people, bug their conference rooms and executive suites, or hack into their computers. We don't misrepresent ourselves, conduct ruse interviews, or have specially molded masks to impersonate others. We really don't need to. In America, where a great deal of our work is done—working for one firm against another irrespective of national pedigree or ownership—we encounter what we call a "target-rich environment."

This target-rich environment gets its name from the comments of a former adversary, a former Soviet intelligence officer who defected to the United States in the late 1980s. We became acquainted a year or so later and have maintained a fairly cordial relationship now that we no longer have professional constraints. He worked against the United States while I worked against his former homeland. Every once in a while, he and I get together to tell each other lies about how successful we were.

On one of these evenings a few years ago, he told me that he'd just finished a great book that really captured the essence of the East-West intelligence competition. Oddly, he said that it was written by a former U.S. Navy pilot. I had no clue what a pilot could have known about our old business. My colleague went on to tell me that the pilot recounted some of his experiences over North Vietnam. The U.S. pilots would take off for missions over the North, and large numbers of North Vietnamese aircraft would rise to meet them. The navy pilot described the aircraft as inferior Soviet export models, flown by inexperienced and undertrained North Vietnamese pilots. Rather than viewing the environment as hostile and threatening, the navy pilot commented that he and his colleagues viewed it as a "target-rich environment."

My former Soviet adversary then said that that really captured the essence of how we competed, he and I. While I worked against a xenophobic and suspicious people who were extremely hard to meet, he had free rein in the United States against an open, trusting people that never really met a stranger. For him, the United States was—and remains—a target-rich environment.

I must admit that our experience bears that out.

In our efforts on behalf of clients to collect useful information that helps them make decisions that impact their financial and technical performance, we follow a standard that requires us to identify ourselves by our true names, and by our company. We do that in every contact with a source or potential source of information.

It maybe be helpful to share a statistic with you—one that we began compiling in 1992 and that has remained fairly consistent since that time. Each time our researchers, our diggers as we call them, contact a source—whether a new one or an old one—they fill out a form that describes the person, their information, and their reactions to the approach. It's their reactions that I'd like to share with you.

Let's say we call one hundred people. We say exactly the same thing to each of them. For example, "Hello, my name is John Nolan, from Phoenix Consulting Group, in Huntsville, Alabama. I'm working on a project involving X, Y, and Z and wonder if this is a good time to speak with you." Depending on how cynical you are, you may or may not be surprised that *fifty* people out of that one hundred will say, "Sure, this is as good a time as any" or "Could you call back in an hour after I've had a chance to clear my desk?"

The other fifty are somewhat less cooperative. Most of these remaining fifty will ask at least one, but usually two, questions. The first usually is "Before I talk to you, what's this about?" Our answer is fairly standard as well: "We're a research firm in Huntsville, Alabama, and we're working on a project on behalf of a client." The second question is a little more focused: "Well, who's your client." Our response is consistent as well: "Sorry, I can't tell you. You see, we have confidentiality agreements in place with every one of our clients and they prevent us from being able to disclose the name of our client."

You would think that anyone with an IQ above room temperature would respond, "Hey, if you can't tell me who your client is, there's no way I'm going to talk to you." Indeed, fifteen out of that remaining fifty hang up at that point. Fifteen. The remaining thirty-five people say something like "Oh, yeah. I've gotta put up with confidentiality agreements at my place too. I understand. So, what can I do for you?" That means eighty-five people out of a hundred agree to talk to us. That's just the starting point. It's what they say afterward, knowing what they've just learned about us and our reasons for calling, that sometimes amazes us.

We'll be spending the first part of this book showing you the ways we keep those conversations going—and enjoy repeat calls to the same people in subsequent projects as well. As you adopt these methods, you'll be joining the thousands of intelligence professionals—government and nongovernment alike—whose approaches to information collection have changed radically and for the better because of the way they've added elicitation to their tool kit.

ELICITATION ITSELF

Intelligence professionals have their own peculiar set of skills and techniques: techniques that have been honed, refined, tested, and applied in settings around the world. Skills and techniques that have withstood the test of time, have transcended national and cultural boundaries. Skills that have significantly contributed to getting the information from those who have it to those who need it, in the right form, and at the right time.

One of the more esoteric of those skills is *elicitation*. When people hear the word, they generally define it as a certain way of asking questions—a variation on interviewing or perhaps interrogation. Both of these sets of techniques have their place and purpose. Yet both are based on the proper framing of questions—questions that often raise more concerns and suspicions and engender less cooperation than the information collector wants or can afford.

Elicitation, for our purposes, is defined as that process which avoids direct questions and employs a conversational style to help reduce concerns and suspicions—both during the contact and in the days and weeks to follow—in the interest of maximizing the flow of information. The purpose of an elicitation session, then, is to obtain the information you want from someone who probably has it, has not necessarily admitted having it, who may or may not be willing to part with it, and who may or may not know—or even care—who the elicitor is.

Typically, it involves collecting information without asking questions, or when you do ask questions, you do so for specific reasons as part of your planned approach to the conversation.

Yet this is not to say that we avoid the use of the question altogether. Indeed, when structuring a conversation, as I'll discuss in chapter 3, questions are intentionally posed at certain, preplanned locations to achieve certain, specific purposes. Nor is this to say that we are attempting to be deceitful or dishonest.

Most people, perhaps yourself included, never actually think about planning a conversation. To some, it's simply not something that's ever crossed their minds. To others, planning a conversation somehow smacks of trying to manipulate another person in some evil or malignant way. Yet, if we consider that effective communication rarely takes place without some organization, some coherence, perhaps even some rigor, then conversations wander aimlessly, may or may not achieve anything, and may leave both parties with a sense of frustration.

Intelligence professionals the world over seek to minimize suspicion and encourage openness. They seek to be more effective, more organized, more directed. They seek information that a decision maker needs—information that can provide you a lead, or a head start, in a fast-moving, volatile competitive marketplace. That's what the rest of this book is about.

Along the way, I'll present the kinds of people who serve as sources of information of Business Intelligence value: how to identify them, how to find them, how to approach them; why they'll cooperate and what you can expect to get from them.

Sources of information roam across the marketplace. Sources you may have thought of in the past but have never approached. Sources you haven't thought of before but who will now become part of the way you collect and use the Business Intelligence process. Sources that you'll come to know enough about that you'll be able to decide which approaches or techniques will be used with one set and not with another. Techniques that you will use in one setting or another.

And lastly, for those people within your own firm who might serve as sources for one of *your* competitors—either wittingly or unwittingly—we'll also provide some of the more effective countermeasures—countermeasures that will help you to protect your own information and allow you to maintain your own competitive advantage.

CHAPTER 1

Transfer Intelligence Community Techniques to the Commercial Sector for Competitive Advantage

And therefore, only the enlightened sovereign and the worthy general who are able to use the most intelligent people as agents, are certain to achieve great things. Secret operations are essential in war; upon them the army relies to make its every move.

—Sun-tzu, *The Art of War*, XIII:23

"There's virtually nothing new under the intelligence sun." That was the opening statement made by the senior faculty member on our first day in training as young intelligence officers. It was his way of telling us that despite the odd marginal and technical changes from time to time, the conduct of intelligence operations was fundamentally the same as it had been for thousands of years.

Moses sent Joshua to lead a group of twelve spies into Canaan; later, Joshua sent two other men into Jericho. They were to work with Rahab the harlot, obtain the information she'd been collecting for Joshua, and get back to him. They promised her that in return for her cooperation and confidentiality, they would take care of her family in the event of an Israelite invasion. That's the short version that most people know already.

Yet for the intelligence officer, there's far more to the tale than that, including any number of "intelligence firsts":

- The first use of operational cover.
- The first use of a safe house.
- The first use of bona fides.
- The first suggestions of a counterintelligence service—one that was working for the king of Jericho.
- The first use of secrecy agreements between an agent and the intelligence officer who was running the agent.
- The first—and some would say the last—time that an intelli-

gence officer actually kept his word when it came to caring for an agent's family.
- The first use of an escape and evasion plan for intelligence officers.
- The first record of intelligence reporting to a decision maker.

With the exception of the last, the notable thing about this list is that virtually none of these intelligence firsts apply to the Business Intelligence model as practiced by most companies in the United States today. While these elements remain part of the mainstream of operational intelligence activity around the world—as practiced by nations—they have not been made part of the Business Intelligence lexicon. The reason is quite simple. Not everything that is commonplace or traditional in the intelligence community is transferable to the commercial arena. Recruiting someone to betray his country and divulge its secrets for money is the heritage that culminated in the 1980s as the Decade of the Spy; yet in the Business Intelligence world, there is no such thing—or at least there shouldn't be. Developing esoteric covers for status and action help to protect the lives of officers and the secrecy of international intelligence operations is part of that same heritage, no matter which country; yet, in the Business Intelligence world, it's not only inappropriate, it's largely unnecessary. And no matter how abrasive one's boss or business rival, it's also highly undesirable to try and plant explosive-laden cigars or poisonous doughnuts in front of them.

Nonetheless, a variety of tools and techniques common to the traditional intelligence community have been, and should be, transferred directly into the marketplace. Tools and techniques that are legitimate, effective, and appropriate. Tools and techniques that are actually found in, and appropriate to, a variety of other disciplines as well: the intelligence cycle, as an organized and well-developed process; intelligence analysis, using any one of a dozen or more techniques ranging from link analysis to time-event analysis to conflicting hypotheses, to name a few; intelligence processing of raw data into a body of knowledge that can be evaluated, analyzed, and distributed; intelligence-specific tasking and allocation of collection resources to actually obtain the information.

ELICITATION TECHNIQUES

Another of those sets of techniques is called elicitation. And although elicitation has been most rigorously developed for use by the intelligence community, it can also be found elsewhere—literature, film, television. If you know what you're looking for, you'll see elicitation occurring almost naturally, sometimes even elegantly. Yet for the most part, those who read or view the use of such techniques fail to appreciate how elicitation is done.

For example, in the following extract taken from *The Complete Sherlock Holmes,* Sir Arthur Conan Doyle depicts what we call a "stacking of elicitation techniques." In fact, Sir Arthur has Sherlock artfully "stack" several different techniques in this short conversation taken from *The Sign of Four.*

The Sign of Four

It tended down towards the riverside, running through Belmont Place and Prince's Street. At the end of Broad Street it ran right down to the water's edge, where there was a small wooden wharf. Toby led us to the very edge of this and there stood whining, looking out on the dark current beyond.

"We are out of luck," said Holmes. "They have taken to a boat here."

Several small punts and skiffs were lying about in the water and on the edge of the wharf. We took Toby round to each in turn, but though he sniffed earnestly he made no sign.

Close to the rude landing-stage was a small brick house, with a wooden placard slung out through the second window. "Mordecai Smith" was printed across it in large letters, and, underneath, "Boats to hire by the hour or day." A second inscription above the door informed us that a steam launch was kept—a statement which was confirmed by a great pile of coke upon the jetty. Sherlock Holmes looked slowly round, and his face assumed an ominous expression.

"This looks bad," said he. "These fellows are sharper than I expected. They seem to have covered their tracks. There has, I fear, been preconcerted management here."

He was approaching the door of the house, when it opened, and a little curly headed lad of six came running out, followed by a stoutish, red-faced woman with a large sponge in her hand.

"You come back and be washed, Jack," she shouted. "Come back, you young imp; for if your father comes home and finds you like that he'll let us hear of it."

"Dear little chap!" said Holmes strategically. "What a rosey-cheeked young rascal! Now, Jack, is there anything you would like?"

The youth pondered for a moment.

"I'd like a shillin'," said he.

"Nothing you would like better?"

"I'd like two shillin' better," the prodigy answered after some thought.

"Here you are, then! Catch!—A fine child, Mrs. Smith!"

"Lor' bless you, sir, he is that, and forward. He gets a'most too much for me to manage, 'specially when my man is away days at a time."

"Away, is he?" said Holmes in a disappointed voice. "I am sorry for that, for I wanted to speak to Mr. Smith."

"He's been away since yesterday mornin', sir, and, truth to tell, I am beginnin' to feel frightened about him. But if it was about a boat, sir, maybe I could serve as well."

"I wanted to hire his steam launch."

"Why, bless you, sir, it is in the steam launch that he has gone. That's what puzzles me; for I know there ain't more coals in her than would take her to about Woolwich and back. If he's been away in the barge I'd ha' thought nothin'; for many a time a job has taken him as far as Gravesend, and then if there was much doin' there he might ha' stayed over. But what good is a steam launch without coal?"

"He might have bought some at a wharf down the river."

"He might, sir, but it weren't his way. Many a time I've heard him call out at the prices they charge for a few odd bags. Besides, I don't like that wooden-legged man, wi' his ugly face and outlandish talk. What did he want always knockin' about here for?"

"Ah, a wooden-legged man," said Holmes with bland surprise.

"Yes, sir, a brown, monkey-faced chap that's called more'n once for my old man. It was him that roused him up yesternight, and, what's more, my man knew he was comin', for he had steam up in the launch. I tell you straight, sir, I don't feel easy in my mind about it."

"But, my dear Mrs. Smith," said Holmes, shrugging his shoulders, "you are frightening yourself about nothing. How could you possibly tell that it was the wooden-legged man who came in the night? I don't quite understand how you can be so sure."

"His voice, sir. I knew his voice, which is kind o' thick and foggy. He tapped at the winder—about three it would be. 'Show a leg, matey,' says he: 'time to turn out guard.' My old man woke up Jim—that's my eldest—and away they went without so much as a word to me. I could hear the wooden leg clackin' on the stones."

"And was this wooden-legged man alone?"

"Couldn't say, I am sure, sir. I didn't hear no one else."

"I am sorry, Mrs. Smith, for I wanted a steam launch, and I have heard good reports of the—, the—, the— Oh, let me see, what is her name?"

"The *Aurora,* sir."

"Ah! She's that old green launch with a yellow line, very broad in the beam."

"No, indeed. She's as trim a little thing as any on the river. She's been fresh painted, black with two red streaks."

"Thanks. I hope that you will hear soon from Mr. Smith. I am going down the river, and if I should see anything of the *Aurora* I shall let him know that you are uneasy. A black funnel, you say?"

"No, sir. Black with a white band."

"Ah, of course. It was the sides which were black. Good-morning, Mrs. Smith. There is a boatman here with a wherry, Watson. We shall take it and cross the river."

"The main thing with people of that sort," said Holmes as we sat in the sheets of the wherry, "is never to let them think that their information can be of slightest importance to you. If you do they will instantly shut up like an oyster. If you listen to them under protest, as it were, you are very likely to get what you want."

Most readers would accept at face value the lesson from Mr. Holmes at the end of the quote, in which he teaches Dr. Watson—and us—about the ways in which our everyday foibles and frailties can be used to great effect in the hands of an accomplished information collector—an effective *elicitor.* More to the point, however, most of us do not even recognize the individual techniques as we read them in print and almost certainly never recognize them when they are being used in seemingly casual, non-threatening conversation.

Learning to use these techniques in an organized way will significantly enhance your ability to obtain information from those who have it. Learning to recognize these and other techniques will also allow you to be forewarned and forearmed when the same kinds of techniques may be employed in conversation with you.

These points—and many more throughout the next few chapters—are regularly and routinely taught to hundreds of mid-career federal intelligence professionals each year. How do we know what they are being taught? Because it's my firm that does the teaching.

Moreover, there are others who receive essentially the same training, with some parts not appropriate to transfer to the private sector taken out. How do we know what's being taught to Business Intelligence professionals? Because for the past decade we have been the primary provider of this kind of training—both at public seminars and at in-company training programs for the Business Intelligence profession around the country. Indeed, around the world.

CHARACTERISTICS OF EFFECTIVE ELICITORS

Here, Sherlock Holmes teaches us some of the characteristics and traits that are peculiar to an effective elicitor. He appears at once to be innocent, friendly, unafraid to make a misstatement, and curious—at least within certain bounds and limits. These are important characteristics inasmuch as they contribute significantly to the appearance that is most effective in conducting elicitation meetings; an appearance that is, at once, casually, nonthreateningly curious.

Yet there are many others as well. They include a seemingly natural gift for making friends or establishing rapport; being an effective manager of human relationships and the underlying, practical psychological insights that are such a large part of any social interaction; an understanding of the subtleties and intangibles in personal relationships; and an understanding or appreciation for national and cultural differences that might otherwise stand in the way of effectively eliciting the information you want and need. Other characteristics include an ability to listen well, a certain amount of flexibility to cope with changes in the conversation, tact, a good memory (since there are few things that stunt the progress of elicitation like whipping out a pad and starting to write notes), and a broad knowledge of general topics, since there are times when it is necessary to simply fill in the conversation with relatively unimportant issues. In following chapters, we'll discuss some of these characteristics in a little more detail for those who may not feel that they have yet mastered them.

And, by the way, Sherlock used eight different techniques during this short conversation. By the time you finish this book, you'll be able to recognize them as they were used. Recognizing how a master uses them is a great example. Recognizing them when they're being used against you is also very useful when you want to protect your own information. In fact, we've included "An Annotated Sampler from *The Complete Sherlock Holmes*" as one of the appendices. It contains extracts from several of Sherlock's adventures, and in each we insert notes about the individual elicitation techniques Holmes uses.

EGO SUSPENSION

However, the single most important characteristic for an effective elicitor is also one of the most difficult to achieve for some of us. I call it "ego suspension." Indeed, I consider it so important and fundamental to the success of an elicitor that it's worthy of separate treatment before we go any further into the structure and nature of elicitation.

Many of the techniques you'll be learning will require you to truly understand a simple concept: *Whatever your position, your job is to collect the information from those who have it.* Your job is not to impress the other person with your intellect, your savoir faire, your experience, your education, your income level, or the greatness of your children. Granted, sometimes you'll find it useful and helpful to say some things about yourself, based on which techniques you'll use. But you'll only be using them sparingly—and as little more than an accelerant, in the same way that fuel is added to a fire.

Sometimes, in the interest of capitalizing on another person's characteristic to be your teacher, assuming the position of student can be arduous—yet highly profitable in the end. In the interest of allowing someone else to talk about how great his new position is, you may well have to subordinate your pride in your accomplishments and recent promotion. You'll see how this plays out in many of the techniques to follow.

At bottom, you should not be the focus of the conversation; that's the other person's role. Your role is to develop the kind of balance that allows the other person to feel comfortable enough with the course of the conversation to not be diverted away from the topic you need to cover—even if it means "one-downs-manship" when your natural inclination might be toward "one-ups-manship." Wait until later, when you've collected what you set out to get, to stroke your ego; wait until the project is completed and you hear the kudos from the people who sign your paycheck. For the moment, suspending your ego will open so many additional opportunities to collect information that you'll wonder if your mother wasn't correct after all when she told you to "never blow your own horn."

And while we're still at the level of pragmatism, we might as well get past some potential vocabulary issues. Instead of some facile or politically correct descriptor or construct that will only confuse things, I'll be using mostly straightforward, traditional intelligence vocabulary throughout. For example, I'll use the word *source* to describe the person on the other side of your conversation. You may wish to substitute words like *client* or *target* or any number of other terms as we begin to consider how to use elicitation to collect information—information that can be turned into useful, timely, and effective intelligence.

Finally, a couple of words about style.

In John Madden's football classic, *Hey, Wait a Minute. I Wrote a Book!* he talks about an experience he had at the end of his first year as an offensive line coach for the Oakland Raiders. He attended an NFL coaches conference and selected one of Vince Lombardi's seminars. Lombardi had taken the Packers to two consecutive Super Bowl victories, allegedly with only twelve offensive plays—six running and six passing. Madden wanted to know how he did it. Lombardi lectured on *one* play for eight solid hours. And he still wasn't finished with all he could have taught about that play. That's how well he was able to break down the play into its many component parts—all of which together constituted a winning play. And an understanding of which led to excellence, Lombardi's only real standard.

We won't be spending eight hours on each technique, but we'll have the same kind of approach in mind, breaking down elicitation into its component parts as you approach excellence in collecting information.

CHAPTER 2

What Good Does It Do to Ask Questions?

By our manner toward a witness we may have in a measure disarmed him, or at least thrown him off his guard, while his memory and conscience are being ransacked by subtle and searching questions, the scope of which will be hardly apparent to himself.

—Francis L. Wellman, *The Art of Cross Examination*, 1903

How's your sex life?

What a question!

If you're with a bunch of your chums after your weekly basketball game down at the gym, and you're hanging around having a few adult beverages afterwards, the question might be acceptable. Maybe even a regular topic of conversation or the basis of a long-running joke.

On the other hand, in a business context, especially in today's politically correct and litigious atmosphere, it's not an especially appropriate opening question. Indeed, you'd probably never start a conversation with it—particularly with someone of the opposite sex—because you recognize immediately that it's on the other side of acceptable behavior.

In fact, it's precisely because this is such a sensitive and emotionally charged issue that it's the question I've used to start this second chapter. It gets us to thinking about the nature of questions and what happens when someone asks a question. In this case, we typically get a defensive, sometimes a highly defensive, response.

A *defensive response* is one that causes the person who's on the receiving end to ask a variety of questions, mostly internally. Questions such as "Why is he asking this question?" "How's he going to use the answer?" "Who else is going to know what my response is?" "Why should I answer?" "What's in it for me if I answer X or Y?"

A major contributing factor that influences how you'll respond is the identity of the person asking the question in the first place. If it's one of your chums after a basketball game, your response might take a completely different form than the answer you might give to your mother—especially if you're a teenager.

In the case of a question about your sexual preferences or activities, it's obvious that you'd start asking yourself this kind of follow-on question before ever coming up with an answer, if you're going to answer at all. Yet, in most cases, we don't consciously form questions on this level.

Take, for example, a question such as "What's two plus two?" We expect—and usually get—a *data response* that is completely devoid of any higher level questions. If you're asked this kind of a question, you see nothing to be concerned about. Unless, of course, you're being asked by the accountant who's just sent off your long form to the IRS—but that's an entirely different matter.

A Question of Sensitivity

The more sensitive the area we're interested in learning about, the more guarded our partner in the conversation becomes. This is true in a business context, it's true in a social setting, it's certainly true in the political setting, and it's true in many others as well. Social workers, ministers, doctors, recruiters, bosses, parents, business and government intelligence collectors, all have legitimate interest in obtaining information. Yet it is often difficult to extract that information from those who are resistant, guarded, or simply unwilling.

For example, do you have any idea how difficult it is to ask an abused or molested child a direct question? Fairly predictably, the child withdraws, avoids the question altogether, reacts angrily or in some other defensive way. Not the intended outcome, but an outcome nonetheless.

Yet the more complex the question, the more potential there is for emotional loading; the more sensitive the issue, the greater your guardedness and suspicion and the greater the number of questions you ask yourself before you ever decide on your answer. There's also the matter of what the circumstances are. The question may not be as potentially explosive in a business context as "How's your sex life?" but the situation may be one where you're reluctant to retort with "That's none of your business." And the questioner has—probably unintentionally—raised your level of concern, your level of suspicion about him and his motives, beyond what he'd intended.

We encounter those kinds of situations every day. We want to get information from someone. We've been taught from childhood how to frame better and better questions to get that information. We've developed a pattern of questions and the ways we ask them in order to get as much of the information we want as possible. Sometimes we're successful and sometimes we're not, based in large part on how offensively our question is asked and how defensive the other person becomes.

If we stop to think about it, almost everyone has a need to get information in today's world. Often, that information is in the hands or minds of people who for a variety of reasons aren't always the most cooperative. Sometimes the people with the information are what the psychological and psychiatric communities refer to as "resistant" patients. The more resistant the client or patient, and therefore the less effective the intervention, the greater the chance that the response will be defensive, misleading, untruthful.

If we're limited to one or two sets of skills, our chances of collecting the information decreases significantly. The most common styles of obtaining information are *interrogation* and *interviewing*. Both styles are question based. The less elegant the question, the greater the degree of suspicion, uncooperativeness, or downright dismissal. These are separate and distinct from *elicitation*. Let's define a term or two before we go much further.

For our purposes, let's define *interrogation* as obtaining what you want from someone who possibly has it, who has not admitted having it, and who knows who you are and why you want it. Most often, an interrogation session is adversarial in tone as well as in character; indeed, it's often deliberately structured to appear that way. Typically, your authority as an interrogator derives from the governing institution you represent. For example, if you're a federal agent with a badge and credentials at the outset of the interrogation, there is an implied or explicit demand for the subject to cooperate. In other cases, of course, when parents conduct the interrogation, the authority is often much greater.

Reactions—Part One

One of the best descriptions of how people react under these conditions comes from the novelist—and former British intelligence officer—John le Carré. In *The Night Manager,* Le Carré says that,

> *Under interrogation, nobody behaves normally.*
>
> People who are stupid act intelligently. Intelligent people act stupid. The guilty look innocent as day, and the innocent look dreadfully guilty. And, just occasionally, people act as they are and tell the truth as they know it. Of course, they're the wretched souls who get caught out every time.
>
> There's nobody less convincing to our wretched trade than the blameless man with nothing to hide.

Naturally, the subject's reactions to your interrogation style will have an impact on the quality of the information you get.

In defining *interviewing,* let's say that it's the process of obtaining information from someone who probably has it, who has more or less admitted to having it, and who knows who you are and why you want it. Typically, interviewing is nonadversarial in tone, although it might be in character. For example, the so-called nonstress job interview is supposed to be nonthreatening and nonchallenging; the stress interview, on the other hand, is both threatening and challenging. As another example, there are puff questions for some politicians from friendly media interviewers; Mike Wallace and camera crew in the door to your office, on the other hand, create all the stress you could hope for—and more.

How do people respond during an interview? In some cases, a good interviewer will structure the flow in such a way as to get the person to cooperate more, to provide more, and sometimes even say things that are not in his or her own best interest.

Responses—Part Two

Most interviewees will begin a session feeling somewhat uncomfortable, lapsing eventually into normalcy—whatever that may be—based in large part on your skills as an interviewer.

Often, depending on what's in it for them, interviewees can be expected to tell the truth as they know it.

Because they know that *something* is on the line, they can be expected to restrict themselves to those answers that don't appear to injure them.

If it does injure them somehow, it will rarely happen a second time.

Interviewees, indeed almost all of us, mentally "replay tapes" of conversations we have had at some point.

We tell ourselves things such as "I wish I'd thought to say X or Y," but the chance is gone. The same thing happens when it comes to questions, which by their very nature are more memorable; the responses are often different.

Cognitive psychologists who have spent time studying communications and mental processing have found that we tend to remember questions far more clearly and for a longer time than the points that are raised in a casual conversation. That's all well and good if the person is open and has nothing at all that they'd prefer to keep to themselves. But when interviewees are less than cooperative, are more circumspect, are unwilling to actually discuss a point or two, their recollections can become problematic.

Upon reflection, an interviewee who has become concerned about what he or she may have said to an interviewer is more likely to remember the questions that were asked—those questions that provoked the response the interviewee might not have really wanted to make if the circumstances had been different.

We can easily see where this becomes especially difficult when the interviewer is hoping to have multiple contacts with the interviewee—which is almost always the case in business or government intelligence collection, a social-work or counseling environment, a media project, or undercover law enforcement.

- The intelligence professional finds previously "cooperative sources" to be suspicious or uncooperative or both, simply because they have thought over—what we might legitimately call having second thoughts—the conversation and concluded that they said far more than they should have.
- The social worker or counselor finds that reluctant clients have become even more distant after replaying those tapes of previous interviews in their minds and find that they are now vulnerable to someone they only marginally trust in the first place.
- The journalist finds that a previously well-placed and moderately forthcoming source is no longer willing to provide the same kind of information as before, either directly or on background, simply because the

source has reconsidered his or her previous answers to questions that are easily recalled and has vowed not to respond similarly again.

- The undercover officer, hoping to be able to make a case in an underworld money-laundering investigation, knows that the more direct the questions he asks of the crooks, the better his chances of dying of lead poisoning—of the 180-grain variety.
- Then there's the parent who needs to have some clue about what's going on in the life of a child's—especially a child of the teenage variety. Clues that the teenager might be somewhat less than willing to leave lying about. Clues about friends, activities, and so on.

So the question at this point becomes: "What good does it do to ask questions?" For the thousands of professionals who have pondered this point during our training programs—whether at government training facilities, at professional association seminars and workshops, or at in-house programs at companies across many different industries—the answer is clear. There must be a better way. We suggest that eliciting the information provides additional arrows for the information collector's quiver.

Reactions—Part Three

How do people respond to the process of elicitation? As you might now expect. Since the conversation starts off as, and continues to be, nonthreatening and comfortable, the level of cooperation with the source is relatively high.

There is a declining concern about the information being transmitted because the elicitor attaches little or no significance to it.

And the use of multiple techniques in an elicitation session further diminishes the source's concerns and increases his comfort level.

Elicitation, for our purposes, is the process that avoids direct questions and employs a conversational style to help reduce concerns and suspicions—both during the contact and in the days and weeks to follow—in the interest of maximizing the flow of information. The purpose of an elicitation session, then, is to obtain the information you want from someone who probably has it, has not necessarily admitted having it, who may or may not be willing to part with it, and who may or may not know—or even care—who the elicitor is.

Typically, it involves collecting information without asking questions, or, when you do ask questions, you do so for specific reasons as part of your planned approach to the conversation.

Yet this is not to say that we avoid the use of the question altogether. We're not trying to be surreptitious, sneaky, or below board either. Instead, we are seeking to be more effective, more organized, more directed. Indeed, when structuring a conversation, as we'll discuss in chapter 3, questions are intentionally posed at certain preplanned locations in order to achieve certain, specific purposes.

Exploding Old Myths and Succeeding at Elicitation

Living agents are those who return with information. These are people who can come and go and communicate reports. As living spies we must recruit men who are intelligent but appear to be stupid; who seem to be dull, but are strong in heart; men who are agile, vigorous, hardy and brave; well-versed in lowly matters and able to endure hunger, cold, filth and humiliation.

—Sun-tzu, *The Art of War,* XIII:11

Now that you've seen how many problems are caused by direct questions in the course of intelligence collection, you probably think it's time to jump right into elicitation techniques. However, like any process, like anything that has a system, elicitation has a number of building blocks. *Planning* for an elicitation session is one of those building blocks; understanding some of the *human dynamics* underlying successful elicitation is another. Leaving either of them out is just as defeating as leaving out some of the blocks in the foundation of your house.

Intelligence professionals don't leave the course of a conversation to chance. Highly effective information collection demands planning, yet most of us never really plan an outcome to a conversation, let alone follow a step-by-step process.

THE VALUE OF A WELL-PLANNED CONVERSATION

People have been telling you for years that conversation is an art form. This folklore has been reinforced by beliefs that either we're born with a conversational tongue in our heads or else we're condemned to a life of social isolation. All too often, some of us find ourselves constrained by preferences for introversion or extroversion. "I'm not very good at conversation" is a common, personally limiting refrain. We hear it all the time from people who attend our elicitation seminars. Their assignments require them to obtain information from a host of different subjects, and yet they may be only moderately comfortable talking with their own spouses.

I've found, however, that this doesn't have to be a permanent condition, even among those who have opted for careers in which they are insulated from having to deal with other people: those who've chosen the rigors of science and the relative quiet of the laboratory; those who apparently choose to live on diets of peanut butter and highly caffeinated cola beverages while writing software code into the early-morning hours; those who follow the mousy lifestyle that our extroverted society has generalized to include accountants, librarians, actuaries, and astronomers.

Indeed, I'm now rarely surprised when one of our more highly introverted seminar participants goes off on an exercise to gather some specified information from a person they have never met before and returns with more—and better—information than their more extroverted counterparts. They might be a little surprised, but most often they return with much more confidence. I've got a hunch that it has to do with the nature of introverts in general. The characteristics they enjoy and appreciate, even strive for, are order and predesign. This is in contrast to those structurally ambiguous situations where the typical extrovert often seems to thrive. In fact, the more introverted people seem to have an additional leg up, as far as I'm concerned. They, unlike the typical extrovert, seem to have a much better developed ability to listen, a trait that is of incalculable value in elicitation.

What we're talking about here is a learned behavior. We teach that elicitation is the art of inducing another person to talk, of guiding a conversation so innocuously that you make the person on the other side feel comfortable. In fact, since the relationship is established as—and continues to be—nonthreatening, both participants typically remain at ease throughout.

When you plan the conversation in such a way that you can obtain the separate component parts of what you're seeking, an interesting thing occurs. Simply, most sources don't see that the seemingly inconsequential pieces they provide are all that important. And, by themselves, the individual pieces aren't that important. Sources rarely recognize the intelligence process at work. That is, they hardly ever see the relationship between the pieces and the puzzle they are helping to put together. The nearby sidebar illustrates this principle in the defense and aerospace industry.

Intelligence Bits and Pieces

If I'm working on an intelligence project for a government contractor who is competing for a multimillion-dollar federal project, one of the likely collection objectives is to determine what their billing rate structure is. That is, what is the multiplier for overhead and general and administrative costs? Everyone already knows what the going rate for the various personnel categories is because they all know their sector of the industry. They also know what percentage of fee the government will accept. So, the only real mystery—and the only really valuable intelligence—is the multiplier: the number you multiply the employee's base labor rate by in order to actually price the proposal; a number that is generally expressed in terms like 1.751 as an overhead rate, for example, and 0.27 for G&A costs.

Can you ask any one person for that information and have a reasonable expectation that they'll provide it? Not in this lifetime. Most people have no idea what their firm's rate is. And even if they do, they know that it is some of the most valuable proprietary information the company has. Those who *do* know it would sooner have their hands and heads chopped off than reveal it.

So how do we obtain such fine-tuned numbers? Largely from people who know many small things—small things that they don't think are important. Naturally, we get some data from government agencies through the Freedom of Information Act. Yet there are some 160 variables that go into calculating rates, many of which are not available through source documents; variables that can only come from source people, who can provide current data on benefits, insurance, building and facilities costs, company paid vacation, equipment costs, number of people involved in the administrivia of a company, et cetera.

For example, an employee responds well to you as a sympathetic inquirer about her insurance package. "It was wonderful five years ago when I got medical, dental, optical for myself, my husband, and my children without any contributions. Now, I'm paying $62.50 per pay period for the most basic coverage." Does that one variable exert a significant downward influence on the firm's overhead structure? You bet. Does the employee consider this to be especially sensitive or proprietary information that she needs to protect? Certainly not. And so, this elicited information becomes one piece of the puzzle after we've confirmed this a few other ways, compared it to prevailing costs of insurance in that marketplace, and find it to be accurate.

Another employee complains to one of your researchers that while during the Christmas season he used to get ten days of paid vacation that came out of overhead, the bean counters have now taken over. The new policy is only two days of company-paid vacation. Does that have a significant, and downward, impact on the overhead rate? Absolutely. Again, the employee doesn't appreciate the value of that one bit of information. But as it is added to the mix of information that you're collecting and verifying from multiple other sources, you are able to ultimately reach a highly accurate number for their overhead rate.

PLANNING THE CONVERSATION

When we say that we "plan a conversation," somehow that seems a foreign concept—manipulative, if not downright un-American. Yet if you remember that the purpose of communication is to exchange information—which means a transfer of information from one person to another—it simply becomes a matter of economics. You will be much more effective if you start off knowing what outcomes you want and what steps you must take to achieve that outcome. This is really a way of reorienting our approach to carrying on a conversation.

For introverted types who have never really preferred, or even had an interest in, dealing with other human beings on a one-to-one basis, developing a specific outcome allows them to know where they are going. They have a system, a program, an outline, maybe even a checklist of coherent steps to organize their minds and achieve results from conversation that they've never previously enjoyed.

Extroverted types, on the other hand, usually don't bother to dissect and analyze the elements of conversation. And why should they? After all, conversation comes so easily and so naturally to them that it scarcely seems worth the trouble. Yet when even the most gregarious extroverts organize their otherwise random and somewhat ambiguous patterns of conversation, they recognize significant improvements in their ability to collect information from virtually all those they deal with in the course of a project. Just as Lombardi's natural athletes and stars, after breaking down their natural techniques and talents, and understanding just how they did things, became a team of champions.

SHAPING THE CONVERSATION

The process of shaping an elicitation session comprises three primary, sequential parts.

First, we've established in our minds what we want to achieve, what that objective is. Once that's been established, we set the various milestones and what will be covered at those milestones. These milestones will be matched up with specific techniques and the exploitable human characteristics peculiar to the source. Naturally, one of the first questions that arises at this point is "How do you control the other person's contribution to the conversation so that you remain on course?"

The answer is really quite simple. Being able to reflect on what objectives you had in the first place allows you to remember what you've covered already and what remains. If the conversation gets off track, as it almost inevitably will, the time you spent in planning and organization will help you to be aware of what still has to be collected. Most often, when there hasn't been any planning you forget what you were there to collect. The conversation just wanders.

The second part of the process is deciding which elicitation techniques you're going to employ and to what end. Some of the dozen different techniques provided in chapters 6 and 7 will feel comfortable to you immediately. You may want to defer using others until later, when you've become more comfortable with the *process* of elicitation itself. Then, you'll be able to match your new techniques to the person on the other side of the conversation. Once we've completed parts one and two, we're ready for the actual structure of the conversation, a structure that most closely resembles an hourglass.

THE CONVERSATIONAL HOURGLASS

At this stage of your planning and execution you learn how to ask the right questions in the right way, at the right time, for the right purpose, with the right person, mixing preplanned questions to focus more on something other than what you want to learn. This stage also forces us to remember to put larger, nonthreatening issues at the beginning and the end of a conversation.

Recall from chapter 2 that the cognitive psychologists tell us that people remember questions much more clearly, and for a longer period, than they do the casual elements and topics of a conversation. Other research shows that we tend to remember the topics at the beginning and the end of a conversation much more readily than the muddle in the middle. When no apparent importance is attached to one topic over another, we have no reason to store those topics or elements in our minds.

Just like any other hourglass, our conversational hourglass has wide openings at the top and bottom and a narrow waist in the middle. But, unlike those other hourglasses, this one has conversation flowing through it instead of sand: conversation that starts at the top with general questions and discussion about what we call "macro" topics. Conversation that continues to narrow to those topics or issues you really want to explore in detail. Conversation that is narrowed by the elicitation techniques you select from those you will learn about in later chapters. Conversation that broadens out toward the end and returns to the kind of general questions and macro topics we used at the beginning.

Yet we put a number of other things into this hourglass. Of course, we put in the outcome we've chosen to achieve; we'll just keep that in the back of our minds for the moment. We also put in the various techniques we'll be learning in chapters 6 and 7—or that we've used successfully with this source in previous conversations. We put in the various human factors, or characteristics, that we'll be learning in chapter 4—or that we've recognized from previous conversations to be this source's reasons for speaking with us. We'll also put in the things that we already know about the subject we want to learn more about; this will aid us immeasurably in guiding the conversation in such a way that ensures we get what we came after. And, finally, we'll put in the background and personal information we've previously developed about the source.

As you'll soon see, the mix becomes a very volatile one. It can provide you access to much more information than you'll get through casual, unstructured, catch-as-catch-can wanderings about the conversational landscape. It helps you to ask the right questions, in the right way, at the right times, for the right purpose—and to avoid questions when they'll only cause you trouble or draw undue attention to the things you really want to learn about.

Most often, it's the target who makes the move as he carries the conversation from the abstractions found at the macro level. A target who is properly encouraged by a technique or set of techniques such as disbelief, naïveté, or opposition cannot explain himself in abstractions. The easiest way for a target to illustrate his point is to describe his own experience, a tendency we might call an inability to resist "the lecturer's temptation."

THE CONVERSATIONAL HOURGLASS

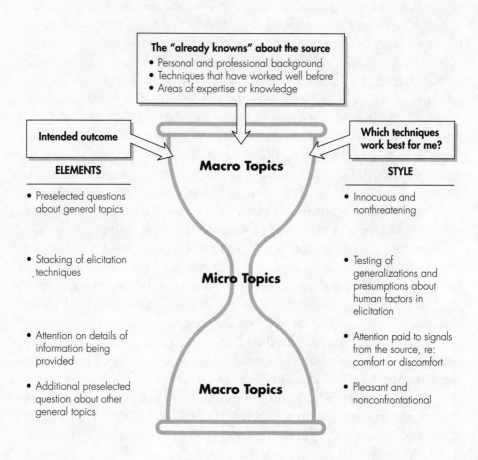

The "already knowns" about the source
- Personal and professional background
- Techniques that have worked well before
- Areas of expertise or knowledge

Intended outcome

Which techniques work best for me?

Macro Topics

ELEMENTS

STYLE

- Preselected questions about general topics

- Innocuous and nonthreatening

- Stacking of elicitation techniques

Micro Topics

- Testing of generalizations and presumptions about human factors in elicitation

- Attention on details of information being provided

- Attention paid to signals from the source, re: comfort or discomfort

- Additional preselected question about other general topics

Macro Topics

- Pleasant and nonconfrontational

You'll know you are a skilled elicitor who has chosen the right technique, and that the sought-after information is about to flow, when the subject says, "Well, take my company, for example. . . ." Once your target has gotten to this point, the specifics get easier and easier to obtain. And then, when you've gotten what you've planned to collect during this contact, it's time to return to the nonthreatening level of macro topics, those relatively unimportant and nonsensitive issues you want the target to recall.

You now have the payoff for the planning that has gone into the conversation. You selected an outcome, you organized what you already knew, and you had a plan or a checklist of topics. You established what your "throwaway" questions are going to be about. You thought enough about the personality characteristics or foibles that your subject has displayed in the past or that you are currently testing: one-upsmanship, ego fragility, a lack of recognition, or inability to keep a secret. You either tested specific elicitation techniques if this is your first time with the target or you've selected one or more from among those that have worked with this target in the past.

What's the Compensation Program Like?

If you're interested in finding out about a firm's compensation program for its sales force, you might start off with general comments about current world economic conditions. Talking about inflationary pressures or balance of payments will obviously be nonthreatening. Gradually, you'll move the conversation downward toward the narrow waist of the hourglass, from the macro to the micro, from the general to the professional/personal.

The abstractions at the macro level will only occupy a certain amount of the conversation. It won't take long before the source—perhaps one of the sales force people—is relating these abstractions to the only real-world example he knows or cares about: the situation in his firm.

Combining the flow with any of the myriad characteristics that help influence people to talk when guided professionally allows you to learn what you wanted—and often more than you expected.

During our training seminars, we send people out to practice collecting personal financial data, precisely the kind of information that would otherwise be considered threatening and private. We task them to obtain income levels, the amount of money they have in the bank, how much their homes are worth, bank account numbers, and if they're really good, they'll get such information as Personal Identification Numbers and other access information. Not to use the information—and certainly not to misuse it—but to build their own confidence in obtaining the very information most people would never reveal to a stranger.

From there, developing business financial information becomes ever so much easier.

In every class we teach, we tell students up front that they're going to be assigned an exercise in which they're going to have to get that kind of information. Inevitably, there are many in the class who respond, "No way."

Later, they almost invariably come back from such an assignment having successfully obtained all they were asked to collect and more. Confident. Somewhat surprised, with a whole new appreciation of how much people will say with what seems to be the least provocation. How much information people will reveal about themselves when they are approached with a plan, with specific objectives, and with selected and practiced elicitation techniques.

THE DETACHED OBSERVER

And, by all means, you'll want to maintain a consistent and apparent detachment. It shouldn't be brain surgery, but there will doubtless be those who read this approach and then, for reasons known only to them, undo all their good preparation. They'll do what my grandfather warned me against when he was teaching me to box many years ago: "Don't telegraph your punches."

Consider the different approaches that some businesspeople take when gathering information in the course of their normal efforts to understand their marketplace. Take the sales and marketing types, for example. These are people who thrive on closure, people who consistently move toward one objective and one objective only: the sale. But frequently the customer walks away feeling violated.

When they're in the information-collection process, they approach it the same way: get the information, and get on with the rest of the job. Do sources dry up very quickly for the collector who consistently takes this approach? Of course they do, and with the results you'd expect. It's almost always apparent what they come after. In their normal way of doing business, they guide a conversation to the point they're after, the information they're after, and the conversation ends with the source remembering the last thing they talked about. Yet salespeople aren't the only ones who get this unwanted result. In virtually every area of human endeavor we encounter the same principle in operation.

On the other hand, as an accomplished and aware elicitor, you get what you want, you control yourself and attach no more significance to the topic you want than you do the other dross of the conversation. You now close off the conversation with another, preselected general topic, using directed questions so that your subject will remember the inconsequential and nonthreatening. You can come back again because, overall, your subject doesn't feel as if he's just been through a wringer.

BACKWARD CHAINING

The concept of backward chaining has application in a variety of industries and business practices. It's also quite useful in developing your plan. Plainly, backward chaining is little more than working backward from a preestablished goal instead of bumbling toward an ill-defined one.

For example, if you were interested in the effect that personnel departures were having on a competitor's ability to develop new technologies, because the real brain trust is leaving—and you wanted to get an idea of who they were and where they'd gone as well—the process might follow this mental checklist.

Final Objective: Discussion of the internal situation and effects.
Step Four: Discussion of the company in relation to the industry.
Step Three: Discussion of general and specific industry issues.
Step Two: Discussion of regulatory issues.
Step One: Give-and-take in a question-based format about national economic issues.

THE SETTING AND THE SITUATION

It's often remarkable to me that this basic and elemental factor is overlooked by novice as well as mature collectors. In trying to satisfy the voices in their heads that tell them to hurry and get the information right now, they not only lose the opportunity but also close the door to future collection opportunities.

How happy were you the last time a telemarketer called just as you sat down to dinner? Is this the best time to call someone and try to engage them in casual conversation? Of course not, but then again, telemarketers are a different level of life form—and certainly they're not interested in becoming professional information collectors.

If you're interested in trying out some of your newfound elicitation skills on the cashier at the supermarket on the busiest grocery-shopping night of the week, is there any reasonable chance for success? Or, what kind of a conversation do you think you can have with a booth maven at a trade show when he's standing in the middle of his booth, surrounded by six of his associates who are all making sure that they all parrot the company line?

Neither of these situations represents the most effective use of your time—and they say nothing at all for your planning process. Each of these situations clearly argues against success, against collecting the maximum amount of information.

In the intelligence world, one of the very first questions we ever ask at the beginning of a meeting is "How much time do we have?" There are a variety of reasons for asking this, many of them relating to unexpected and last-minute changes in the source's schedule, even if he *is* working for you. There's a business counterpart to this as well, especially when the elicitation is going to be conducted over the telephone. It's not only a nice thing, a polite thing, to do—it's the only thing to do. Ask up front whether it's a good time to have the conversation. If it's not, offer to call back when it's more convenient. Practically nothing you're going to be talking about involves world peace or the future of mankind as we know it. And, we already know that elicitation does takes a bit more time than a quick question-and-answer session.

MEASURES OF SUCCESS

Interrogators, interviewers, and elicitors all measure their success by the amount and quality of information they collect.

Interrogators measure their success in signed confessions, jail time for offenders, and closed cases. Interviewers measure their success in the quality of the articles they've written, or the quality employees they've hired, or the social interventions they're able to make in someone's life.

Elicitors measure their success in other ways: how third-party observers to an elicitation session, as well as the sources who are immediately involved, react to the conversation. If a third party comes away from witnessing an elicitation session and finds it singularly boring and inconsequential, that's success. If a source comes away from a conversation and is still fully comfortable and not concerned that anything of a reasonably valuable nature has been communicated to the elicitor, that's success too.

This kind of success can be further assured when you combine this structure, this process, with the human factors that contribute to effective communications, combining these elements to dramatically increase your ability to collect almost any kind of information from almost any kind of source.

CHAPTER 4

Human Characteristics in Elicitation

Normal is only a setting on a dryer.

—Sigrid Ahlmark

When dealing with normal people, perhaps dozens of human characteristics come into play when information is exchanged. We'll focus on those we consider to be the most common and yet important. These are characteristics associated with elicitation that we encounter over and over in assignments, whether the assignments are domestic or international; whether the people we speak with are in industry or in government; or whether the people are among the intelligentsia or among the less educated.

We won't be making any special claims to brilliance or insight in developing these characteristics and presenting them to you. Instead, these are the characteristics that are stored somewhere in the primal recesses of our minds. We rarely think about them as ways to help us organize our approach to a particular source and to get the most from that source. Sometimes, it's those apparently simple things that appear to be profound when we actually think about them for the first time—raising them to a level of awareness where we normally don't bother to operate.

These characteristics don't have any special order or ranking. In practice, you'll feel more comfortable with some approaches than others. Some of these characteristics depend on your individual personality and preferences. Some are peculiar to individual sources and may not be present in the population at large; others are so widespread, cultural, and common that they can be generalized across entire industries.

Fulfilling a desire or need for recognition: If asked to respond to a question about how much we need recognition, most of us would probably answer that while we all like to be appreciated, it's not an overwhelming factor in causing us to talk with another person.

Now that we've gotten past the seemingly correct thing to say, let's get down to our experience, supported by numerous—perhaps even thousands—of studies, papers, and theories about how we all respond to recognition. Of course, some of us are more prone to need recognition than others. In our experience in the business world, the people who seem to appreciate it the most are those who would least agree that they need it.

In this respect, we're not talking about the kind of artificial recognition that comes from having our name in the paper or getting a plaque as the sales leader of the month. It's that recognition that comes directly from another person, especially when it is sincerely given. I think it was George Burns who once said that acting was all about sincerity and that once you could fake that, you had it made. Yet, whether the recognition is sincerely expressed or manufactured solely to encourage someone to recognize the source as a cut above the common herd is irrelevant. The simple fact is that when a source is recognized as being perhaps a cut above the rest, he responds in a variety of interesting ways. This includes saying more in a conversation than he might otherwise. And the flip side of recognition can be just as powerful a tendency.

Tendencies toward self-effacement: Almost equally powerful is the obverse—sources who are uncomfortable taking credit for something whether a successful result can be directly attributed to them or not.

For example, there's what I call the "aw shucks" response. A variant is the "'tweren't nuthin'" response. And we don't just find it in Alabama. In both, the underlying principle is that those who are not total egomaniacs—and that's most of us—seek to explain why we were so blessed with that talent, skill, or other attribute that is being recognized.

Compliment someone on their performance and very often their response is not only to downplay their role in the project or accomplishment but frequently to go into the details of how it was done by the team or other people. As they talk about the topic in this vein, it's likely that they'll discuss many of the elements that are of interest to you. It's even more likely that they'll provide you additional sources of information about the topic under examination. The job will be even easier with the second, third, or fourth person because of what you've already learned from the first source—both about their role in the project and the project itself.

A secondary response a source may offer you is to talk about how easy the project was. In describing how easily it was done the source discusses the new financing that allowed the project to go forward, the new equipment that made the job possible, a new bar-coded *kanban* replenishment solution, a *kaizen* rapid continuous-improvement process, or any one of a hundred other elements.

In the hands of someone who recognizes and appreciates this need in others and can satisfy it, it becomes a powerful mechanism for encouraging someone to be more and more verbal.

A natural tendency to correct others: Recall the importance that we placed earlier on the characteristic all good elicitors share—*suspension of ego.* Nowhere else is ego suspension more profitably employed than in this area. If you're able to remember that your principal purpose in business is to gather information and not to have your ego stroked for your knowledge, wit, or wisdom, then capitalizing on the tendency some people have for correcting others is custom-made for you.

Who are the kind of people who exhibit this correcting trait? Teachers? Certainly. Supervisors, inspectors, auditors, coaches, parents. You name it. Anyone who is formally or informally engaged in helping someone learn a trade, a professional, a calculation, a language, or which fork to use. When they see or hear something that is in error, their inclination is to correct misimpressions, misunderstandings, and misstatements of fact. Not being psychically afraid to say something that you know is wrong, or even possibly wrong, means that you can accept correction. And in so doing, sources give you the accurate data you need to complete a project.

A natural tendency to prove someone else wrong: An extension of a tendency to correct others can be found in those argumentative types that dot the landscape. If you're up for the bombastic style that some sources display, this characteristic can be especially fruitful in elicitation. You can find this tendency in the more messianic parts of the population: the true believers in their companies, organizations, enterprises, occupational groups, religious societies, sports or fan clubs, or social/political causes. All those people who know that what they hold dear is better—often far better— than the things anybody else believes or experiences.

Of course, this is more than just mere correction of a misstatement. This gets down to the level of real substance, down to the level where someone really lives. And as they defend the institution in which they have made an investment, they are very often capable of waxing eloquent about the many superior characteristics of that institution, its processes, its people, its functions, its successes.

A natural tendency to discuss things that are not their direct concern: Later, in the chapters where we talk about finding and using specific kinds of sources, we'll talk about such things as other knowledgeable competitors. For the present, however, we'll focus on people who get information in the course of their normal activities but for which they have no responsibility.

It may be the new-product launch data for something that's being developed in another division of the same company. The source heard about it in the cafeteria but is not working with it directly. Since the source has no real investment in what's going on in that other division—or in that company down the street, or in that neighbor's company—there is a declining interest in protecting that information *even if they have been told that the matter is sensitive.* And, of course, in most cases, they're not told any such thing.

The lack of listening ears in the world: Bartenders, social workers, psychologists, and many others make their living by listening to the slights—real or imagined—endured by disgruntled employees, former employees, unsuccessful job applicants, vendors who competed but not well enough to win the business, and hundreds of others. Simply being a sympathetic ear in a world filled with voices of complaint allows you to learn much of what's going on in a firm without having to resort to any of those highly distasteful and inappropriate activities such as theft, bribery, burglary, or waste archeology—the nice phrase for Dumpster diving.

Business Intelligence professionals know to always pay attention to those who are dissatisfied—most of the time, dissatisfaction may cause some sources to be less than dedicated to the company's purposes. This kind of dissatisfaction can be either chronic or situational.

- Chronic dissatisfaction can be developed into a long-term, mutually rewarding relationship in which the disgruntled employee and you find it in both your best interests to have repeated conversations over a long period.

- Situational dissatisfaction is found in sources who don't complain all the time. It requires you to be alert to the possibility of a certain, transient level of dissatisfaction surfacing during a conversation.

Since dissatisfaction may never be the case with a particular source, it would certainly be limiting if you were to restrict yourself to the use of this characteristic to the exclusion of all the other factors. Furthermore, even if you did find someone whose level of dissatisfaction had turned him into an excellent source of information, you may still want to depend on other characteristics—and use other techniques—because there's simply no way to expect that you'll encounter this characteristic every time you speak with him. At bottom, the only way to be prepared for as many situations as possible is to understand as many motivators as possible. And a cautionary note here might be worthwhile. Just because someone is dissatisfied or disgruntled doesn't necessarily mean that his information is going to be reliable or accurate; indeed, unless you're careful, you may become the victim of an angry exaggeration that'll be more misleading than you would want. This is just one of many reasons why you want to follow Ronald Reagan's joking quotation of the "ancient Russian proverb," *Trust, but verify.*

A natural tendency to gossip: As deplorable as it may be, people have been talking about other people and things since time immemorial. The bane of any organization, gossip and rumor remain some of the most elusive and unsolvable management problems. And in today's hypercompetitive environment, the result is often far more than just wasted time and confusion around the water cooler. Very often, gossip and rumor provide the first indications about mergers, acquisitions, new products, hirings and firings, financial changes—all of which are passed along both inside and outside the company.

Domestic politics and the "Springerization of America" provide a rich and fertile soil for salacious and lurid detail that help to fuel this tendency toward gossip, making it either blood sport or food for common discussion. As the participants in the exchanges become more jaded, the tendency to believe that nothing is off-limits extends to proprietarily sensitive or privileged information. The electronic water coolers provided by inexpensive telephone connections and e-mail make the size and shape of the opportunity all that much greater for the collector, all the while becoming even less manageable from an information protection perspective.*

A general inability to keep secrets: Benjamin Franklin once observed that the only way for two people to keep a secret was if one of them was dead.

---

* The flip side of this is the way in which some companies like to capitalize on something they can't change. They recognize and use gossip, rumor, and innuendo to spread false or misleading information—in the interest of misleading the competition without having to worry about the SEC stepping in, as would be the case if the misinformation had been officially produced.

In today's business environment, which reflects the commercial world as a whole, there are fewer and fewer secrets as society becomes more and more open.

Not only is there the almost natural personal inclination many people have of wanting to be included among those "in the know," which can only be demonstrated by sharing the secrets to which they have gained access, there are cultural shifts occurring that exacerbate this tendency. In decades gone by, a government official's claim to withholding information on the basis of national security considerations meant that no one asked for it again; in today's environment, it's interpreted as a venal means of covering something up.

The days of the "Loose Lips Sink Ships" posters on company walls are long gone, replaced by a culture that extols and celebrates the transmission of information in all its forms. It has long been a problem in government scientific circles to protect the secrecy of a technology, project, or program in the face of strongly held beliefs that science should be for the benefit of mankind; correspondingly, the knowledge that science brings us should never be bounded by national or cultural borders. This same kind of concern exists in our increasingly information-rich, technological environment, where technological advances are so swift that information-based advantages are seen as highly transient and not really worth protecting. For example, the technology that brings us today's most advanced personal computer will be replaced so quickly that it becomes tomorrow's doorstop or boat anchor.

And the phenomenon of unprecedented transience in the marketplace corresponds to a general lack of loyalty to a firm. Protecting the information that underlies a company's competitive advantage is hardly on the mind of an employee who anticipates job cutbacks and is actively out shopping himself—and his most recent experiences—in the workplace.

Tendencies to underestimate the value of the information they are providing or the ability of the recipient to understand it: This bilevel tendency is especially interesting to and for us. Quite often, the person with whom we're speaking has no real understanding of the value of the information they are providing. In part, this relates to the nature of the intelligence process, as we've described it previously. Seemingly insignificant points, when taken all together, are of great importance; yet the source, who can't see the larger picture, as the researcher often can, fails to understand the value of what they're saying. Even in the case of those who might appreciate fully the value of individual pieces of information, they don't consider the aggregate to be especially important either. As a result, they're often completely open about things.

On the second level, however, we see the other side of the coin. There are times in each of our lives when we are trying to explain the intricacies of a particular matter to someone who is somewhat slow on the uptake. Our reaction, depending on how patient we are, can range from careful explanations to immediate frustration and surrender.

In our business, when some of our researchers who work from our Alabama offices call potential sources in the Northeast and introduce themselves by name, company, and location, they often find that the people on the other end of the line act as if they are so intellectually superior that they think can say just about anything and the importance of what they say will be lost on our researcher. That's fine with our callers, because they long ago learned how to check their egos at the receptionist's desk as they come into work. While it might be assumed that the first response from such an "intellectually superior" source would be to hang up, it is our experience that they stay on the line long enough to underestimate the ability of the researcher to actually understand. Far more often, the "superior" person provides even greater enlightenment.

The tendency to want to be recognized as an expert in their field, no matter what the field: We have rarely encountered anyone—no matter what their occupation, specialty, or career choice, who admits to having to close their eyes in order to accept a paycheck. Welders or chief financial officers, secretaries or scientists—no one wants to acknowledge that their role is unimportant to what happens in the company, rarely are they unwilling to take the least little credit for things that have gone well, and equally rarely are they unwilling to suggest solutions that only they can understand to make the enterprise perform better.

Thus, no matter whether we're talking to a welder or a scientist, they are among the best—if not the best—in their discipline. They also, not infrequently, have the best answers in other disciplines as well. It's just that no one ever asks them about how they'd solve the problems; no one ever seeks their wisdom or counsel. And if they do, they only sometimes follow it. What they know would fill a truck—if only someone would listen.

Occupationally derived habits of advising, teaching, correcting, substantiating, or challenging others: Many professionals have additional roles, such as the formal and informal mentoring process, representing other employees as union stewards, or reviewing the work of others.

And it becomes habit forming. So habit forming in fact that we find people who cannot resist the opportunity to give their best advice; people who simply have to teach what they know because their specific knowledge is important and needs to be shared; and people who are so accustomed to argumentation that it's their natural way of life.

In fact, so many people share this set of traits and tendencies that they are found almost everywhere. The traits are so pervasive in our experience that we find two out of every three sources to have this kind of orientation; thus, when we consider which of the traits we'll plan to employ in a conversation with a person we've never contacted before, this is one of the most commonly tested approaches. It's almost as easy as singing words from the child's song, "Lead me, guide me, walk beside me."

Tendencies toward indiscretion when not in control of one's emotions: At first blush, you might think that we're only talking about people who get angry and speak out of turn when they're upset. While that's true enough, recall that the very nature of elicitation is that it works best in comfortable, nonthreatening circumstances. So, unless handled quite deftly, introducing anger or fear into the elicitation equation is generally counterproductive.

However, there are many other emotional highs that we can and have employed to great advantage. Think about the amount of excitement shown by that manufacturing consultant in the seat next to you on your last flight, or a similar person who was so caught up in their work that they could hardly stop talking about the last major success. Similarly, think back to the people who perceive their firm to be under attack by unions, newspapers, legislators looking for an election-year cause—and who become so energized in the defense that they unconsciously or unwittingly step over the line of propriety. This characteristic, when considered and used as the backdrop against which one of the actual elicitation techniques in chapters 6 and 7 is employed, can be especially powerful.

Tendencies of some professionals to share confidences with, or to show off expertise to, another professional: This last trait is one that allows some of us the most fun. Professionals such as lawyers and doctors are believed to have the highest awareness of the sensitivities of their clients or patients; such professionals have such supposedly high degrees of discretion that they wouldn't even be considered vulnerable to questions about their practices. Certainly, they are so smart that they would never violate a client's or patient's trust and confidentiality in response to an elicitation technique.

Right.

Not only do doctors and lawyers often represent a mother lode, so too do many other professionals who might otherwise be considered models of discretion and propriety.

And why does this happen? How does this happen? On a number of levels, really.

On one level, they're so ever ready to be nonresponsive to direct questions that they can't imagine that there's any other way of obtaining information. Absent the questions, they are no more alert than any other group in the population.

On another level, there are situations and circumstances where merely listening to a conversation between two professionals in the same business—whether it's medical, legal, scientific, technological, consulting—allows a third party the opportunity to guide the two principal parties to open discussion of things they might not otherwise talk about. One of the more effective ways to take advantage of these opportunities is to orchestrate a competition between two professionals in the same area—two heart surgeons, for example—in getting one to explain a particular approach and then encouraging the other to offer his approach; similarly, pushing two scientists together at an international symposium can yield the same basic results. In competitively sharing their professional experiences, they tend not to pay much attention to the "moderator" of the event.

On a third level is the case where being recognized by a professional because of your association with their industry is just as fruitful as being one of the source's peers. For instance, using a sufficient amount of the vocabulary that is peculiar to an industry allows for the elicitor to be treated as if she were a fellow professional when indeed she is only operating on the periphery of that discipline. Clinical researchers in the pharmaceuticals industry are but one of literally hundreds of possible examples of this application, where the professional courtesy of open discourse in the name of science and mankind tends to accelerate the flow of information.

On a fourth and final level is the hubris that so often affects those who believe that the rules under which mere mortals have to operate do not apply to them. All in all, the tendency to gain professional recognition from their peers is too strong a lure for some to resist.

We'll be talking more about professionals—and many others—when we discuss the types of people who are most susceptible and those who are least susceptible to elicitation as we turn to chapter 5.

Who Is Most Susceptible to Elicitation— And Who Is Supposedly Most Immune

Rank times IQ is a constant.

—**Norm Augustine, former chairman and CEO,
Martin-Marietta Corporation**

In our elicitation training programs, we have asked literally thousands of people two questions: "Who is the most susceptible to elicitation?" and "Who is the least susceptible to elicitation?" The answers are fairly uniform. Not very scientific, but nonetheless, uniform. So uniform, in fact, that we've stopped asking the questions and now we just present the answers. It always sparks a somewhat lively discussion of why the respondents put certain people at the top of their lists in either category.

In this chapter, we'll take a look at the findings from these surveys and discussions. Not only will it help you understand why some people say the darnedest things, but you may also start to broaden the pool of sources that are the heart and soul of intelligence collection.

THE MOST SUSCEPTIBLE

In the "most susceptible" category, the winners are factory workers, minor government officials, professors, and sales and marketing people. There's no real rocket science here if we think about it for a moment.

These folks have one thing in common: They generally don't deal in especially sensitive information. As a result, their employers don't spend very much time encouraging them to be discreet about what they know. This isn't to say that the people in these categories have no discretion in their own right; it's just that they're rarely told or reminded about the value of what they know.

Essentially, either employers underestimate the value of the information these people deal with each day, or they themselves underestimate it.

Either way, these people—or more correctly, these *kinds* of people—consistently top the list.

Factory Workers

Sources at this level can be counted on to have a considerable amount of valuable information at their disposal. Admittedly, it's sometimes a little difficult to reach out to factory workers, since they're generally not sitting by a telephone at work, waiting for your call. But getting to them is something we'll be talking about in chapter 11. For now, we'll examine why we consider them to be susceptible.

When we talk with sources in this category about their work, we generally find them to be proud of what they do and quite willing to talk about it. They're important, but their management rarely tells them they are—either explicitly or implicitly by asking for their advice or just talking to them. They're also quite aware, very often, of even the most arcane and insightful inner workings of the enterprise.

Often, by talking to them as if they really are important to the business, really important to the project we're working on, really important enough to have someone listen to them without dismissing them as just another common worker, we are able to learn a considerable amount about some of the most important things in a company. New equipment, new processes, factors and elements that impact costs, production rates and problems, inventory issues—all these and more are within the knowledge base of the person who falls into the category of factory worker.

And virtually none of them have ever been told that what they work with every day has competitive value or sensitivity. Indeed, in one firm, one supervisory employee related to us that his management had directed the supervisors *not* to tell employees how valuable the information was that they worked with everyday. To the manager's mind, if they knew how valuable the information was, the employees would go out and brag about how important they were. Little did he realize that while he was covering for one side of the equation, he was completely missing the other: if the employees had no idea that they had information that was worthy of protection, they would have no reason whatsoever to remain silent about it.

I use this phrase "factory worker category" because it doesn't apply solely to blue-collar, disgruntled union workers, as some might suspect. These factors exist in white-collar workers just as widely.

Consider the accountant who works hard and smart and imaginatively. He reaches a great financial conclusion after days or weeks of grunt work down in the numbers. He produces a wonderful document, with backup spreadsheets that outline everything that he's moved from one place to another, and he has improved the financial performance of the enterprise considerably.

And he delivers it to yawns. He hears, "Can you leave it for a little while and if I have any questions, I'll call?" He knows that this is code for "You'll never hear from me unless there's something seriously wrong." And he's one of the people who know virtually everything about the company because of the Business Intelligence principle that "Wherever money moves, information moves along with it."

At the end of the day, the same principles and conditions apply to hundreds of employees. People who know the details of what's going on in the firm. People who have not been conditioned to appreciate the value of what they work with, the value of what they know, the value of their everyday efforts from an outside viewpoint. And very often, their pay, location in the company's food chain, and other indicators of their treatment by management contribute to this conditioning.

With this viewpoint, it's clear that while many managers and leaders attempt to develop harmonious relationships with the rank and file in the interest of operational efficiency, they have other serious incentives to form relationships in which they trust employees and encourage them to think and act for themselves. Or, in the words of a wise man with wide experience in leading organizations in perilous times, "We teach them correct principles and let them govern themselves."

Minor Government Officials

Have you ever met a *minor* government official? They know—and you should too—that there is no such thing in the mind of one of the lower paid government employees. In fact, if there ever was a population that felt oppressed by common perceptions of laziness, venality, or incompetence it's your basic government worker at whatever level: federal, state, county, local, village. The electorate can put these people in their crosshairs on any given day as the butt of jokes in Letters to the Editor or in everyday conversation anywhere in any town. And they are largely incapable of responding because their Masters—the bureaucrats who run their offices or divisions—have told them to avoid angering the public that pays their salaries.

When was the last time you had a kind word for a minor—or even major—government functionary? When was the last time you allowed your focus on the job of collecting information to be superior to the loathing that you might have otherwise felt for the bureaucrat when you reached the head of his forty-five-minute queue? A focus on your job that caused you to be nicer, more decent, possibly even saccharine sweet toward the person who is the exact opposite of a "civil" servant.

The professional intelligence collector has an opportunity to do more than suspend her ego in this situation; she must also be prepared to suspend her inner fury or mere disdain for the functionary in the interest of doing the job.

The Intelligence Officer and His Obnoxious Source

Ushered by Jason to the dining room, we lunched at a twenty-foot oak table and drank barley water while Ockie Hodges successively dismissed intellectuals, Jews, Blacks, the Yellow Peril, and homosexuals with a benign and universal hatred. And Tim Cranmer, he just smiled his rent-a-drool smile and munched his fish, because that was what he had been doing for Ockie Hodges these fifteen years: stroking his little man's vanity, riding out his insults, turning a deaf ear to his bigotries, and paying court to his disgusting calling, all in the service of a safer, wiser England.

"Flawed from birth is my view. Subhuman. I'm surprised you boys don't have them shot."

"There'd be no one left, that's the trouble, Ockie."

"Yes, there would. There'd be us. And that's all that's needed."

(From *Our Game*, by John LeCarré)

But how can you do that? Of all the espionage novelists, John le Carré is the one who most adroitly captures the essence of what the intelligence professional's life is like in many different circumstances. In the situation in the box above, Le Carré notes the way that the tale's case officer, Tim Cranmer, focuses on the mission and not the personality.

Why does he do this thing? He does it because it advances his mission, his purpose, his assignment. He does this because at the end of the day, he knows that a greater good is being done by his flexibility than by trying to take the bureaucrat to task.

Considering the exceptional value of information that government agencies and activities possess about companies, doesn't it make sense to cultivate relationships with minor government workers? Granted, the Freedom of Information Act should make all the information you should ever want available to you. But we're talking about getting to the people who administer that stuff—as well as the additional things that other government people have access to that is not necessarily available under FOIA. And besides, one of the things that we know about government people is that as inexorably as the tides, government workers will continue through the promotion scheme that is largely designed to reward mediocrity. It always helps to have sources who continue to progress in responsibility and access.* Allowing yourself to be impressed with a government worker's skills, dedication, hard work, maturity, responsibility, and perennial underpayment can yield all manner of benefits.

And like the factory worker we dealt with up front, there's more to this than meets the eye. Aren't there similarities between the minor government official and many other, bureaucratically engaged employees—in nonprofits, not profits, public-interest groups, and even the bureaucrats in your own industry, those who are working in some sort of establishment-imposed drudgery that's really roughly akin to that enjoyed by the government worker. Take a moment and think about how many others in your experience exhibit these traits or live under these conditions.

Professors

What are the characteristics of the professorial type, and why is he especially susceptible to elicitation? Clearly, he has a need to teach, and the more studentlike you are, the greater the opportunity. This doesn't mean that you have to misrepresent yourself as a student, though. It just means to portray the part of a studentlike personality, one who is a sincere inquirer after that knowledge which may repose only in the mind of a registered genius such as the professor.

---

*Just in case you, as the reader, happen to be a government employee at some level, this section *does not* apply to you—it applies only to that person sitting down the aisle from you. You know who I'm talking about.

Being interested in knowledge for knowledge's sake—and to be seen as the primary purveyor of that knowledge—is often the primary characteristic of the professorial type. The mixture becomes even more volatile when you add in the tendency of many in academia to chafe under the constraints that administrations try to impose upon them. After all, if a professorial type is interested in knowledge for knowledge's sake and certainly opposed to any restrictions on the growth of wisdom and science, then he is rarely interested in such abstractions as proprietary information.

Additional elements include the publish-or-perish requirement in the academic community and the nature of advancement. And, lest we forget, the character of the faculty ego. Of course, we find these traits and characteristics only in a university setting, correct? Play with this in your mind for a few seconds and you'll surely come up with half a dozen other groups of people who share the same orientations—and thus, susceptibility—toward serving as a source of information.

Just in case you think that we're advancing the professorial type as a category only, thinking that we find the type and not the actual academic useful in collecting competitively valuable information, please hold that thought until we discuss the types of sources in chapter 10. There, you'll find that even the people in their ivory towers are potentially very useful to you.

Sales and Marketing Types

The first shot out of the barrel whenever we ask groups of seminar participants why they put sales and marketing types at the top of the list is "because they always talk too much" and "because that's what they're paid to do: talk." Certainly these characteristics exist with the sales and marketing type, but there are a couple of other dimensions to their personalities, even if the ones in your company resemble *WKRP in Cincinnati*'s Herb Tarlock and his plaid sports coat.

They're not all the mindless chatterboxes that Herb presented to us. In fact, they are very often some of the people who know the most about what's going to happen in their company weeks, months, or even years out, since they have to prepare the market for whatever's going to be happening. So, they're very much in the know rather than being behind the information curve. Since their compensation formula is probably tied far more to product and service performance in the marketplace than nearly anyone else's in the enterprise, it's to their advantage to impress the market as much as possible with what is going to be happening. Impressing the people in the market with how smart, how clued in, how clever, how simply wonderful they are as sales people, as marketeers, is really of secondary value. Sometimes.

Taken overall, these are the kinds of characteristics that contribute mightily to the contributions that salespeople can make to your information-collection activities. And if we back up just a little into some of the personality traits that we've been able to capitalize on thus far, we see that many of them exist in spades in the sales type: high energy, higher levels of extroversion, less orientation toward planning, and more comfort with the ambiguity of give-and-take situations. They provide another wonderful mix of potential sources.

Think about the planning aspect for just a moment. If you have someone who's very confident that he can deal with the world without notes, as it were, what is the degree to which he is susceptible to the well-planned approach? There's no rocket science here. In fact, there's a lesson that goes back to the ancients: hubris, that wonderful yet tragic Greek element that allows one person to think that he's superior to all others.

Of course, by now you've become accustomed to thinking about those other groups of people besides sales and marketing people who exhibit these characteristics. Congratulations on your initiative. How many other people—either by category, occupation, or name—have you added to this group?

THE (SUPPOSEDLY) LEAST SUSCEPTIBLE

> *No generalization is worth a damn—including this one.*
> —Mark Twain

Of all the generalizations about susceptibility to elicitation, the belief that lawyers and doctors are the least likely to say too much is one that simply doesn't hold water.

We're conditioned to believe that such professionals as these have ethical and legal obligations to safeguard the information that could compromise a patient, client, delicate business relationship, or ongoing intelligence operation. Just as with many other presumptions and shibboleths, this falls by the side of the road in actual practice.

In the first instance, doctors and lawyers are especially prone to the concept we spoke about earlier—the tendency of professionals to share confidences with other professionals, particularly when there may be the seeds of competition between them.

Lawyers

As a company, we often work for law firms so that many of our efforts are protected under work-product conditions, particularly when we're doing protection projects. As an individual, I've been shepherding my oldest son through the pits of undergraduate prelaw work and law school and have learned much about process, vocabulary, approach, and conditions. Thus, the common language value that we alluded to in earlier chapters certainly comes into play when dealing with these folks. Very often, it only takes that common vocabulary for an attorney to begin to treat your conversation as one between peers.

This is not to say that it's especially easy, nor that it works all the time without fail. Yet it's our experience that when we speak their language, instead of the haughty aloofness that lawyers are supposed to maintain when dealing with the lesser classes, they become more and more open as the conversation progresses. Bearing in mind, of course, that these are the kinds of conversations that don't occur in their offices or on the phone while they are on the clock. Billable hours are not a joke for these folks, and the setting- and situation-dependent nature of successful elicitation we spoke about earlier certainly applies here.

What are some of the approaches that are especially helpful when dealing with attorneys who are, after all, particularly knowledgeable in many cases? In the first place, it's not especially difficult to find out which companies are on a particular firm's client list. Once you've determined that the company you're interested in is represented by the law firm, it becomes a matter of finding the right lawyer to talk to. And it may not be the one who is handling the case for the target company. Indeed, in many cases, it's better when he's not. Why? Just link the characteristics together: professionals sharing confidences with others plus the tendency of some people to diminish the value of something in which they do not have a direct personal or professional stake.

After identifying the attorney—or paralegal—you want to speak to, you know the drill by now. Plan your outcome, plan your approach, plan the techniques you wish to use, learn as much as you need to in order to support the techniques you're going to be using, and set out. One of the few guarantees that you'll find in this book is this: Once you have scored some especially important and valuable information from an attorney, the feelings will be exhilarating—especially if you have had lengthy and painful experience with lawyers in your personal or professional past.

Doctors

In addition to the lawyers who populate our lives, there are also doctors we meet on social and other levels whose dedication to principles of confidentiality are a basic article of faith. Notice that I didn't suggest that we meet them professionally in order to build the structure of an elicitation session. I actually enjoy, and foster, building contacts with doctors almost as much as I enjoy dealing with attorneys outside the workplace. Those with whom I deal on a quasi-personal level are those whom I enjoy practicing on, to get them to violate something as simple as patient confidentiality. Indeed, most of the time, my goal in such practice sessions is to learn the identity of specific patients. Not for the purpose of using the information in any way—either personally or professionally. In the first instance, it has no practical use on a personal level, and in the second, precious little that we can ever learn from a medical doctor can be used in a professional situation.

Except, of course, in dealing with those medical types who are engaged as clinicians in drug trials. You'll be bound to ask, "Aren't they all covered by nondisclosure agreements?" The answer is, for the most part, yes. A better question, however, is "Do they abide by those NDAs?" The answer to that should be fairly obvious by now.

If we're going to be dealing with doctors, there's really only one way to become conversant enough in the vocabulary, and that's where social contact comes in—developing that broad general knowledge that will represent the concrete that ties the conversation together. Once the language has been developed, and you can make judicious decisions about its use, you begin to consider some of the other factors we've mentioned. For example, virtually all medical doctors consider themselves scientists on one level or another. What have we said about science knowing no boundaries, having no limitations, having no constraints when its dissemination can only be for the good of mankind? Or ponder the doctor as teacher and professor, with the myriad approaches that can be used in such a pseudo-academic setting.

At bottom, we've looked at the people who—in our culture at least— are supposed to represent the most discreet, least forthcoming, and smartest elements of the potential source universe. There certainly are others, many in your own experience. As you've thought about the traits that people in the highly susceptible category share with others in your experience, apply the same approach to those whom you might think share reputations for discretion and probity that you had attached to lawyers and doctors. You may add to your list such potential sources as senior businesspeople, senior government officials, and intelligence officers of the national or commercial stripe.

And you'll find that they all have certain class characteristics that make them susceptible to elicitation when you combine those characteristics with the techniques in the following chapters.

CHAPTER 6

Your First Six-Pack of Elicitation Techniques

Good Pitching will always beat good hitting–and vice versa.

—**Yogi Berra**

You now have an appreciation of the various factors associated with elicitation. Factors that relate to how you can plan to collect information. Factors that relate to the target personality—those basic human characteristics that can be found in people across industries, cultures, and languages. Factors that relate to the environment. Factors that include the psychological and personality traits specific to the individual source you'll be dealing with. Factors that all set the background for the techniques that you'll now begin to learn about.

Notice that I didn't just say "learn." That would be presumptuous of me, since it suggests that you have no clue about interpersonal communications. Instead, we'll couch it in terms of learning *about* elicitation techniques: what they are, who is more susceptible to this technique than to that one, which ones to match to the source at hand.

For some of you, this whole matter of elicitation will be completely new. Yet I will be the first to say that as some of you go through the techniques, you'll feel a certain familiarity with some of them already. Either way, some of you will echo the sentiments of intelligence professionals and others who have undergone the formal training program in elicitation. Often, while they acknowledge having learned many new things, they recognize that some of the techniques presented to them are things they have seen themselves using—usually in hindsight, and usually not very well across the board. Indeed, it's quite refreshing and rewarding to hear a career intelligence officer say:

I actually learned a few new techniques during this program, even though I'd thought I knew this stuff cold. But, what I really learned was that while I was already using some of these techniques, I did it in a haphazard and unorganized way. Now I know how to do it like a master.

Or, on the other hand, to hear a career law-enforcement officer say, "Not only did I add a couple of new arrows to my quiver of tricks, now I know how those defense attorneys used to eat my lunch. I know *that'll* never happen again."

By the time we get finished with this chapter, you'll have the tools and understanding necessary to employ a half dozen different techniques that I consider to be among the most basic and easiest to learn. In the next chapter, you'll find six more techniques that may be somewhat more complex for you.

Although there are about three dozen techniques that we could provide, it's the basic mastery that we're trying to achieve here. Most people, we find, will begin by mastering the first few they feel immediately comfortable with, adding one or two more at a time as they feel more confident.

Just consider that most people have very few, if any, of the techniques; once you've gotten a mastery of this dozen, you're going to have more than enough ammunition to deal with most circumstances.

A final word of introduction. There will be a couple of techniques that you'll find relate very well to others. Techniques that complement each other very closely. Techniques that almost seem designed to be used together. And, in fact that's the case. As you become more proficient, more aware of the mechanics of your conversation, you'll find that you move from one technique to another with increasing facility. That's really where we're headed, because after all, using one technique over and over becomes noticeable—and problematic. You're heading into waters where you'll want to learn about, practice, learn, and then almost automatically use the techniques that follow. One of the basic and most fundamental techniques is the first: the Provocative Statement.

1. PROVOCATIVE STATEMENT

This technique can be as simple as one sentence—placed either at the outset of a conversation or at a point of your choosing in the middle. Or it can be a full paragraph or even a short story or commentary. Despite its title, it's not meant to be offensive, although sometimes and under some conditions it can be if used for a specific purpose with a particular source. The purpose of the Provocative Statement is actually twofold: to engender a question directed toward you from your source and to set the stage for your use of another technique. Used at its best, the Provocative Statement can be highly disarming and deflecting.

Now, you may sense that we're smoking moss extract or some other powerful pharmaceutical. What's this deal about "to engender a question"? Aren't we here to learn how to avoid using questions? Certainly. In fact, you've just seen this technique operate. It's just like those billboards that really draw your attention and then say "Made You Look!"

Let's examine the dynamics.

On one level, where the question is being raised, it has great value. In the unlikely event that your source becomes nervous or too curious about why you're having this conversation, on this particular topic, your natural and innocent response is quite simple. "Well, I don't know. You're the one who asked me about X, or Y, or Z." In this way, most people will remember that, indeed, they asked *you* and not the other way around.

On the next level, and it's by far the more valuable and frequent use, the Provocative Statement sets up another technique. Now this doesn't mean that the Provocative Statement can be used only at the outset of a conversation. It can be used at virtually any point. It can be used to either introduce another technique or to change the nature, tenor, or focus of the conversation. The most common use, however, is to introduce, to set up, another technique. The techniques that are most commonly set up by the Provocative Statement are the Quid pro Quo, Naïveté, Disbelief, and Criticism. In the boxes, you'll see how they operate in a typical conversational style. In all the technique boxes from now on, the letter *E* will stand for Elicitor and *S* will stand for Source.

Provocation and Quid pro Quo

E : You know, it's at times like these that I really wonder why I've stayed with this company so long.

S : Well, why did you?

E : That's a good question. I guess it's because I came here right out of college, when just getting a job was a big deal and holding on to one was an even bigger deal. Besides, I've been with them now so long that I guess it'd be foolish of me to start looking around for something else.

S : You know, that's what happened to me. I came here right out of school and . . .

What happens at this point is that the elicitor has already decided he wants to gather some basic information about the source, then use that as a springboard to learning more about the attractions or disincentives for staying with the company. We'll talk more about the Quid pro Quo in a little while. For now, just keep in mind that the Provocative Statement gets you to the point where you have apparently been provoked into this line of conversation by the source.

Provocation and Naïveté

E: I'm really glad that I don't have to work on the pricing side of these proposals. It always seems like black magic to me. I'm not sure that I've ever understood this kind of thing.

S: Well, it doesn't have to be black magic. What don't you understand?

E: Well, just the other day, one of the accounting guys was telling me that he was able to reduce our company's overhead rates by about 30 percent in just one year without laying anybody off. He tried to explain it to me, but it went from English to gobbledygook in about a heartbeat.

S: Well, it doesn't have to be. It's a matter of being creative with the numbers, like when we were able to cut 22 percent from the . . .

When we start discussing the use of Naïveté, you'll see how basic human characteristics can be recognized and combined to get an accountant—who is really a frustrated teacher or mentor—to talk about cost accounting. Bearing in mind that when this happens at the outset of a conversation or is being used to initiate a new line of conversation from an existing one, you can see how we'll capitalize in fairly short order. You can move from accounting practices in general, allowing you the opportunity to guide the conversation to the specific points you're really interested in developing. Your source starts to talk about things that relate to his own experience in moving from the macro to the micro, moving from the general and abstract to the personal experience that gives meaning to what you're being told—so that indeed you *can* understand.

Provocation and Disbelief

E: I just can't believe that the market in animal toiletries is ever going to recover from this latest hit from overseas. What's more, I can't believe that we allowed ourselves to get into this kind of a fix.

S: What do you mean?

E: Well, I mean we had a pretty good presence in almost every country in the world, the margins were getting better, and then the government has to step in and try to regulate how we're doing things both domestically and internationally. The government guys just seem to be there to hurt business instead of helping it and the economy.

S: You know, the same thing happened to us in China. Not only did the Chinese negotiate like capitalists, but our own Commerce people really screwed up when they . . .

In using the Provocative Statement to set up the technique we call Disbelief, the process is roughly the same. As you may imagine from the sidebar conversation, this could go in a variety of directions, with you steering, augmented by whatever investment your source has in the matter. In this case, perhaps you're speaking with someone who has been similarly affected in their own company, in a business that it is completely unrelated to your own. Or your source may a midlevel government type who has some information about processes that you'd need to understand better.

Provocation and Criticism

E: You know, Jim, for such a high-tech environment as this, the Internet service providers here could really take some lessons from the people in Dubuque.

S: What's wrong with it?

E: Well, the servers always seem to be down; when they're not down, the in-bound lines are always busy, tech support is almost nonexistent, and when you do get them, it's some pimply-faced kid who thinks that microchips are what's left in the bag after all the big chips have been eaten.

S: You've gotta be talking about our competitor *alwaysbroken.com* because we've just put $1.5 million into new hardware, we've just signed a new relationship with . . .

In setting up to use the Criticism technique immediately afterward, you provoke a question that will in turn allow you to explain your criticism. The reaction to this criticism, then, is to defend the thing that you already know the source has an investment in. Once you're along this path, you can continue to use whichever other techniques you have in mind and over which you've developed some mastery.

As a final point before we get into the other techniques, there is always the matter of constancy and consistency. It's important to understand that if you're going to use a particular approach—Naïveté, Disbelief, whatever—you have to be consistently naive, consistently disbelieving. Without question, there are some things you should certainly avoid, for example, jumping forward and getting excited with a phrase like "No kidding? Really? Tell me more, tell me more, tell me more!" You can certainly see that such a response would have a somewhat chilling effect and would certainly reduce the elegance of your elicitation approach.

2. QUID PRO QUO

This is an old Roman Legion Intelligence Service elicitation technique that translates as "I'll show you mine, if you show me yours." In using this technique, especially when preceded by the requisite planning and introduced by the use of a Provocative Statement to provide some acceleration into your chosen topics, you can enjoy the greatest latitude with the least amount of suspicion and concern.

Planning entails not only the advance decisions about outcomes and topics to be explored but also the techniques that you'll feel comfortable using. Since most of us have, at one time or another, said some things about ourselves—and sometimes more than we think—this may be the easiest of all the techniques to use and to master. If you think very much about it, however, you'll recall from these instances that you didn't really think much about how far you'd go. This is where planning comes into play.

For example, if you're interested in determining someone else's personal background and you choose to use your own heritage as a Quid pro Quo, there'll be several parts to your decision.

First, you'll need to decide what you want to talk about so that you can transition to the point where the other person—seemingly naturally—becomes the logical topic of the conversation while all the while remaining essentially oblivious to how you've gotten it to this point. This means deciding how you'll get to the point of shaping and directing the conversation so that the focus is really on the other person. For instance, if you know you're going to speak with someone who is a retired military officer, some aspects of your own military career may serve as the opening gambit that allows you to get on to *his* career.

Second, there's the issue of what is called "backstopping." This refers to how well you can appear to be the person with the history that you say you have; how well this pseudo-history can withstand the harsh light of day if someone decides they want to check you out, to see if you are who you say you have. This is not for the faint of heart, and in our experience in the United States, it's almost always impractical and unnecessary as well.

Turnabout Is Fair Play

In using the Quid pro Quo technique, you've decided to offer something to your source about your company. Your expectation is that your source will respond with a similar degree and type of information about his or her company. And then, life is what happens when you have other plans.

You've been talking for a while about general topics, and you're down to leading economic indicators, perhaps. You're ready to begin the elicitation part of the conversation. You expect that since your target has been fairly responsive and comfortable so far, it's time.

Your next verbal move is the Provocative Statement: I guess that just about every business in town is being hit in some way. His response can be fairly predictable. It'll be something like, "What, is yours in a hurt?"

You respond with an organized, maybe even rehearsed, statement about what's happened to your organization. Not too exciting, not too compromising, yet enough to get him to the point of reciprocity— something about his company that you can guide, using other techniques that you've stacked up.

But instead of telling you about what's happening at his place, your source, either in all innocence or well-placed curiosity, asks you about some further detail. You realize suddenly that you really shouldn't go much further into the topic than you already have. You want to say to the source, "Don't you realize that it's your job to tell *me* something now?"

Of course you can't do that. At least, not if you still want to get some information from the source. You're actually in a trick and it could get worse. If you don't know beforehand what you can offer up to further

---

the conversation, you're going to have to be thinking about too many things while you're on the defensive.

Now, instead of sitting back and listening as you press his "push to talk button," you become a little frantic. Does he suspect something? Is that why he's asking more questions about me? What should I say without compromising something I shouldn't? What other technique do I have in my arsenal that'll help me regain control of this conversation? Or, I really wish I'd paid attention to Nolan when he said elicitation requires some planning.

There are always those who think they have to go to this extreme of building some sort of cover to get the information. Usually they reach this decision because they're either lazy or foolish or both. At best, they generally have little confidence in their interpersonal skills. We know that it's not illegal to misrepresent who you are while collecting business information. It may well be unethical, immoral, and distasteful. But it's not illegal to misrepresent your identity in the business world. If it were, 50 percent of the people we know in the headhunter business—as well as a battalion of other sectors of the economy who use ruses to get what they want—would be making little ones out of big ones on a chain gang somewhere.

It might even be well to think about the damage that you might do to your company from the inside if you were to encourage the use of misrepresentation, ruses, and cover stories. We have provided elicitation training in quite a few companies for the express purpose of allowing researchers to have alternatives to such approaches. These companies reached this point from different directions: Some had young and idealistic researchers who object on personal grounds and who simply don't perform to expected levels; others had lost valued employees to competitors because of their disagreement with the company's approach to information collection. Perhaps surprisingly, only a few of these have even been in the Business Intelligence department. They've mostly come from other departments and functions such as human resources, sales and marketing, purchasing, and everywhere in between.

The Truth

Remember what John le Carré said many chapters ago about no one being less convincing to our wretched trade than the blameless man with nothing to hide? We have all developed, to one extent or another, abilities to identify falsity and deception in others. Sometimes, we're even accurate about it. But that's another matter. For the moment, let's suppose that you decide to use something that you've made up out of whole cloth, a complete out-and-out fabrication.

Unless you had some very special training—perhaps in the Mistresses of Deception Course that is called "Girls' Health Class" in high school— you've never really been trained to be an accomplished liar or dissembler.

There are professional programs, usually sponsored by government agencies at different levels, that help intelligence officers, undercover officers, and the like to maintain an identity of some sort in order to remain alive and do their jobs. These programs focus on helping these people maintain the fiction that constitutes "cover."

And the best way to develop, maintain, and live a cover is to make it as close to the truth as possible. Because even if you're being trained to be a professional dissembler, you have to simply accept the fact that you'll make mistakes about your cover life if it's considerably different from your real background.

Third, there's the same issue that confronts teenagers almost every day it seems: how far you'll go.

In another part of my life—the lay religious part—I spend quite a bit of time with young men and women who sincerely want to know about the appropriate timing of their first sexual experiences. How old should they be? Who should "it" be with? Let me just say that while my personal tastes and recommendations run in the direction of abstinence and monogamy, I'm not the one they should be asking; and neither should their peer friends be their primary advisers. They should be making such decisions in their family room, in conversation with their parents, far from the event. The absolutely wrong time to make that decision is in the backseat of a car two hours after they've pulled into the parking space under the moon, where the hormones are in full rage and roar.

Similarly, the best advice you can get when you're developing your approach to use the Quid pro Quo technique is to decide well in advance what you're going to say as the opening gambit. Then, decide on those additional things you'll be willing to contribute to the conversation to keep it from becoming one-sided. Avoid the backseat decisions that may prove far more revealing about you than what you'd intended to get from your source.

Fourth, topic knowledge. Let's use the military guy again, since we're getting to know him a little. Maybe you've decided to refer to your family's long history of military service going back to your fourth great-grandfather's service in the Irish Brigades during the Civil War. Your intent is to get him to talk about himself. Since you've already figured out from his accent that he's a Texan who'll probably try to one-up you, you hallucinate that in mere moments the focus will be on him and his family, and then on him, for the rest of the conversation. But he also happens to be a Civil War buff. He asks—with great interest and in all sincerity—whether your forebears fought in the 64th, the 65th, the 69th, or the 113th? You have no clue. What are you prepared to say at this point?

Are you going to make something up? Are you tempted to create something out of whole cloth simply to avoid looking like someone who doesn't really know what's going on? Don't be—just say you don't know, or that you don't know enough, and learn from the experience. The next time perhaps you'll have prepared yourself better. I hope.

Yet, in addition to preparing yourself better in the future, there are some other things you might consider doing as you plan your approach and select the topics you're going to use. And bear in mind that just because you've used a particular approach with someone already, it doesn't mean that you can't use it in whatever situation presents itself in the future. If you play chess, think about how many various openings you have at the outset of a game, which gambits and countergambits you have in your arsenal. And how many variants you have developed on your own.

For some of us, a variant that I call the *Reflected Quid pro Quo* may be the best approach. In this approach, you are referring to someone else's experience, and it becomes even easier for you to claim ignorance of the actual details—details you would be expected to have some mastery of if you had been claiming the experience as your own.

To illustrate, let's go back to the military officer example. If you have no military history in your personal background, you may well have a father, grandfather, great-grandfather, brother, uncle, or even neighbor who did. Acknowledging that, referring to the things that you learned about military life at your father's feet, and introducing that part of your background into the conversation almost always pay off with some degree of reciprocity.

And the beauty of this approach is that you can make all manner of mistakes in the construction of your relative or friend's experience. Mistakes that are natural in someone who hasn't actually had the experience; mistakes that can be especially useful if you're using this technique as a foundation upon which to stack some other techniques such as Naïveté or purposely False or Erroneous Statements. It also somewhat reduces the amount of planning and preparation that you might have to do. You don't really have to worry about how far to go, since to a large extent the matter is not going to come back to haunt you later—you don't have any real investment in it.

3. SIMPLE FLATTERY

The basic principle that operates here is that "Everybody enjoys a little bit sometimes, and many would like it all the time." No matter whether your potential source is a welder or white-collar worker, secretary or scholar, clerk or CEO, simple flattery can be a particularly effective technique for gathering information in the marketplace, especially when used as one of the techniques in a stack. Flatter the CEO with a remark that seems to be directed at the company's recent success, and how is it accepted? On a subtext level, he takes it as a compliment to his brilliance, leadership, vision, and personal courage. Granted, we often hear that "Aw shucks, 'tweren't nothin'" kind of response described in the section on self-effacement in chapter 4. But frequently that's little more than the opening through which we begin to touch the CEO and his repository of information.

Let's consider the margins of flattery for a moment.

On one end is the great American philosopher and *Dilbert* creator Scott Adams. He might portray simple flattery in the workplace as the pointy-haired manager's dream of himself come true. In his mind, somebody actually thinks this manager has done something correctly—and maybe even well—however unintentional that may have been. From the outside, we can see the venal manager accepting the less-than-heartfelt applause of his subordinates and mistaking it for sincerity. I'm not suggesting that you're working for—or are—a *Dilbert*-strip sort of manager, but how many people can you recognize when you look at that cartoon strip each day? Don't you recognize them for their unsuspecting acceptance of flattery that is directed toward them? Don't they almost always provide the opening for a more detailed discussion of the things that you're really interested in learning about?

On the other end of the flattery scale is the genuine and heartfelt sincerity in comments about something that is well done, looks good, works well, and so on. I'm grateful to report that in my experience, more people respond positively to this kind of an approach, this kind of applause, for something that's truly well done and deserving of recognition. The response of the person at this end of the scale is significantly more self-effacing; the source attempts at least once, if not more, to deflect attention away from himself in favor of advancing another person's role in whatever success is being attributed to his action or intervention. One or two more simple, straightforward, complimentary statements gets you to where you're able to narrow the aperture to view the things you set out to get in the first place.

Making It a Big Production

Perhaps it's a compliment to a manufacturing plant foreman, whose production rates have increased considerably over the past six months while the rejection rates have gone down by 40 percent. What's his first response in most cases?

S: Wasn't anything special that I did personally. We've got some really excellent people and with the new equipment that the company put in, it was bound to happen.

E: Come on. That couldn't have happened without somebody knowing how to make the people work together with the equipment. If there's anything I know about dealing with man-machine interface it's that the whole magillah falls apart if there's no leadership at the line level.

S: Well, yeah, I guess you're right. I did spend quite a bit of time having to get to know the ins and outs of the equipment. I even spent two weeks at the plant where they make the stuff just so I'd be able to help through the setup and first few problems that always arise. And, you're right about the problems at the people level. When somebody is afraid that the equipment means that they're on their way out in the next downsizing, they aren't really too encouraging.

E: And, I guess you've got a couple of horror stories about that.

S: You betcha. I remember the first day we were up, it was almost like a nightmare. We'd been moving at about eighteen-hour throughput and the new line was supposed to drop it to around four hours. But, that first shift worked at about a twenty-two-hours rate and that made us all crazy. It took me two weeks, but I got it to three hours, twenty minutes and I don't think we're where we can be yet. In fact, I'm thinking that if we just . . .

Obviously, in the case of some of the members of the political class, we can stop this intermediate step and go right to the heart of repetitive flattery. Yet by and large, we can almost expect that the initial response of a source to flattery is to minimize the impact of their contribution, or to make a seemingly difficult job appear easier and less of a challenge. Of course, there will always be those who use this initial response as part of the process of fishing for more compliments, more flattery.

No matter. Once we've gotten someone to this point, where they don't react to the flattering statement, it's not difficult for them to get into an explanation of what mitigating circumstances made the achievement somewhat less difficult.

What is happening here? Simply, we're operating in the world where people want to downplay what they've done or how well they've done it. We don't want to let them get away with that, because if we do, they won't explain things; they won't tell us what we're after. And we can't have that.

It doesn't have to be just performance in the workplace, either. I've found that Simple Flattery is another arrow in the quiver that can be fired at almost any time as we move from nonthreatening areas into the personal/professional area quite quickly. It's one of the easiest things to do, particularly when it's set up in advance.

In our workshops, the use of Simple Flattery is demonstrated in a video clip of a conversation with a woman. Since I'm the one who is actually doing the elicitation, the question often comes up about the impact of gender.

In my experience, the least problematic combination for the use of Simple Flattery is woman to woman. I really do respect Mark Twain's comment earlier, "No generalization is worth a damn—including this one." Nonetheless, I maintain that there is far less suspicion of, and far greater acceptance of, a flattering statement made by one woman to another than from a man to a woman, for example.

A flattering statement made by a man to a woman can have all manner of unwanted overtones that defeat the purpose of attempting a nonthreatening, largely unmemorable approach to information gathering. Leering, while using flattery, is definitely out. Yet flattery doesn't have to be eliminated altogether. If done with a certain amount of deftness and when it's included in a stack of techniques, it can be very effective in getting to the point you want to reach. Just for argument's sake, for example, the video clip that I referred to earlier contains nine flattering statements in a row—a process that doesn't seem to hinder the conversation in the slightest. So, it really does become a matter of degree, of paying attention to those subtle changes that occur in any conversation, and knowing from those changes when to move on to another technique as you go about collecting what you want and need.

Simple Flattery used by one man to another man, again with the nature of generalizations in mind, tends to be one of the most problematic. Why? Simply because guys don't expect compliments or flattery from another guy without waiting for the other shoe to drop. "Okay, whattaya want?" is the usual response when one man flatters another—unless the elicitor/flatterer decides well in advance to practice the approach until every and any Simple Flattery appears normal, natural, and nonthreatening to the recipient.

And, forgetting political correctness, a woman flattering a man provides the immediate mental image of a dog rolling over to have his belly rubbed.

4. EXPLOITING THE INSTINCT TO COMPLAIN

We've become a Nation of Whiners and Snivelers. Think about the last time you were around the water cooler at work. Were you talking about how wonderful the benefits package is? Were you commenting on how great a manager your boss has become? Were you doing anything else besides drinking water?

What does this mean for us as information collectors? It means that an already target-rich environment has become even more so. And in such an environment, more and more people turn a deaf ear to the tribulations—either real or imagined—of others. In a variation of an age-old phrase, in the land of the deaf, the one-eared man is king; in other words, as you listen easily and well, you'll become an excellent collector.

Sweet Retirement

During a visit to the lobby of a manufacturing plant, we came across copies of the past few months of the company newsletters. The back page had a section on retirees—people who had retired recently from various departments and what they were doing. Unless of course some of these retirees had been put out to pasture before their time—in their minds—and might well want to feel of value again. A fairly common condition among recent retirees.

When we called one of the men on the list, he was especially bitter. Not because he'd been retired too early but because of what had happened to his son. It seems that his twenty-five-year-old son, who'd been unemployed and living at home, was a constant drain on the father. After much string-pulling, the father had been able to get the kid a job at the plant about three months before he retired. Finally, the kid could move out on his own and leave the parents to the retirement they'd anticipated. Then just the previous month, the kid had been laid off—following the last-in, first-out formula—when the plant was upgraded with some new equipment. The kid was back home, just as much of a burden as ever.

Thinking that perhaps the son had told the father some things about the new equipment, we continued the conversation. The son hadn't been especially knowledgeable about the equipment, and as a relatively new employee, hadn't understood very much anyway. The father, though, maintained close contact with many of his friends from the plant and even continued to bowl on the company league team with some of his former co-workers.

He'd actually learned quite a bit from his colleagues, and it was easy for him to share his knowledge with us—especially since he was being treated as an expert and not an exile. Naturally, we got to the limits of his knowledge. He volunteered to call us with anything else he might remember or come across, and so we provided him with a name and telephone number to call in such an event.

Within a week, he called back with all the answers we'd asked about and much more. It seems that he enjoyed the conversation so much that the previous day, with nothing much to do, he decided to take a trip out to the plant and see some of his old chums. He spent the better part of the day being shown around the new equipment, seeing how fewer pieces of the new equipment not only produced more but reduced rejection rates because the tolerance shared by fewer machines allowed much better assembly further down the line. The bulk of his information was right on the money, as later events were to prove.

And this part of the story still has no end. Although this project was completed almost three years ago, we still get monthly to bimonthly calls from the retired worker, who still pays visits to the plant and goes bowling and fishing with his old friends. He tells us all manner of new things that are happening at the plant. We have neither encouraged nor discouraged him to do this. In fact, this has been repeated in seven or eight other cases, where people have effectively "self-recruited" and gain a great deal of satisfaction from "keeping their hand in."

Naturally, we continue to pass the information he provides to us to our client, despite the fact that we haven't undertaken an assignment against that facility in quite some time.

We're not talking here about the difference between gruntled and dis-gruntled workers. There will always be workers who are disappointed, dis-mayed, and dyspeptic. They are natural sources for information collectors, whether the collectors are working on behalf of another company or union-organizing attempts. And where do we find such people? Among the present employee force, certainly, but among other populations as well: former employees, temps who worked in the firm and were dismayed over their lack of benefits when compared with full-time employees, suppliers who haven't been paid on time, real estate agents who thought they had a lock on a property that the company was looking at, only to find that somebody else took the sale away from them at the last moment. These and many other kinds of disgruntled sources have provided information of considerable competitive value.

And at no time have we ever sought out or run some kind of a fifth-column movement inside the company for the purpose of fostering discontent, or anything like it. Indeed, companies are doing such a good job of making their employees unhappy that no outside influences could ever hope to better the job that companies are doing on themselves. How do we know this? From two angles: the angle of the information collectors who identify, deal with, and listen to people with an ax to grind; and from the perspective of being asked by companies to help them design programs to protect information when significant personnel turbulence is expected.

Of course, the only people from whom we receive information through our sympathetic, listening ears are line workers and the like.

Right.

There is a different motivation operating for the leadership. People talk at the management level about employee performance, unreasonable boards, recalcitrant unions, intrusive public-interest groups, political and regulatory actors. The things they say are at a higher level, have a different perspective, and are rarely considered in the light of how much of an insight they actually provide into their companies' operations.

In a recent collection project, we learned that the comptroller of the firm had left shortly before we began our activities. At first, it appeared that he had left for another position at another firm. But soon it became apparent that while he had left voluntarily, he had not done so "to pursue other interests" or to join another firm. When we were finally able to find him, our suspicions were borne out quite rapidly. Something wasn't right at the company and he left rather than continue to sign financial docu-ments that were false and misleading. His instinct was to complain about the situation at the company because he had, indeed, been asked—and then told—to put his signature on documents that were highly inaccurate. As he complained to a sympathetic and listening ear, the only way he could provide context to make his situation clear was to speak with a high degree of specificity about the true financial conditions at the target company. As you might imagine, the kinds of information he has access to were about matters at the highest levels of the company and related to possible problems that could reverberate as far as the Securities and Exchange Commission. Frankly, we could've cared less about the SEC ever finding out; it was our client who needed to have the information. If the SEC ever got the information, that was just the luck of the draw.

Further, the company had made no effort to continue his compensation and thus ensure his silence or even discretion. As a result, he felt no loyalty to the firm for what they had tried to get him to do and he had signed no confidentiality agreements. You may leave it to your own imagination as to which options the client in this case had at his disposal. What would you be doing right now if you had learned of similar things about your publicly traded competitor?

5. WORD REPETITION

For those of you who've taken an active listening course of one sort or another, you know that repeating a key word or phrase, or another person's last word or phrase, is supposed to send the message to your partner that you're paying attention to their important message. It's also designed to encourage them to say more than they've already said, so as to encourage them toward greater openness in your exchange. Sounds a little like elicitation, doesn't it?

Well, it is to a degree. We want the other person to provide us with as much information as we require to answer the tasking that we've received. Anything that speeds us along in that direction must be good. But just like any good thing, too much of it becomes problematic. On one level that's why we encourage you to develop numerous elicitation techniques. Techniques that can serve as bridges from one topic or one emphasis to another. Techniques that can afford you a range of flexibility in your dealings with sources.

Word Repetition allows us to achieve many of these objectives quite easily and simply. But there are some issues associated with Word Repetition in the active listening model that do not fit well in the elicitation model.

In the first place, there's the matter of how many people have been through a certain level of training that emphasizes word repetition as a management device. Word Repetition in the active listening model is specifically intended to overtly signal your partner in the conversation that you're interested in what he's got to say. Even if they don't get that overt message, if your employees have been through the same course, they'll no doubt recognize that you're using what you've been taught.

The downside from an elicitation perspective is obvious. Clearly, one of the foundation blocks of elicitation is that we really don't want the source to feel that we're attaching any specific importance to what he's saying. Then there's always the danger driven by employee (or, source) suspicion that it's just another one of those "management things" that's rooted in getting the job done and not necessarily something that's in the employee's (or source's) best interest. Using Word Repetition in this light is also sometimes problematic because of the condescension, or even paternalism, that some attach to it. Since we're dealing with people—as sources of information—who've probably had the same kind of exposure to active listening, we have to expect that there would be a corresponding problem at some level.

Secondly, Word Repetition in the active listening framework is suggested as a method to be used over and over—especially as you get deeper into the conversation and your partner is responding more fluidly. Yet for us, another of the hallmarks of elicitation is that we learn many techniques so that we don't have to rely on just one. And that's what Word Repetition is for us—just one technique among many. That it's simple and uncomplicated, can be used quickly and for the most part discreetly, is true. That there are many variations on Word Repetition from the elicitation standpoint may not be immediately clear. But, that's the reason we're here.

In Word Repetition as an elicitation technique, we find it much more useful to think about what the other person has said instead of just finding the key word or phrase and parroting it back. Thinking about what they said means that you can come up with synonyms for the words, synonyms that take the place of the word itself and yet are not the same words. This significantly reduces the potential of a source recognizing the repetition of their own words, all the while achieving the same effect. The same can be true of restatement of the phrases that are central to what the source has said, those phrases that you want the source to expand upon with the least degree of provocation.

For example, if I'm interested in learning some things about an individual's background and yet I don't specifically want to ask him about his education, we may be talking about how he got into his present position. He relates that it was on the basis of "that assignment in East Podunk, plus advanced degrees, that got me to the place I am now." Rather than repeating "advanced degrees," the reformulation could become a slightly whimsical statement such as "Ah, graduate school. A good time had by all."

Do you see what's happening here? It does a variety of things. It gets the same thought across without parroting the source's words. It also helps you to build into your relationship with the source that you've been there, done that, gotten the tattoo. It also doesn't say anything about you that you haven't already decided to use. It thereby saves your experiences in grad school for a Quid pro Quo exchange you might want to use later. Using it now would just be a gratuitous waste of breath and information that may have greater utility later on.

Enter another human characteristic, one so tied to Word Repetition that we didn't address it in chapter 4, where we described the others. The characteristic is this: *silence.* In the example above, leaving the whimsical statement just hang there in the air by itself for ten, fifteen, or twenty seconds will surely get your extroverted source to expound on what graduate school was like, what he studied and where, what he liked and what he didn't. You see, people can become very uncomfortable with silence—especially extroverts. Do you have any idea how long ten or fifteen seconds of silence can seem? Try it the next time you're in a practicing mood.

Emphatic Loading is what we call the other major part of Word Repetition. In our training seminars, we use a variety of basic statements or questions to illustrate this principle.

For example, I might ask someone to say the phrase, "John, did you know that Jim Johnson won the Congressional Medal of Honor in Vietnam?"

My simple response of "Jim *Johnson*??" with the sentiment that Jim Johnson ever doing anything at all heroic is simply too ludicrous to believe, is designed to engender a response. A response such as "Yeah, I know he doesn't look it, but that's the way some heroes are. He was a career guy who got out and went into business and has exactly that same kind of courage leading his company as he did leading a platoon thirty years ago."

Or, a response like "Congressional Medal of Honor" that's tinged with the right amount of awe can result in another kind of an explanation about what kind of experiences led to that award.

Or, a response like "Congressional Medal of *Honor*" that sounds dismissive or denigrating is certain to elicit another kind of a response, especially if it's someone who has a deep respect for the award and those who've earned it.

Or, any other responses that capture by emphasis or inflection the various emotions or attitudes that can be attached to whichever word you choose to repeat. Again, try using this add-on element in a variety of settings for practice and you'll see quickly that Word Repetition will become one of your favorite —albeit not repetitively used—techniques.

You'll also see the use of Quotation of a Reported Fact as another technique in the middle of this progression toward the objective, thus ensuring that we don't use one technique so repetitively that it becomes apparent and problematic.

6. QUOTATION OF REPORTED FACTS

In a world where information is accessible at virtually every street corner and family room in the country, it's hard to remain ignorant of the world around you. In fact, we're sometimes almost saturated with information, much of which we not only don't want but don't need either. Unless, of course, your job requires you to be able to get all kinds of information from all kind of sources.

It's precisely because of this information glut that this technique works so well on several levels. In our modern world, nothing demonstrates impotence more than "being the last one to know." It's the case in marriages; it's the case in politics; and it's the case in business. No one wants to be the last to know. And in a business world where knowledge is power, nobody wants to be seen as an information eunuch.

A basic principle that serves as the foundation for this technique is Quotation of Reported Facts. It operates in the mind of the prospective source. "If the information is already out there in the media, then why shouldn't I talk about it?" The principle operates whether the quoted information exists in the public domain or not. As long as the source believes it does, that's all that matters in terms of their deciding whether to talk about something or not.

Legions of journalism students are sent out each year with this as one of their basic approaches to information collection. They ask, "Will you please comment on reports that your company is going to be laying off ten thousand employees?" They're taught to ask the basic question, relying on the "reports"—whether they really exist or not—as a way to get the person from the company to comment. Of course, there are several problems with this approach, as we've spoken about already. With this general lack of subtlety, it's perfectly clear what the reporter wants to learn; as a question, the source will recall a direct question for quite some time; and generally, it's very often asked in a demonstrably confrontational setting rather than a comfortable and disarming one.

How, then, can this be used in elicitation? Simply, in the same way that any other elicitation technique is used. It's placed in the right temporal location within the conversation instead of standing out there all alone with the light focused on it. It's been set up by one or two other techniques and reduces the impact as the source becomes more comfortable talking about it.

For example, let's assume that you've just read something about Acme Fertilizers. In chapter 11, we'll be talking about getting the most out of the media, so we won't cover that group of sources at this point.

Instead, let's go to the people at Acme Fertilizers. What do we know by now about those human characteristics that can contribute to someone being open and useful as a source? We know that some people like to teach; some people like to be seen as important, based on the information at their disposal; some people are of a mind to correct people who have made foolish or unwise or even incorrect statements.

We also know quite a few other characteristics by now and how they can affect the ways in which some people simply can't resist sharing their knowledge with others. People at Acme Fertilizers know as much about their company as you do about yours. People at Acme Fertilizers, just like the people in your company or in your industry, will react quite predictably when given a set of circumstances.

In the Know

After having set the stage with a conversation that began on a macro level and has been winnowed down to a company-specific level:

E: I was reading the other day where the analysts expect your quarterly earnings to be off by 20 percent and that it was because of production problems at your Kuala Lumpur facility.

> S: Well, as usual, the media gets it all wrong. Sure, we're probably going to be off a bit, but probably around 8 percent. And, it has nothing to do with KL. It's the plants in Thailand that are killing us. We'll probably wind up having to kill off three of those places, just because they can't get the job done there.

Engage the person from Acme Fertilizer who's been in the job for ten years. Mention that you were reading an article about Acme's new product line in the paper last week or last month, or whenever you read it. There's only a small chance that the employee will have read the article in the first place. At the same time, chances are very good that employees who've been around for a while don't want to show—or even suggest— that they don't know what's happening inside their own company.

We basically get three kinds of responses when we use Quotations from Reports. The first is from those who know and want *us* to know that they know something; the second are those who are marginally aware of what's going on but whose expertise and knowledge is in a different area—and whose problems are of a different sort; and the third group is made up of those who really don't know much about the subject at hand but are aware of much else that is of consequence. This latter group wants to be part of a group that is doing stuff that's just as important as any other part of the company.

Either way, in the hands of someone who knows what they want and how to get there, there are quick returns on an investment in time.

Slightly out of the Know

Using the same background and approach, with a different person with a different perspective and access, can yield just as valuable information:

E: I was reading the other day where the analysts expect your quarterly earnings to be off by 20 percent and that it was because of production problems at your Kuala Lumpur facility.

S: Well, I really don't know anything about the earnings stuff, but I will tell you that those clowns in KL haven't got a clue about how to run a plant. I was over there for three months, and they still didn't have the hang of the equipment or any concept of fabrica-

> tion. We sent them the latest machinery from Blacque and Whyte—almost $3 million I think—and they are still having a hard time opening the shipping crates.

It doesn't have to be something taken from the written media. It could just as easily have come from the electronic media, where a talking head could have said just about anything. And then we get into the issue of accuracy of your quotes.

So far, we've spoken about actual quotes. But there's more. Quite a bit more. In this information explosion, we can get all kinds of information. Sometimes, we even get the quote wrong. And sometimes the quote doesn't exist at all. If pressed for the source, the typical response that a reporter uses may simply be that she doesn't recall where she'd seen the article, but is fairly certain of the facts. We all misquote things. Sometimes we do it because we only have a passing understanding of what was said in the first place. In other cases, it's specifically done in order to capitalize on the tendency that some people have to correct others.

Out of the Know

And, with the same background and approach as used in the two other cases, we'll now see what happens with a person who knows little about the topic at hand but doesn't want to appear to be a complete information eunuch:

E: I was reading the other day where the analysts expect your quarterly earnings to be off by 20 percent and that it was because of production problems at your Kuala Lumpur facility.

S: I don't know much about Kuala Lumpur, but we've got more than enough problems right here. They've had to bring in Stepp, Fetch and Wheedle to completely reengineer the manufacturing process for the piston ring lines. We're going to be down for at least another two weeks and I have no idea how we're going to meet the schedule for the Italian government job.

This technique is commonly used by reporters; you can use your own variant. Reporters will cite other sources as having commented on, or other media outlets having reported on, a particular topic. Sometimes, those other "knowledgeable sources who've commented recently about X" are none other than their pals in the newsroom who were conjecturing about the topic. In your case, you may find it useful to apply the "my friend John" variant. This allows you to capitalize on the experiences of that friend or associate who has told you about something, whether it's correct or incorrect. The object to be kept in mind is your selected outcome: the source providing you additional information beyond what you have heard or read somewhere.

There's also a tactical dimension to the use of the Quotation of Reported Facts. If you start off with a real but only moderately related quote from the media, you establish your bona fides as someone who actually reads. That may not seem like a big deal, but if you think about it for a second, it makes a lot of sense. So few people actually spend time reading these days that you automatically gain credence and value in the eyes of the source. This additional credibility then attaches to the item that never actually appeared in print, fostering the potential for comment by the source.

REVENGE-BASED TRAINING

Now that we've been through the various human characteristics associated with elicitation, a half dozen techniques, selection of the right places and times, and a variety of other issues, it's time for you to put some of these things together before you start to implement them in the business world. Armed with this first group of six techniques, you can venture out onto the practice field where the risks are small and benefits for confidence building are great. And I know this from personal experience.

When I was first undergoing my training as an intelligence officer, I used to leave the training facility in the Dundalk section of Baltimore for a couple of hours on as many afternoons as possible. For additional experience, for additional practical exercises. I would go to bars in the working-class neighborhoods that were frequented by the workers from the steel mill, the GM plant, the soap factory, one of the distilleries. I would get there a few minutes before the whistle blew, for no other purpose than to be on a stool at the bar when the regulars came in. This kept me from having to penetrate their "space," since I was already there; they'd pile in around me and never really give me a second thought.

For the next few hours, I would use the techniques I was learning during the day with these fellows as my own, self-imposed homework assignments. Frankly, I could've cared less about the substance of what I learned from these folks about their problems with money, girlfriends, wives and girlfriends, cars, houses, and neighborhoods. Neither did I care very much about the problems that the companies were having, at least those problems that were apparent from the worm's-eye view that most of the workers had. This doesn't mean that they weren't interesting—in many cases they were extraordinarily interesting from a competitive point of view that I didn't much appreciate in those days.

I haven't changed very much since that time. I still practice these techniques and try out new ones as I think through the dynamics of interpersonal communications, as I think about ways to get people to tell me things. And so I ask you to consider practice sessions yourselves.

I refer to this section as Revenge-Based Training because it's just wonderful to pay back all those people you have reserved a special place in your heart for: brothers-in-law who have just become insurance salesmen; used-car dealers; telemarketers; the ladies in curlers and muumuus who run the garage sales your wife forces you to visit on those days when there are important football games; the dregs of humanity that your husband brings home for cigars, beer, and poker; and of course, teenagers.

There are so many people available for your practice sessions.

Decide what you want to learn from someone, and decide which technique or two or three you feel most comfortable using. Practice a few provocative statements in your own mind as you drive to the auto dealership, bound and determined to find out what their absolute bottom, definitely-lose-money-on-the-deal price is. Master the techniques that you've chosen and that are matched to your personality—the ones you feel most comfortable with at first. Later, you'll find it easy to match a couple of your favorites from your increasing stable of techniques to different kinds of people.

Then, you'll be more than ready to seek out, contact, and extract information from some of the hundreds of potential sources of competitive intelligence that you'll get to meet later in the upcoming chapters on collecting information.

For now, though, you've got the option of taking a while to practice techniques from this first set of six or going through the second set of six and deciding which ones you feel most comfortable practicing. Build on them incrementally until you're comfortable stacking two or three together in the same conversation; then to the point Sherlock Holmes reached, where he's "stacked" multiple techniques and moved—seemingly naturally and seamlessly—from one to the other.

If you were to attend one of our one-day elicitation training seminars, you would go off on a noontime exercise. You'd be paired with someone who would serve as an observer while you sought someone out and attempted to collect certain kinds of information. The observer's job would be to watch and listen, with the intention of giving you some helpful feedback—that of course you couldn't get from the unwitting target of your affections. Then it would be your turn to watch and listen as your partner sought out another person.

What are the kinds of things you'd be attempting to glean from this exercise? Naturally, they would include such things as the person's name, age, occupation, where they worked, what they liked the most about their job and what they liked the least, what kind of education they had and what they made a year in compensation. Too difficult? Hardly. We've never—not once in literally hundreds of cases—had people come back from such assignments over the noon hour without the majority of the information, and most come back with all of it.

Who do they target? Typically, they work on waitresses and waiters, clerks in bookstores and department stores, florists and pharmacists, fellow customers while standing in line. Others have gone back to eat at their desks, called clients or others, and used the opportunity to flesh out what they know. And we've had our share of interesting responses as well: the police officer who gave one of our students a ticket, all the while providing the information that the class had been asked to gather.

If you go out by yourself to practice these techniques, make sure you know what you're going after. Decide which of the techniques you've been exposed to so far would appear to work for you—those techniques that seem comfortable to you. One of the pretty consistent comments from our attendees is that they found it much easier to do this than they thought, simply because they spent a few minutes actually planning for something they'd never sought to do before. Knowing what they were going after and preselecting which approaches they would try are always of considerable value. If you're going to practice at this point, good luck.

And, when it turns out to be fun as well as rewarding, I'd really enjoy hearing about it, just as I do when hearing post-exercise debriefs of seminar elicitors. The addresses are in the back of the book. Thanks.

CHAPTER 7

Your Second Six-Pack of Elicitation Techniques

Good Hitting will always beat good pitching–and vice versa.

—Yogi Berra

Now that you've had a chance to consider some of the preceding elicitation techniques, we'll introduce the second set. Perhaps you've had a chance to practice a couple. Possibly you've already seen some that you feel comfortable using and those that you'll put on the shelf for a little while, with the intent of mastering some others before you go on.

If you've decided to try a couple of the techniques over a noon hour, as our seminar attendees do, you'd be involved in a debriefing right about now. We'll just hallucinate for a moment that you've done just that. You've come back with most of the information you sought. As you run a replay of the videotape in your mind, you'll probably notice that you still relied on questions to a large extent. That's quite common and quite normal. After all, you've been taught since childhood to ask for what you want. A little reading isn't going to change that overnight. You've also noticed that even having used questions more than you might've planned didn't get you into any trouble. Your target in all likelihood will not have demonstrated any discomfiture or concern anyway.

You'll have also gone over in your mind's eye what kinds of reactions you got to the elicitation techniques you did decide to try and your level of comfort in using them. You'll have a whole new appreciation for just how much people will say about themselves that you've never noticed before. You might even put the question to yourself: Am I like that too? Do I say these kinds of things without thinking to near or total strangers? Just a thought, as we get started on your next installment.

1. NAÏVETÉ

Of all the techniques, some people find this to be the most difficult to master. Yet this technique proves the natural law that the harder you have to work for something, the greater value it has. We'll talk a bit about why before giving you a bunch of examples about the use of Naïveté.

First and foremost, this is the technique that really requires the application of first principles. By first principles, I mean those that we spoke about at the very front of the book, the most important of which is *ego suspension*. Remember ego suspension? Remember where it has great payoffs if you're capable of focusing on your job as a collector of information and not as a collector of ego strokes? Remember that it may mean suspending all the wonderful things you'd like to say about yourself—education, experience, wisdom, knowledge, intelligence, athletic prowess, and your amazing offspring? Good. Your having remembered it means that I won't have to review it for you.

Second, it's helpful to bear in mind that to do a credible job of appearing naive—when indeed you do have a fairly good clue—you simply have to appear as something less threatening, less accomplished, less knowledgeable, less sought after than you otherwise are. It may even be a variant of the George Burns comment about sincerity in the acting profession: that once you can fake sincerity, you've got it made.

I Was Wondering

E: Explosive welding? I've never heard of such a thing. It sounds like something that could get you killed and made into something else all at one time.

S: Well, it's not really that complicated. And it's not scary either. It's just a way to make something really hard, using laminates and high energy together.

E: This sounds a lot like kids doing home chemistry projects in the kitchen: Formica countertops and glue explosions all over Mom's clean floor.

S: No, it's nothing like that at all. It's a process for creating a lot of small explosions in a pretty small place and allowing those powerful, small explosions to weld steel plates onto such things as tank hulls and ship hulls. Let me show you how our company is getting ready to . . .

But since we're going to be more straightforward and less venal than actors, it becomes a matter of feigning Naïveté, not faking it. We see examples of this every day when, without getting too awfully sexist, we watch as some blond-haired vixen runs her fingers up and down the accountant's lapel and coos something like "Oooo, it must take a really smart person to remember all those numbers and where they go." If that makes your teeth ache, as they might after listening to three uninterrupted hours of Karen Carpenter music, then good. Because that's so far out on the edge that it doesn't really constitute Naïveté. We can do ever so much better than that.

Another element of successfully employing the Naïveté technique is remembering that naive doesn't mean stupid. We all have gaps in our knowledge—some of us have larger gaps than others. Not everyone can know all things, in all technologies, in all industries, in all the sciences and the arts. Not unless you're the perennial brother-in-law who's starting a great new job next week as an insurance salesman.

Is it possible that you can go through life really not knowing very much about laser optics? Certainly. Can you talk to a laser physicist about kilojoules and plasma without appearing to know very much, if anything at all, and be able to carry that lack of knowledge around without shame or discomfiture? Sure you can. Most of us can. It's just a matter of degree, then, isn't it?

A third element to using Naïveté successfully is the actual opposite of naïveté: knowing some of what you're actually interested in. If that sounds upside down, please bear with me for a moment. The principle is really quite simple. You're going to be after certain kinds of information. You'll have to have some understanding of the topic already or else you won't be able to understand where the conversation is going. You'll have to recognize the things that will be of importance to you and be able to orchestrate, to guide, the conversation in such a way that you get what you need out of it.

And this element is not without its risks. While I consider it an article of faith in our business that "Knowledge never kills, but ignorance does," there are always exceptions to a rule. The box that follows shows an exception to this rule. Indeed, it's possible to know too much when you're employing this technique.

A final note on Naïveté. When one of our trained elicitors at our Alabama office is calling someone in another part of the country, they're likely to maintain their identifiable, regional accent. Does it accelerate their ability to employ the use of Naïveté when they're dealing with one of those clearly superior New Yorkers? Absolutely. In fact, the New Yorker type often acts as if it's a challenge to raise up those of us who are among the less fortunate—and to allow us the opportunity to recognize our very own inferiority at the same time. You can almost hear them thinking: "It's a good thing they have wheelbarrows down there, or else this guy wouldn't be able to walk upright." That's okay with us. Our folks are able to remember, at the end of the day, that their job is not to impress New Yorkers but to get the information the client wants and needs.

Too Clever by Half

An attendee at one of our in-house seminars had to unexpectedly leave in the middle of the training program. He was in town for the next program, so a month or two later he came back in where he'd left off. In the first program, he'd gotten a bit of exposure to the use of Naïveté but had left before we got to the caveats.

He recounted for the class, when we got to these warnings, that he'd just victimized himself the previous week at a trade show. He'd used three different techniques to set up and then guide the conversation to where he thought using a certain naive approach would do well with the source.

Indeed, he was correct, and the source opened up quite quickly and fully. Things were going along quite well until our man used a very industry-common but otherwise unusual jargon phrase.

As soon as he said it, two things happened: He realized that he was now out in front with a phrase that an industry naïf would have never known; and he saw in the eyes of his source that the source realized the exact same thing at precisely the same moment.

It's wonderful when fellow students help to teach attendees from their own experiences. During the debriefings after the exercise, none of those who chose Naïveté as an approach came even close to stepping over the line of ignorance.

---

2. OBLIQUE REFERENCE

The phrase Oblique Reference must immediately raise the question in your mind "Aren't all these things we've been talking about oblique?" Good question. Indeed, for the most part they are indeed oblique, since they are not direct. However, in using Oblique Reference we're going a step beyond avoiding mere questions. We won't be using direct questions, obviously, except for those things at the beginning and end of contacts, and then only about macro or general topics. We established that a long time ago.

Oblique Reference relates to the process of making comments about a related topic that really takes fullest advantage of the tendency we described earlier of people making the transition from general to specific. Recall from chapter 3, where we presented the conversational hourglass, that when a source is speaking in the abstract with you, after a while he's able to describe the finer points only in terms of his or her own experience—moving from the abstract to the personal and giving clarity and meaning to the topic.

For example, our basic life experience provides us an awareness of many general matters. We can combine these experiences with another basic principle: The only way for your source to fully describe something to you is from his own professional situation. The major principle here is that the opening and oblique topic is apparently so unimportant and general that it does not present any kind of a challenge or threat to the source. And it makes little difference whether the oblique topic chosen is mentioned either positively or negatively. The following example is a partial transcript from a real-world vignette we captured on video and use in our training programs to illustrate this technique. The source in this case is an engineer who works for an electronics manufacturer.

OSHA Ain't for Everybody

S: Oh, yeah. OSHA. Their job only seems to be to mess you up.

E: You sound like you've got some experience with them yourself.

S: As a matter of fact, yeah, I do. About three weeks ago, OSHA came in for a routine inspection and found that we were using a product similar to Freon in our manufacturing process. They just had a fit. Shut everything down. We've had to reengineer a whole bunch of our production line even though we've been doing the same thing for at least three years and they never had a problem with it before.

E: What you're telling me is that my assistant coach isn't blowing smoke at me. That he really is up to his armpits in alligators.

S : You're not kidding. We've got all this dead inventory sitting there. We've got people scheduled to work that shift that we have to pay for just sitting around. And, worst of all, we're going to be at least a month late on this new chip technology and the $12 million contract that goes with it. It seems like OSHA's only job is to mess you up. To cost you a lot of money.

E : So, on top of everything else, it's costing you money too.

S : You said it. When all this is over, it's probably going to cost us $200,000 or so.

E : They might as well have gone ahead and fined you $200,000 and let you go on with the project.

S : It would've been easier.

E : Well, I hope it gets easier for my assistant. I'm really looking forward to getting his help, especially before we get close to the play-offs.

S : You think your kids are going to make it to their play-offs? What level, majors or minors?

The foundation for this was laid by a Provocative Statement on my part about getting burned out in a Little League baseball coaching assignment. The engineer asked why, naturally, and I told him that one of my assistant coaches was a safety engineer at one of our local defense contractors and that OSHA had come in and found wholesale violations. As a result, my assistant coach had been unavailable for three weeks while trying to get his facility back up to snuff. My presumption going into this part of the conversation was that he'd probably had some experience with OSHA, that it probably wasn't very good, as is the case with most employers, and that his only real frame of reference with OSHA was the plant where he worked. His movement from the abstract to the professional/personal could only take him in the direction of his company. My intent was to determine if OSHA had had an impact on plant operations, and if so, how.

As you look at the conversation, please notice that as it goes on, we get to the point I was interested in reaching fairly quickly. But I've got a little problem. Ostensibly, I could give a fig about his company and its problems with OSHA. But I surely can't exhibit too much interest in what I want to know more about, or he'll quickly catch on to what I'm most interested in. It would simply be an anomaly if I started asking him questions or probing around his company. So, what's the response to this situation? The only one is to remain consistent in my apparent interest. Just like maintaining consistent naïveté, it's important to maintain the oblique angle of your attack on the topic. In this case, you see that we went right back to the opening. The "so he's not blowing smoke at me" comment is designed to do just that: saying that I'm really only interested in Little League baseball. Once we've gotten a fair amount of the information, we guide the conversation back to where the clear emphasis is on baseball and not plant operations.

Think back on some of the objectives we had when we started our discussion about elicitation. One of the primary objectives was to be sure that a source left the conversation with the impression that we really didn't speak about anything of importance. In this engineer's case, what do you think his recollection of this conversation was? A conversation that had five minutes of fairly common talk prior to the OSHA discussion, and then five more minutes about his kids' baseball program, my situation, and the prospects for our team and such. Plant operating problems? Hardly.

3. CRITICISM

This highly effective technique is mostly useful with employees at the other end of the spectrum, especially management types who have a considerable investment in the firm—employees who are loyal, have a significant career or financial investment in the firm, or whose options outside the firm are especially limited. In fact, the Criticism technique is useful in dealing with a wider range of people than might immediately leap to mind.

Rather than going through a list of those kinds of folks, let's look at the range of criticism that's possible. In each case, what we're expecting is that we've developed a sufficient amount of rapport to allow for some pushing on the edges of the envelope, perhaps even in a jocular way. Of course, if you've developed a source over time, you may have a pretty clear idea of how far you may be able to push something—you've practiced criticism in a variety of other areas already and seen how he responds.

The range of potential criticism can start at the level of the most casual and friendly, poking fun at small or inconsequential things at first. In this vein, you might chuckle when a source is describing his military service as a helicopter pilot. Your response refers to the general apprehension that you'd have if you were to be flying around in an aircraft that is constructed of twenty thousand parts assembled by the lowest bidder. Your source will give you a fairly quick and accurate reading on whether he deals well with criticism of something in which he has an investment. Based on that reading, you'll have calibrated his responses and you'll know whether or not to put that into your bag of tricks the next time around.

We can extend the range of criticisms a bit further when you get that broad understanding we spoke about a few chapters back. As an example, take a look at an actual approach made to a senior manager at a cable company. We chose to test a range of potential criticisms to which we believed he might respond. Based on previous projects on the periphery of the cable industry, we knew that the largest hot button cable people have is programming and content. Not service. Not competency. Not necessarily price. The description of that approach is nearby in *The Cable Guy* box.

The Cable Guy

We set the stage with a Provocative Statement that relates to the general low quality of cable service in the city. He can be expected to respond to this opening gambit, if for no other reason than he hopes you're about to bash his competitor, with the question we wanted him to ask so we could launch off on our preplanned course through Criticism-land. When he asks, "What's wrong with it?" we're quite ready with a list that becomes slightly more acute until we get to the hot button. "Well, the cretins who come around to do the installation are never on time; they never seem to bathe regularly; outages when you'd least like them to occur." No response yet.

Then you add "lousy programming" to the list. The response is a sort of "Well, hold it right there, partner." He begins to talk about the new programming that's already in the bag for the upcoming season. As he defends the content choices that he's going to be adding, the conversation quickly gets to how much it's going to cost six months out—in a rate hike that hasn't yet been announced.

He acknowledges that programming is going to be a driver for increased rates, and using another technique, you determine the rate that they're going to be shooting for. You get that information six months before the company is ready to ask for permission from the local governing board. Is that information of any competitive value?

You'll be surprised at what you actually know from your life and work experience if you take the time to plan your approach. As you set up your objective and how to achieve it, take into consideration the various things you've heard about the person, his or her industry, his or her company, and so on. What do you know about that can be used in the conversation to provide the cement that holds it together? These and many other elements that'll help you organize your approach will come from the data you maintain within your own organization. Data that you and your colleagues have accumulated over the course of other projects. Data that relate to the individuals you have spoken with in the course of previous projects. Data that is maintained and updated after every contact. Basic background data that represents the heart and soul of any primary-source research activity. Basic background data—and many other details associated with keeping things straight—that you'll find in Appendix F: "The Job's Not Done Until the Paperwork Is Complete."

4. BRACKETING TECHNIQUES

In collecting any kind of information that is quantifiable, Bracketing is an especially useful technique. Simple in its execution, it does require a bit of prior planning, just like any other technique. Yet most of the time Bracketing is one of those techniques that you keep in the back pocket of your mind until it's time to use it. Very often the timing of the use of Bracketing is ambiguous at best, and surprising at worst. If you're prepared, however, the pain of ambiguity for those who dislike it can be lessened.

Let's go back to the conversation in *The Cable Guy.* Prior to sitting down and talking with him, we chose certain intended outcomes: What changes in programming were going to occur and what, if any, rate hikes were going to occur? Clearly, there was going to be a quantifiable element to this conversation at some point.

Based on what we've read up to this point, and what our life experience has told us, we'll be hard-pressed to start off the conversation with a discussion about rate hikes. That's why we chose to use criticism of service, quality, and finally content as the entry point that could eventually lead to the topic of price increases. Price increases that will be described in numbers. Deciding on the *range* of numbers is critical to the use of Bracketing.

The basis of good Bracketing follows the Goldilocks model of Not Too Big, Not Too Little: provide your source with a realistic range of numbers. Realistic in terms of both width and narrowness. Now, doesn't that seem confusing? It's really not.

When setting up the bracket for the Cable Guy in the box entitled *The Cable Guy—Part 2*, you see that the range of the *initial* bracket is between $5 and $35 per month. You've decided beforehand, with an arbitrariness born of experience, that the number has to be somewhere in this realistically broad range. You've thought about this for a nanosecond before the conversation takes place. You already know that no cable company is going to go to the trouble of working the approving authority for a rate increase of $2 a month, just as you know it's not going to be $50 per month, yet it probably isn't going to be $35 either. But $35 *seems* realistic for somebody who is not necessarily in their industry. So the acceptable range starts at a floor of $5 and tops out at $35.

The Cable Guy—Part 2

E : So, this new programming is going to be a good deal for everybody, including us. We'll probably be seeing a nice rate hike for all these lovely new programs.

S : Well, we've got to pass along the cost of program content to the customer.

E : Sure, program content costs like between five bucks and thirty-five bucks.

S : More on the lower end, I'd think.

E : Lower end like $15.

S : Well, closer to ten or eleven.

E : So, if it's ten or eleven, you'll pick up the difference for the increase in my cable service.

S : Actually, probably more like $13 or $13.50.

At the same time, you don't want the range to be too narrow, because it really limits your options. Think about how much essentially nonthreatening conversation you can have if you guesstimate the range between $5 and $7. Two scenarios develop: Either you're awfully far off and the source won't feel any reason whatever to get you closer to the correct price, or you're right on target. Dead on, in fact. So dead that the source immediately gets hyperdefensive and turns off the information flow valve right away. Better to be wide ranging at the initial bracket, because if the number is acknowledged as being inside that realistic range, your next step is the *interim* bracket.

In the case with our friend the Cable Guy, he can still feel somewhat comfortable with the openness of the range, yet he's not going to give anything up right away. You wouldn't expect him to, would you? If this was easy, you wouldn't be reading this book, would you?

So, he says, "Probably on the lower end of that." He's already accepted the floor of $5, so our task is to find what that "lower end" means. But instead of making the lower end $7, which would be on the lower end, we need more commitment, more investment from him. So, almost as if a challenge, we respond with the $15 figure—challenging inasmuch as that's really closer to the middle than to the lower end. That's when he responds with the $10 or $11 range. You see, he's still comfortable with the concept of bracketing and is agreeing to the narrowing. But is there anything else we can do to get a better sight picture on this target number?

Here's where a little more prior planning, broader knowledge, and a bit of hallucination come into play. Up front, one of the things we determine from this fellow is some personalia data, to include his electrical engineering undergraduate degree. What do we know as a general rule about engineers? That they like precision is one of those generalities I'd like to test for a moment. That might help us get some focus on the actual numbers. What else do we know? We know, for example, that many engineers are living proof that 7-Eleven stores have men's clothing departments; places where hundreds of thousands of baby polyesters give their lives each in the interest of long-lasting, quality, *and inexpensive* clothes. Maybe he's like other economy-minded and stylish engineers. Maybe he'll respond even more precisely if we appear to be getting into *his* pocket.

Thus, when he says "Maybe $10 to $11," we give him an opportunity for personal growth and involvement in the transaction. If it'll be more than ten or eleven, then he'll pick up the difference? His economical side kicks in. He doesn't want to have to come up with anything out of his pocket, that's for certain. That's when you know he's sincere—when you can get a personally based piece of commitment.

Now, how do we use this in other pursuits besides finding out about price increases? Again, in virtually any area or dimension that can be quantified: new product rollout dates, compensation ranges, production rates, personnel turnover, rejection rates. The lot.

For those of you with any kind of a background in sighting weapons—whether rifles or artillery pieces—you'll recognize the Bracketing technique in the shorthand: Fire Long, Fire Short, Fire for Effect. No matter what your background or interest, you can see that Bracketing will get you closer to the numbers than you might have ever thought possible.

5. FEIGNED OR REAL DISBELIEF

What do you know about your source? Is she someone of high personal and professional standards and integrity? How does she react when her veracity is being challenged, if even the least little bit? Defensively? Sure. And in that defense, she wants to make certain that there's absolutely no doubt that what she said before is true. The best way to show that is by giving a sufficient amount of background data and detail. Data and detail that you're after in the first place.

Of course, that's just for starters. Nearly everyone has a desire to be believed, regardless of whether or not they have high standards. In fact, it's an old interrogator's trick to accuse someone of something they haven't done, knowing that in proving that they didn't do one thing, they implicate themselves in the matter that's really under investigation.

But you can't just walk up to someone and directly challenge them with your disbelief about a topic or issue. Again, you've planned what you want to get from the source. You've planned which steps you want to pass over in the unimportant phases in order to increase the level of comfort as you near the topics you're after in the first place. The time for disbelief is well into the conversation, once you've established that elusive condition we refer to as rapport. Which is another, entire book in itself.

One of the great things about Feigned Disbelief is that it can be embodied in a Provocative Statement. It can be used as a follow-on as your disbelief mounts along certain, preplanned lines; it can certainly be tied to an emotional investment in the topic should you think that's appropriate.

Let's say you've been engaged in a conversation for a few minutes. You've gotten to the point that we call the Headhunter Two-Step—a part of a conversation with an executive recruiter. As you reflect on what you read about next, you'll no doubt come to the conclusion on your own that there are probably hundreds of others for whom this two-step gambit could be named.

In this example, we've gone from a general conversation about changes in the recruiting industry to a particular placement the headhunter had been involved in a few months previously. We were in the middle of doing one of our remote psychological profiles of an executive who had taken the helm at our client's competitor. The executive was new to the industry, few people knew anything about him, and the people in his previous firm had a strict policy against saying anything about previous employees.

The Headhunter Two-Step

E: Speaking of winners and losers in your business, I just couldn't believe that Hogbreath International let Jones get recruited away by ASA Ice Crystals.

S: Do you mean *Johnny* Jones?

E: Yeah, the guy who was Hogbreath's director of R and D for about ten years. I was reading the other day how the market seems to think he's going to have a real impact on their new technology directions. It seems impossible to think that a techie like that could be the key to turning a company's whole future around, but if he could, I'd think that some shareholders would be hacked off that the people at Hogbreath let him get away.

S: What do you mean?

E: Well, if he'd been that important to ASA, he should've been that much of a key to Hogbreath, and now Hogbreath might not have the edge it did in the past. If I'd been a shareholder, I wouldn't believe that the leadership was doing its job.

S: Well, of course there was a lot more to it than that.

E: Oh, sure, he was probably taking money out of petty cash to pay for pocket protectors.

S: It was a lot more than that.

E: You can't tell me that anybody with that kind of background and essential "geekiness" has ever done anything any more serious than that.

S: I can only tell you that there are some things that are stranger than fiction. Their board just didn't quite see eye to eye with some of his after-hours activities, shall we say.

E: Oh, no, you mean that he got caught wearing something other than black socks with his dress shoes and shorts?

S: Try some home movies that he was making with some summer intern-program kids.

E: Well, if that's true, he'd be in jail somewhere.

S: Not if the events happened at the company and they thought that they'd get embarrassed *and* get sued for allowing it to happen on their time and property.

The source in this instance was a headhunter who had provided the replacement for our current subject. We contacted the recruiter after reading a short blurb that his firm had brought our subject's replacement to his previous company.

What are some of the principles that underlie this approach?

Since the subject of our inquiry was working for someone else altogether now, since this recruiter had nothing to do with the placement at our client's competitor, and since this recruiter had no investment in the executive, the tendency to share information that was not of direct concern to him certainly was one we thought might come into play.

Another was the possibility that we could capitalize on the tendency of some professionals to share information with each other—in this case, that he had learned about our subject's tenure as he had prepared to fill the vacancy.

And a final piece has to do with the behaviors of some people who know a secret, or at least a part of one.

6. PURPOSELY ERRONEOUS STATEMENT

This is another tool that demands the suspension of your ego in order to get the information you need and want. You'll capitalize on characteristics we've already seen: a desire to correct someone, a desire to teach someone, a desire for detail, precision, or closure. Add in the way that some people react to the Feigned Disbelief you just learned more about in the preceding section.

But for some of you, who are still not quite certain that you can suspend your ego long enough or well enough to use Naïveté or to make a Purposely Erroneous Statement, all is not lost. The "my friend John" variant related in the next box is especially useful for you, although others can use it as well.

The Purposely Erroneous Statement allows you to get to many of the hardest pieces of the puzzle without having to attack frontally. Tales about the uses of this technique are absolutely legion in our collection experience.

E: A factory like that couldn't possibly make more than five hundred units a week.

S: Oh, yeah, what if I were to tell you that we've got all new machinery and in the next two months, we'll be at 1,135 units a week?

E: You guys'll be lucky if you hit anywhere near what Doomafleegit Company is going to bid. I've heard that your personnel costs are just eating your lunch and besides you've got those new buildings to pay for yet.

S: Shows how little you really do know. I've seen the advance numbers and they're going to blow your socks off. We've even built a separate cost center to chase this line of business, and our rates are going to be the lowest of any ten companies. And, we got those buildings at a fire sale. That floor space is half what we're paying at the main building and we may even move more people into the new places.

My Friend John

The "my friend John" variant came to prominence under the late great psychotherapist Milton Erickson. While he used it for different purposes and in a different time, the concept is a useful one for the elicitor to keep in mind. For Erickson, my friend John meant ascribing something to someone else altogether—some experience, some frailty, some misunderstanding, some foolish characteristic.

It allowed him as the psychotherapist to remove himself from active involvement in the matter at hand, to maintain a professional reserve as it were, in the interest of getting one of his more resistant clients to open up to him. Erickson's friend John was never a threat to the client, was never present at any meeting, would never be allowed to have anything to do with the client in any way. A completely detached persona.

You as an elicitor can find the same people—either real or imagined. Personally I like to refer to real people because it gives me a far better feel for the story that pertains to "my friend." Of course, changing the names to protect the innocent is mandatory.

And in the case that we spoke about with using the Quid pro Quo without much ammunition or real knowledge, this variant also allows you the latitude to say quite earnestly that you really don't know the ins and outs of it, since it was your friend who had the experience, not you yourself.

Now that you've been exposed to an even dozen techniques, and you've gotten about as much background commentary, examples, and mechanical process as you need, it's really time for you to take a practice session in earnest. If you did one at the end of chapter 6, all the better, since you'll have developed a considerable amount of confidence already. The kinds of things you'll set out to obtain from those you'll meet during an evening session will be somewhat more than what you tried to get at lunchtime.

Perhaps you'll be well prepared and you won't suffer the fate of the young FBI foreign counterintelligence officer who thought he'd go out on the problem alone, in the Georgetown section of Washington, D.C. Thinking that he was quite suave and accomplished, he didn't spend much time figuring out what he would say or do if the tables got turned on him. And so it was a somewhat dejected, but brutally honest, special agent who returned for the next morning's debriefing and told about the striking blonde who was seated at the bar. She had a delightful accent and wonderful personality. Things were going along swimmingly, and she'd told him all about having just been in the United States for four months from Russia when she asked him what he did for a living. This was at just about the same time that a fellow with a bad suit—and no neck—sat down on the other side of the young woman. She introduced him to the agent as her friend Ivan who was her boss and mentor as well, and then asked the question again: "Where do you work, Tom?" You may have some idea of how much of a lesson he learned about preparing himself to answer questions that may come up from a target.

Or, perhaps, you'll be bold and supremely confident. As bold and confident as a few military intelligence officers were in another class. They decided that they would really put their money where their mouths were, so to speak. They purposely went to a biker bar where they knew that falling back on their old direct-questioning habits would become problematic *pronto*. That they not only escaped with their lives but came back with the sought-after information as well as free beers is testimony to something. I'm not sure what that was. Perhaps just excessive confidence. Perhaps something else.

And what was it they were all after? Almost the same things we spoke about in chapter 2: name, age, marital status, number of siblings, number of children, birth place and other origins information, educational level and area of concentration, present employment, greatest likes and dislikes about their jobs, salary or other compensation, current bank, the account number of the bank they used or credit-card numbers—and they'd get a gold star for a PIN number. Again, not for the purpose of misusing the information, but just for the confidence that comes from getting such seemingly private and typically hard-to-get information.

To paraphrase the software company's advertising slogan: What do you want to get today?

Again, if you're out there practicing, you're having interesting experiences. I really would like to hear about them if you've got a moment.

Part II

Business Intelligence Collection

*As business begins to compete on a global scale, corporations, like
national governments, are going to need intelligence systems. Those who
use the product of intelligence will be better prepared to decide and act.*

—Bob Galvin, chairman, Motorola

The preceding chapters have focused on the ways intelligence professionals use their interpersonal skills to obtain information from
primary, or human, sources—the people who know what you
need to know in order to prevail in the marketplace.

To this point, that's all it's been. Tools and techniques without a context. And we already know that for the intelligence professional, nothing
exists without context. Without a focus and purpose, the skills presented
in part I become little more than advanced party skills, some possibly useful in a business setting to be sure. Part II introduces the first part of the
Business Intelligence Process, and subsequent chapters provide the pieces
of the action plan for using it.

The Elements of the Business Intelligence Process	
Competitive intelligence focuses on:	*Competitive counterintelligence focuses on:*
Competitor intelligence	Competitive intelligence collectors
Customer intelligence	Industrial espionage
Technical intelligence	Economic espionage
Legislative/regulatory intelligence	Assorted "ne'er-do-wells"

The Business Intelligence Process is actually a bipolar creature that is
relatively new in the marketplace. It's a process that operates on two distinct levels and with two distinct purposes within one corporate body; a
process that had gone through development and refinement that spans
the centuries and continents; a process whose two parts are called intelligence collection and intelligence protection, or counterintelligence,
which we define as:

- *Competitive Intelligence*—the organized, professional approach to
the collection, analysis, and distribution of timely, accurate, and

useful information as intelligence products—intelligence that contributes materially to the achievement of strategic and tactical business objectives, as defined by the leadership of an enterprise.

- *Competitive Counterintelligence*—active measures—sometimes taken in conjunction with federal agencies–undertaken to identify and neutralize the intelligence collection activities of a business rival.

Once we've developed the elements of the collection side of the equation in part II, part III will focus primarily on the protection of your own information. For the time being, however, let's just agree that the protection of the relationship with sources who provide you with information is important; that the final result of your intelligence collection—the assessment or report—is also important; and that the protection of your firm's operating information is important enough to warrant the most careful measures. This is a natural follow-on, both in the history of intelligence and in recent practice. Perhaps it's best summed up by the frequent, and consistent, responses of corporate leaders who have asked our firm to get the information they need to know about their competition. Once they have the reports in hand and contrast them to what little they had actually known about before, their next immediate question is invariably, "If we can get this about our competition, what's to keep them from getting the same kind of things about us?"

The answers to that question will be in part III. In order to understand those answers, part II will provide the operational framework. And that's where you'll find some differences between this book and others in the competitive intelligence field.

Some books focus on competitive analysis; some focus on building a competitive intelligence infrastructure; some focus largely on listing the different kinds of sources that can provide you competitively valuable information, although most tend to focus on secondary sources of information; and some are very good at giving exemplars of tasking requests, reporting formats, validation instruments, and the like. Virtually all of them are good at serving these needs, which are absolutely necessary to a professional approach to Business Intelligence.

Our purpose is not to replace or replicate any of those efforts. Instead, we've focused on those sources and methods that are not reported or suggested elsewhere in the literature—and to help you find them and capitalize on your newly acquired skills as an elicitor. We've focused on the operational aspects of source identification, utilization, and protection.

CHAPTER 8

Intelligence for Decision Makers

Now the reason the enlightened prince and the wise general conquer the enemy when ever they move, and their accomplishments surpass those of ordinary men, is foreknowledge.

—Sun-tzu, *The Art of War*, XIII:3

Today's business world is rapidly adopting the emerging business practice that is called competitive intelligence. Competitive intelligence has been described in a very limited way as a means of gathering information about a competitor, analyzing it, and using it to gain an advantage over that competitor. That misses the mark by a considerable margin. Indeed, when the focus is on the competitor alone, it is really a subset that would be better called competit*or* intelligence.

Competitive intelligence differs substantially from its illegal, immoral, unethical, and otherwise fattening twin cousins, industrial espionage and economic espionage—both of whom we will encounter again in part III. Further, competitive intelligence differs from market research in that it relates to the entire competitive spectrum and not just to a map of the territory—that is, not just to a description of customer buying habits, trends, or opportunities. Finally, competitive intelligence operates as a cyclical process that allows the forward-thinking business leader to ask disciplined questions, to receive disciplined, processed, timely, and reliable answers in order to avoid surprise in the marketplace, and to prevail.

When we expand the view of truly competitive intelligence, we find that it is not just information about a competitor or set of competitors. Instead, by using the same basic practices and principles, it extends out to cover the competitive universe, one that includes many other actors and factors, such as:

- Examining customers, their leaders, and decision makers and making use of the collected information in pricing, delivery, product development, procurement decisions, and the development of business strategies and tactics.

- Examining merger and acquisition candidates, joint-venture partners, and team partners for competitions that range from product development to defense and aerospace industry procurement actions.
- Examining the various factors in the regulatory environment and being able to anticipate changes that may profoundly impact an enterprise or an industry.
- Examining emerging technologies and their potential impact on the competitive environment—and on your firm's ability to survive and prevail.

INTELLIGENCE PRACTICES ON THE NATIONAL LEVEL

Essentially, Business Intelligence operations cover the same broad spectrum that national intelligence services examine every day in the interest of national survival: political, military, economic, technological. The kind of spectrum that includes not only today's enemies but, in many cases, today's friends as well.

Perhaps the most pragmatic statement about business-related intelligence comes from France, where Pierre Marion, the former head of the DGSE,* echoes the earlier sentiments of Charles de Gaulle. Whereas de Gaulle said, "France has no allies; France has only interests," Marion's formulation about of the conduct of intelligence operations is:

> *I think that even during the Cold War getting intelligence on economic, technological, and industrial matters from a country with which you are allies is not incompatible with the fact that you are allies.*

In the wake of the uproar against the DGSE's *Service 7* for its wholesale penetration of Texas Instruments in 1992, Marion was also quoted as saying:

> *This espionage activity is an essential way for France to keep abreast of international commerce and technology. Of course it was directed*

---

*Department Générale Sécurité Extérieure, the French version of the American Central Intelligence Agency.

against the United States as well as others. You must remember that while we are allies in defense matters, we are also economic competitors in the world.

And his predecessor, Count Henri de Marenches, who served from 1970 to 1981, wrote in his autobiography, *Dans les Secrets des Princes* (1986):

Spying in the proper sense is becoming increasingly focused on business and the economy, science and industry—and very profitable it is. It enables intelligence services to discover a process useful in another country, which might have taken years and possibly millions of francs to perfect or invent. This form of espionage prevails not only with the enemy, but among friends it must be said.

We'll even pay a little professional homage to M. Marion by using one of his titles prior to ascending to the head of that service. You see, while serving as an Air France senior executive in Atlanta for several years, he was a willing and agreeable "Honorary Correspondent" for French intelligence. Throughout the remainder of this book, we'll use the terms "internal sources" and "correspondents" interchangeably; after all, there's little sense in reinventing wheels or vocabulary in this business.

And from the other side of the globe, a spokesman for the Japanese Ministry of Trade and Industry (MITI) commented as far back as 1985:

Japan was defeated in World War II partly due to the superior intelligence network and strategy developed by the American government. Why can't American businessmen develop the same kind of superior intelligence and strategy to cope with Japan today and be victorious? Most Japanese don't understand why American businessmen cannot win this war.

Indeed, one of the reasons that the Japanese businessman *cum* warrior cannot fathom American reluctance to use this most established of all warfare principles is that the Japanese find it so profitable. In fact, Japanese government and industry have approached the collection and analysis of competitive information in such an encompassing and organized way precisely because business competition is viewed as warfare in the finest, traditional sense: cooperating fully for the national interest against foreign interests.

In subsequent chapters, we'll discuss the ways that competitive intelligence is conducted in Japan, France, and other countries. Ways in which the national intelligence agencies in some countries directly support national business interests. For the present, however, this is simply background to the larger picture of the use of the intelligence process by American business.

THE AMERICAN INTELLIGENCE COMMUNITY AND U.S. BUSINESS

American business has shown pretty consistently that it neither wants nor needs the active intervention of the federal intelligence community to collect, analyze, or disseminate information of potential competitive value. The reasons are as many and varied as there are business ventures, yet a few are worthy of direct mention as part of this background.

At the 100,000-foot level, there's Senator Daniel Patrick Moynihan (D-NY), who, as a member of the Senate Intelligence Committee that was considering the Clinton administration's push to assign such activities to the Central Intelligence Agency, asked:

> For a quarter of a century, the CIA has repeatedly been wrong about the major political and economic questions entrusted to its analysis. Why would anybody fight to get their analysis?

At the other end of the spectrum are the intelligence grunts, the Clandestine Services case officers who have to put themselves in the right place with the right people at the right time—and often at considerable personal risk. Having spent most of my professional life at that level, I certainly share the views of those officers who told then-director of Central Intelligence Robert Gates that they would have no compunction about spying and/or dying for the United States, but that there was no way that they'd do it for General Motors.

In between are those businesspeople who have testified openly and directly that they would rather not have the CIA as a potential albatross around their necks while plying their trades internationally. They've learned from sad experience that the man from the government is never really and truly there to help; they inevitably believe that there will always be certain unwanted strings attached, whether that belief is accurate or not; and, that if evidence is ever uncovered that an intelligence operation is being conducted on behalf of *a* company by The Company, woe to the company's chances of gaining popular product acceptance. After all those years of companies being accused by left-wing terrorists of being merely front covers for the CIA, wouldn't it be ironic for an agency officer to be actually caught spying on behalf of a company? On an even more practical level, while a country can certainly handle a couple of intelligence officers getting PNG'd (declared persona non grata) out of the host country, no company can stand that kind of pain very long. And the only guarantee is that the company's fortunes will do even more tailspinning in other countries in the region as well.

Essentially, the answer for American business is that if you want to use the intelligence process to ensure your continued competitiveness, you're far better off developing your own competency. Either build an internal intelligence function or organization or rely on one of the consultancies that have emerged to satisfy those needs.

SOCIETY OF COMPETITIVE INTELLIGENCE PROFESSIONALS

An indicator of how American business has responded to the need for a better and more rigorous understanding of their environment is the growth of the Society of Competitive Intelligence Professionals (SCIP). Founded in Washington, D.C., in 1986, it has grown to nearly seven thousand active professional members by the end of 1998, the greatest majority of whom reside and work in the United States. Although Washington, D.C. is the center of government and the headquarters of much of the federal intelligence community, SCIP's founding population—and the majority of its members even a decade later—did not come from the intelligence community. Instead, they came from the commercial sector, and the SCIP drew its initial membership from librarians and MBAs, not from the federal sector. Gradually, over time, more and more business-oriented, former intelligence officers entered the SCIP population; these were intelligence professionals from both the analytical side as well as the operations side of the services, bringing with them a somewhat different orientation. To a large extent, the influx of former national intelligence officers has contributed positively to business intelligence efforts, whether the individual had his or her origins in the U.S., French, German, British, Soviet, or other national intelligence services.

By and large, SCIP's membership abides by the Code of Ethics (see box), which may seem at first blush to be somewhat Pollyanna-ish to those who think that intelligence officers are little more than midnight skulkers and lurkers in trench coats and bad suits. Always identifying yourself by real name and company before talking with anybody? Always abiding by the law? Come on, who're you kidding? Wouldn't James Bond be mortified?

Code of Ethics

Society of Competitive Intelligence Professionals

- To continually strive to increase respect and recognition for the profession on local, state, and national levels.
- To pursue his or her duties with zeal and diligence while maintaining the highest degree of professionalism and avoiding all unethical practices.
- To faithfully adhere to and abide by his or her company's or client company's policies, objectives, and guidelines.
- To comply with all applicable laws.
- To accurately disclose all relevant information, including the identity of the professional and his or her organization, prior to all interviews.
- To fully respect all requests for confidentiality.
- To promote and encourage full compliance with these ethical standards within his or her company, with third party contractors, and within the entire profession.

Indeed, there will always be those outside the mainstream who will "Do whatever it takes." Yet it's our experience that the information a decision maker needs is almost always available to the quick, to the imaginative, to the dedicated professional without having to break any laws or be surreptitious about it. Remember the statistic from the introduction to part I about the willingness of people to be interviewed? The greatest majority of the people we attempt to interview agree to those interviews; and when we encounter the ones who won't cooperate, the remainder are still waiting for their fifteen minutes of fame and importance.

The SCIP population is as diverse as the worldwide industrial and commercial business base. With twenty-nine organized chapters in the United States and another fifteen in other countries, SCIP is one of the fastest growing professional societies in the world. Estimates of expenditures in the range of $11 billion for competitive intelligence by American firms alone in 1997 provide another metric of the growth of this business practice, which has clearly outlasted the management fads of recent decades. The table on this page, which breaks down the SCIP population by industries from 1994 to 1997, shows both its recent growth and how widely competitive intelligence has been accepted.* Further, the growth in various industries—such as telecommunications and utilities—is a reflection of the environmental factors such as deregulation that drive the changing nature of competition today.

SCIP Membership by Industry 1994–1997				
Industry	1994	1995	1996	1997
Banking and finance	71	117	149	220
Petroleum/Energy	30	73	93	115
Chemical/Pharmaceuticals	221	291	401	525
Transportation/Automotive	54	61	95	131
Communications/Telecommunications	194	384	410	524
Computer/Computer services	105	205	206	256
Insurance	52	110	115	145
Food manufacturing	41	139	79	93
Consulting	236	328	435	585
Defense/Aerospace	85	194	165	189
Educational services	28	58	53	79
Industrial products	99	146	158	204
Information	129	210	273	357
Health care	64	120	164	182
Public utilities	0	75	171	198
Other	288	391	704	1399
TOTAL	2422	3330	3664	5229

---

* SCIP had grown in mid-1998 to nearly 6,700 members, although the industry breakdown is not yet available.

As we've seen, at its inception the bulk of SCIP's practitioners were drawn from the side of the business that emphasized secondary-source research. It was clean and noncontroversial, it clearly focused on open sources of public information, and it was well within the scope of most companies to employ. Many of the original members of the community were drawn from the ranks of market research and library operations, and so a focus on secondary-source exploitation was a natural result of these backgrounds and orientations. A number of on-line companies grew rapidly as subscription services, somewhat in advance of the Internet—several of which remain as important secondary sources of competitive information.

Gradually, over time, as competitive intelligence grew in acceptance as an effective, legitimate, and valuable business practice, it expanded from the exploitation of largely secondary sources into a discipline that more closely mirrored the national intelligence services models: not only availing business leadership of secondary, open-source reporting, but also extending to the use of primary sources. Humans. People in the know.

Remember from the introduction to part II that the typical national intelligence model included both intelligence collection as well as counterintelligence. As you now know, the commercial version of a complete intelligence function is what we term Business Intelligence, which consists of both competitive intelligence and competitive counterintelligence.

As we now turn specifically to competitive intelligence, you'll see how information can be gathered using an operational framework. An operational framework that begins with the section on elicitation techniques that you've just completed. An operational framework that now moves on to actual collection operations.

CHAPTER 9

Operational Business Intelligence— Actually Doing It

It is pardonable to be defeated, but never to be surprised.

—Frederick the Great

For a profession that is often called the world's second oldest, you'd think there would be some rhyme or reason to it. The good news is that indeed we haven't been asleep at the switch, lo these many years, and there's actually been some progress made.

Some kind of organized way of going about this collection and use of information has been developed. Some kind of rigor has been attached to the ways that it gets from one form of raw data into the finished product that we call intelligence. Intelligence that gets to the decision maker in a timely and accurate way. Something that is called, perhaps not advisedly in some cases, *actionable* intelligence. *Actionable,* when used by Business Intelligence professionals, means that it gets there at the right time, in the right way, with useful conclusions. *Actionable,* when used by lawyers, means billable hours because somebody has done something wrong. Something wrong enough to warrant the attention of the courts. Something bad.

What we're going to be talking about from here on out is "good" actionable as opposed to "bad" actionable. A lot like good cholesterol and bad cholesterol. And we're going to be talking about it as an actual process. That will make some readers who like to have things packaged up nicely and coherently very happy.

In my experience, if I ever fail to start off a presentation to a company or any other kind of group about how we do Business Intelligence— especially if the audience is made up of engineers, architects, scientists, technical types—without presenting the process first, I get into trouble quickly. Rather than getting into trouble with you, that's where we'll begin.

THE INTELLIGENCE CYCLE

Most national intelligence services recognize and portray the process of intelligence as a cycle. There are those who would like to portray the intelligence process in a linear way. That's their choice. Rather than reinventing the wheel, so to speak, I'll stick with the cycle. And I hope that you will too.

At Phoenix Consulting Group, we apply an approach to information collection, analysis, and reporting that is captured in the accompanying graphic. An approach that we call the Business Intelligence Collection Model.

You may find that the Business Intelligence Collection Model is best understood when described as discrete elements:

- *Tasking:* When viewed clockwise from the top, you'll start with— and depend upon—specific *tasking* from your firm's leadership as to the specific information that is of particular concern to the decision maker. It will be your job at that point to break those larger questions, issues, and tasks down into manageable subelements, subtasks, direct questions that need to be answered, and indicators that will ultimately provide the useful insights you need.

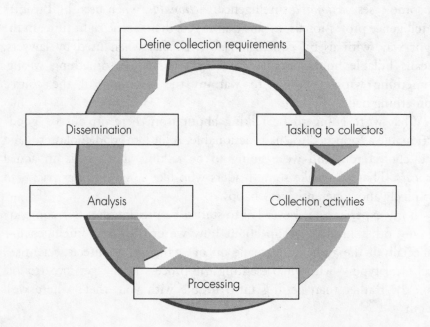

- *Collection Objectives:* Once you've received that tasking in a refined form that you and the leadership agree on, it's then refined further into its very specific items. It's not unusual, for example, for a single question to come from senior leadership, to be broken down into major elements and what would constitute a completed effort in the opinion of the decision maker, and then to be broken down into thirty or forty more very specific questions. These specific questions then become quite manageable, especially when they are matched to the available collection resources. It's at this point that you'll also do your operational needs assessment as the collection planning process gets under way: plans for the time and financial budgets, additional collection resources, milestones, delivery forms and formats, et cetera.

- *Collection Activities:* At this point, you'll be concentrating initially on actually exploiting sources, particularly secondary sources, not so much to obtain current and reliable information but rather to develop background data. That published data may exist inside the company or outside, as we'll go into in some detail in chapter 10. Further, and more importantly from an operational point of view at this point in the cycle, you'll identify, contact, and employ those primary human sources who have the most up-to-date, and often most reliable, information when collected by trained researchers.

- *Process and Report the Raw Information:* Throughout the collection process, information is flowing from the collectors to those responsible for collection management and analysis. Certainly, by the previously agreed-upon information cutoff date, active collection and processing is concluded, although provisions are made for later reporting of information that may not have been rigorously analyzed. Processing may be through any one of a number of channels, depending on whether they involve active debriefing of sources or electronic or other written reporting by sources. Processing includes the management and initial validation of the sources and their information. It also includes the storage of that information, an especially important issue in an era of data warehousing, data mining, and knowledge management across enterprises large and small.

- *Analysis:* Upon completion of the collection activities according to the planning schedule, you'll subject the information to rigorous analysis and comparison with other developed information, particularly as it relates to established assumptions. However, it's a deadly mistake to seek consistency with established assumptions; trying to achieve an outcome a predetermined answer significantly undermines the integrity of the project and inevitably causes you to lose credibility. Arguably it should cost you your job.

- *Reporting and Dissemination:* At this point, you'll be reporting the results of the collection activities and analysis. Typically, it's reduced to a formal report presentation, in both a written as well as an oral format, since experience tells us that there will always be questions that simply can't be anticipated and answered in a written document. From a purely political standpoint, it's also highly useful for the one who managed the collection effort to be there for the follow-on tasking that almost inevitably occurs as iterative tasking.

It's also well to cover a few other important points that are floating around in the background to the Business Intelligence Collection Model. They're not usually found in cyclical representations of the intelligence process, but they are nonetheless the hallmark of an effective program, since most management people in the private sector demand:

- *Iterative Tasking:* Quite often, the results of the project raise additional issues for consideration that were not initially of concern. These results drive additional tasking requirements being levied on either internal or external resources for coverage, collection, and analysis.

- *Interim Reporting and Initial Analysis:* As the collection activity continues, the information is checked and measured against known or postulated data with regular analysis of the accuracy of the information's validity. At specified intervals, collection managers present a review of the objectives and interim findings to the leadership, with refinements of the objectives occurring as necessary and in light of findings.

- *Planning and Budgets:* Perhaps it's a function of the tendency that modern societies have to promote instant gratification; perhaps it's the reason that CNN and McNewspapers are so popular; perhaps it's just plain old impatience. Whatever the reason, our experience tells us that in nine out of ten first-use cases, the tasking leadership thinks that the information should be immediately available. It's these people who learn very quickly about the first rule of consulting: The client can have it fast, cheap, or good—but they only get to choose two of the three. If they want it fast and cheap, it won't be good; if they want it fast and good, it won't be cheap. And that's not just the case with outside consultants either; it goes for those internal intelligence consultants as well—and after all, that's the real role that most corporate intelligence professionals play anyway. That of a trusted adviser, confidant, consultant. It's simply not possible to emphasize strongly enough that there has to be time set aside to plan the collection project and to build in the requisite time for production and analysis. Neither is it possible to overemphasize the need to have established time and dollar budgets up front, particularly for the in-house intelligence professional, since it almost goes without saying that few external providers get to operate with a blank check.

- *Realism:* Sometimes, intelligence professionals get caught up in their own sense of what can be gotten and what should be acknowledged as impossible.

  Please understand that while we'll be talking about the great amounts of information that can be turned into quality intelligence about the marketplace, there are still going to be a number of limits. And it shouldn't take Dirty Harry to tell you that a man's gotta know his limitations. Often, a leader will unwittingly ask for certain kinds of information, and only the intelligence professional knows that it can't be gotten legally. It's her job to tell the boss that she won't do it. In those cases where the leader wants the information "no matter what," it's time to start looking for another line of work—or at least another company. The most that can be done in this kind of situation is to talk about the pros and cons. Without intending any pun, either. It might be helpful to glance at the box *You Can't Get There from Here.*

You Can't Get There from Here

Long ago and far away in another life, I was commiserating with a colleague while sitting in a lounge in a Third World country where we were both working for a season. His specialty was training helicopter pilots for that country's military. He was crying in his beer over the loss earlier that week of his single most promising student ever. In fact, the young pilot had been so good that he'd been recently selected as the personal pilot for one of the country's senior army generals.

My colleague had just come from the crash investigation review. It turned out that the aircraft was in perfect operating condition except for one small factor. It had crashed out in a desert with a completely empty gas tank. The explanation had come from the ground-crew member who'd been present when the pilot had been told by his general to fly him to another location many miles away. Even though the pilot knew that the range of the aircraft was only 60 percent of the distance, his culture did not allow for him to tell the general "No."

Does your corporate culture allow you the opportunity to Just Say No?

The flip side is guaranteeing that you'll get the information that the boss says he wants. The only time any intelligence officer worth his salt offers a guarantee to obtain a certain kind of information is if he's already got it. While that may work in the case of an in-house officer, it becomes more problematic for consultants to offer guarantees. Usually, the only time professionals can do that is if they've already done the selfsame project for another client and they'll only be repackaging it for you at an exceptionally high margin for themselves. Not that it's legally wrong to do that, and maybe not even ethically improper according to some people's lights. It just seems to me that someone goes over the line of professional conduct when they merely repackage a product that someone has already paid for as a one-time. Secondhand goods sold as original and custom work. That sort of thing.

- *Paradoxes of Intelligence and Operations:* Perhaps the greatest, most frequent use of the intelligence product is surprise avoidance, the Art of Anticipation if you will—allowing the decision maker the greatest amount of time before an event occurs, and thus maximizing his range of options, his flexible responses. Yet, this bangs head-on against certainty. If you're waiting for 100 percent accuracy about a competitor's new product—what it is, what it will do, what the price point will be, what the distribution channel looks like, who the target market is—the only time you'll have that complete, and completely accurate, information is once the product has actually been launched. Your leadership has significantly reduced potential responses. Thus the paradox: The greater the reliability of the intelligence, the fewer options you have. So, the question becomes, what's the mix at the decision point? Is your leader comfortable with making a decision at the six-month point before an event with 60 percent of the necessary information which is 75 percent reliable, or does he wait until he has 90 percent of the information, with a 95 percent reliability, ten days before the event—when the time he needs to actually respond to the event is measured in months? Is good intelligence, therefore, going to be the be-all and end-all for business leaders? If your leadership needs to have 100 percent of the necessary information with 100 percent accuracy, he doesn't need an intelligence professional. He needs a historian, because that's what that information is—history. If your leadership can make tough decisions with 40 percent of the information and 50 percent confidence in its accuracy, that's why he gets paid the big bucks—to make those plans, to make those decisions while he has the greatest latitude. And, of course, not to stop the information flow just because a decision has been made. Colin Powell's admonition plays well here: "No strategic plan survives initial contact with the enemy." Whether a military operation or a quick strike against a business rival, the principle remains the same. There's no such thing as a static battlefield; there's no such thing as a static marketplace.

Before we get too much further along, let's also talk for a moment about tasking and uses: that is, the levels at which intelligence is used and is useful.

To some organizations and practitioners, the only place where Business Intelligence is useful—and where it should be housed—is at the corporate level where strategy is formulated. That's absolutely true if the nature of the project is the same as it was for the Eisenhower example used in the introduction. But those are not the only kinds of projects. In fact, if you follow the Eisenhower model to its logical conclusion, you'll find that intelligence in support of military operations goes all the way to the company and even pla-toon level—where the troops are actually being shot at in anger.

Intelligence has a different focus, a different urgency, and a different means of validation, analysis, and communication at the tactical level. Just as the rifleman has virtually no concern with grand strategic designs when he's con-cerned with the fellow who's pointing a weapon at him from across an open field, intelligence consumers in the business unit would have completely dif-ferent interests from the people on Mahogany Row. The infantry company commander needs to know the size, weapons, morale, supporting forces, and equipment of the opposing forces because the lives of two hundred people are at risk. Similarly, the product manager is less concerned with the company's strategic direction and potential acquisitions than he is with a competitor's new launch date, the price point they're trying to hit, or the market segment his rival is seeking to dominate. So it goes, and unlike most analogies that break down at a "laugh point" somewhere, this one really doesn't.

Eisenhower the captain had a completely different intelligence need at the company commander level than he did as Major Eisenhower working on the division staff; General Eisenhower had a completely different need for intelli-gence than *President* Eisenhower did in his later career. The corporate coun-terpart example is yours for the interpretation and application to your own situation. To help you consider that, glance at the different levels and their respective focus for intelligence requirements in the chart that follows.

SAMPLE INTELLIGENCE REQUIREMENTS by CONSUMER LOCATION

	Business Unit	Group or Sector	Corporate
Regional			
Domestic			
Continental			
International			
	• Products • Direct competitors • Pricing • Sales • Services • Customers • Vendors	• Technology sharing • Interbusiness unit concerns • Common customers	• World-wide technology trends • Long-term domain selection • Business unit resource allocations • M&A activities • Strategic relationships • Regulatory environment

The bottom line remains the same for a business company or a rifle company, for a business division or an armored division. Different intelligence needs have to be satisfied at differing levels. An important corollary is that the lower you go in the organization, the less time you have for planning, collection, analysis, and action. And, the lives—or the products—are not abstractions at the lower levels as they might be at the strategic.

In fact, there is a significantly disproportionate interest in the volume of strategic collection assignments we undertake compared with those that are really tactical in nature. We understand, of course, that some people simply can't deal with the possibility that the results of their labors are not being awaited with bated breath in the boardroom. They have to insist that their real mission is to support the strategist. That may be, but there's more to the intelligence business than grand strategic support. In fact, it's our experience that even though some people will couch their requirements in strategic terms, their application is really on tactical, almost day-to-day business issues. While it may be true that business leaders consider themselves above the fray and are focused on the grand strategic design of the future, the reality is closer to what one client realistically refers to as SNOW within his firm. SNOW, in this case, is the acronym for Strategic Notion Of the Week. In a business world that is so focused on quarterly report cards and earnings projections, perhaps it's easy to understand why someone might see their organization engaged in a SNOW job.

In the chapters to follow we'll focus mostly on the collection-activities portion of the cycle, since that's what this book is primarily about: operations. Yet there are still a few things to be said about how the entire process fits together. Later, in chapter 12, where the focus will be on getting the most out of your investment in trade shows and conferences, we'll revisit the Business Intelligence Collection Model as we "ride the cycle." For now, though, we'll enter into the Land of a Thousand Sources: internal sources and external sources. Who they are and how to find them.

CHAPTER 10

Intelligence Begins at Home: Internal Sources—Who They Are and How to Find Them

What is called "foreknowledge" cannot be elicited from spirits, nor from gods, nor by analogy with past events, nor from calculations. It must be obtained from men who know the enemy situation.

—Sun-tzu, *The Art of War*, XIII:4

Businesses are rapidly learning what governments have known for centuries. Early warning without human sources is impossible. To a certain extent it's like the stock market: If you're *reading* about an opportunity, most of the time that only puts you on par with every other investor who is able to read. The real money is made by those who are out in front of a wave, not just on the crest, or worse, in the following trough.

After all is said and done, there are really two kinds of information sources: primary and secondary. We've mentioned both of them in passing already.

Primary sources are those people who know what we need to know. People who will provide you with intelligence information for all the reasons that we've spoken of already, and more. People who know what's going on today, not just yesterday's headlines or summaries.

Secondary sources, on the other hand, are written, generally publicly or openly available, and can be either free on the Internet or available through any one of hundreds of on-line subscription and news services. They can provide incredible amounts of information, and every once in a while they can even produce nuggets of information that are of considerable value.

In our way of looking at the world, secondary sources have only one real purpose beyond providing background data: They help to identify those people, those primary sources, who have today's information. Before we just dismiss secondary research out of hand, a short explanation is in order.

We find that few companies publicly announce or otherwise openly provide information that is of a competitively valuable nature until it's too late for anyone to do anything about it. That means that the greatest majority of published information is of a historical nature, even if you don't count the amount of time it takes to conceptualize, research, write, edit, produce, and distribute the material.

There's also the Paul Harvey aspect: the Ressssst of the Story. Much of what is written winds up on the floor, courtesy of the editor. How much of the actual story is missing from the printed version simply because of space or other factors is hard to estimate. Generally, we find that the most important information, that 10 to 20 percent that is not publicly available, is still obtainable through legal and ethical means if you apply yourself to finding the people who know the things that you need.

That's what this and the next chapter are all about. Identifying, developing, and engaging primary sources of information, both internal as well as external.

INTERNAL PRIMARY SOURCES

The 80-20 rule seems to be the "one-size-fits-all" rule across America. It seems that it's used in everything from personal productivity to hair care. Not to be left out of this great statistical smorgasbord, some of the gurus of the Business Intelligence world tell us that 80 percent of the information you need to make safe and sound business decisions today can be found right inside your own firm. That may even be true. Frankly, we're a bit too busy to try and quantify the amount.

We'll just say that we've found all manner and amounts of information inside companies. The most common refrain we hear from prospective sources of information inside a company is "Well, nobody ever asked me" when they are asked about their knowledge of a particular competitive issue.

Internal sources, or *correspondents,* consist of three primary categories inside the company: knowledge bearers, external connections, and travelers/hosts.*

- *Knowledge bearers* are people who work for your company. They have specialized skills or contacts that have never been exploited, and they typically know very little about the Business Intelligence process, let alone how valuable a role they may play in helping the

---

*Please note that these categories and the ones to follow, do not exist in the literature at this point. Instead, they represent my own classification methods, based on my professional experience.

firm competitively. They may be people who work in one division of the company that has no real interaction with other divisions. Finding them, and linking their areas of expertise, allows the Business Intelligence professional to conduct intelligence-mining exercises throughout the company. This allows you to capitalize on the information that already exists.

- *External connections* are the people whom your firm's employees contact on a regular or routine basis. These contacts can occur through business transactions; purchasing agents, for example, might have contacts with vendors who are in contact with the purchasing agents at *competitor* firms. They can also occur in professional affiliations; your company's HR managers, for example, might meet and converse with their opposite numbers at monthly or annual professional meetings, conferences, and symposia.

- *Travelers and hosts* refer to those people throughout your firm who travel to other companies—both competitors and noncompetitors. They come into contact with people at those other firms who know things that would be useful to your organization. Conversely, your firm is often the host for visitors from outside the company who bring that same kind of information with them. We'll talk more about them in part III, where our concern will be on protection measures rather than collection activities. At this point, however, we're interested in them as prospective sources of information who during their meetings are in close contact with your visitors. They can range from the sponsor of the visit to the person staffing your reception desk. Sponsors can be expected to provide information on specific things in which professional visitors from other companies seem to have particular interest in learning; we have found receptionists to be excellent sources of information about what a group of visitors talk about—as if the receptionist were invisible—before their sponsor or escort arrives.

A number of underlying principles drive our interest in internal sources of information. We'll briefly touch on four of them here. Once you understand the intelligence effort as an ongoing process with some maintenance requirements, then have it in place, you can expect to increase information from:

- *A Migratory Flock:* People migrate from one company to another, carrying information with them about their former employers and their former competitors. The intelligence collector identifies them through an ongoing review of the HR files, builds a database of who they are, meets with them, and essentially recruits them. He then evaluates their areas of expertise, who their contacts are in other companies and industries, and how they can best be tasked to collect competitively valuable information. In essence, he knows who to call to get what.

- *Return on Investment:* Many, if not most, companies have virtually no intelligence ROI on the money they spend sending people to trade shows, conferences, professional symposia, and other meetings. The intelligence collector identifies them through a review of the number of people in the company who attend such programs. She sensitizes them to what the needs of the company are before they ever leave for a professional meeting, and guides them through the process of collecting information in that target-rich environment where competitors, vendors, customers, consultants, journalists, writers, all converge for the purpose of communicating. It becomes far more than just demanding the odd two-paragraph trip report in order to get their travel voucher paid. And it's worth so much to the collector that this is treated separately in chapter 12.

- *Treasures, Even Hidden Treasures:* Employees have contact on a variety of levels with their peers in other firms, many of them competitors. For example, HR mavens meet with their colleagues and discuss common problems and solutions about benefits, recruiting, and other issues. Some of this information points to costs and hence profitability; some to new personnel in fields they've never hired in before that can point to new efforts, products, or ventures; some to future plans and strategies. Task your specialists throughout the company—whether in R and D, accounting, facilities management, financial planning, operations, production—in specific collection objectives. Train them well enough in nonthreatening collection techniques such as elicitation, and they'll reward your efforts with incredible amounts of high-quality information. At bottom, you'll capitalize on the tendency of professionals to share experiences— even confidences—with other professionals in the interest of peer recognition and many other motivations. And that's just what you set out to do. There's always the serendipity that you so richly deserve, if for no other reason than having read this book. To see how pure luck and the law of unintended consequences worked to the benefit of a client company recently, take a glance at the box *The Professional Development Seminar.*

- *Isn't Work All There Is?* Employees have lives outside the company too. They coach soccer with other parents who work for other firms with similar interests. They attended college or university with people who are now working for other companies where competitively valuable information resides. They have relatives or neighbors, or fishing buddies, or even old classmates who may have opted for the quiet life of academia, spiced up with some consulting work from time to time. Identified, softly and deftly recruited, and tasked on occasion for real reasons, you have many additional sources of information—what Mao Tse-tung referred to as the fish in the sea.

The identification and the handling of sources is perhaps the most difficult and time-consuming task in any intelligence-collection and analysis project, and that's true whether you're interested in developing internal or external sources. It's what the national intelligence services refer to as "spotting and assessment"—the process that leads to recruitment of a source.

Depending on the circumstances, this recruitment is either formal or informal. In the formal case, the source knows—or believes he knows—the organization he's working for; in the informal case, it's often an unwitting relationship, where the source doesn't really know for whom he's working or why. That's the case in international intelligence operations. Yet source operations in the business world are considerably different.

The Professional Development Seminar

We were in the process of a typical twofold project—helping a company develop an internal collection system and at the same time setting up an additional level of protection beyond that provided by an already well-functioning security department.

While sitting with the security director, the Business Intelligence manager and our consultant were describing the kinds of things the company was interested in protecting that had not been on the protection list before. In part, the list of protection topics was a mirror image of the kinds of things they were hoping to collect from their competitor. One of those areas had to do with plant equipment upgrades, enhancements, and replacements.

The security director had just returned from a professional development program that was specifically focused on safety and security in transportation. He pulled out his notes and the handout materials from the presentation made by the security manager of one of the facilities that was on the list of the collection objectives. The target company's security manager had spoken at length about the safety and security issues involved with moving three new multiton pieces of machinery into the plant, including the origins (which gave the manufacturer and many characteristics), the routes (including the roadbuilding that had to be done to get the heavy equipment from a main road into the plant), and the issues associated with the actual installation, to include the concrete pads and performance/calibration issues. Within ten minutes of review, terrific insights were made into the new equipment lines that had been installed at the targeted facility.

Had it not been for the fact that the security director had been specifically interested in the kinds of things the BI unit was being tasked to collect, he would've never asked. And the BI unit manager would never have thought to ask him either. The notes and presentation handouts would have been stored away in the security director's office, and the diggers would've had to find other ways to obtain the needed information.

In the world of legitimate business intelligence operations, sources are paid only when they are employees of the firm on whose behalf they are working. Most of the time, their pay is in the form of their regular paycheck and perhaps a meal on the house once in a while. Some firms provide bonus rewards to employees who serve as especially valuable collectors of information in addition to their regular duties. And in some firms that seek to capitalize on the access to multiple potential sources that the sales force enjoys, the BI-oriented leadership has actually changed the sales force's compensation formulas to reflect their contributions. After all, they reason, the salesperson's only real commodity is time. Given the choice between collecting information that may be seen as having only passing or marginal value to themselves and using the time to sell, they'll settle for selling 100 percent of the time. On the flip side, there are those salespeople who recognize that customer intelligence and competitor intelligence have corresponding value and are often collected at the same time—either of which serve as a leg up for sales.

External sources in the business world are virtually never paid for their information, unless you feel like bribing someone—and that steps well over the legal and ethical boundaries between intelligence operations and industrial and economic espionage. Paying sources, blackmailing sources, entrapping sources—that stuff is just as foreign to the conduct of Business Intelligence operations as meeting rules such as "I'll be wearing a mauve and orange fedora, with a black orchid in my lapel and a June 11th, 1947, edition of the *New York Post,* open to page 17, under my left arm. If I'm wearing a Harvard Boolah-Boolah sweater with a patch on the left elbow, it means that we have to postpone the meeting until your forty-third birthday." Rot and melodrama.

Clearly, there are going to be as many motivations for an internal source to cooperate in helping to satisfy your intelligence needs as there are individual choices in ice cream. Similarly, there is going to be an altogether different set of motivations to get the external source to cooperate with you, whether the external source is employed by the target firm or in any of the myriad other locations where they can be found.

FINDING INTERNAL SOURCES

There are as many ways to find internal sources of information as there are ways to invest in your future. Instead of trying to hallucinate how your organization is structured, we'll just give you a few of our favorite mechanisms to provoke your imagination. These may aid you in thinking outside the box and help you to identify all those potential, yet hidden, intelligence resources you may have at your disposal.

The first of my favorite resource mechanisms will also introduce another fundamental and basic Business Intelligence practice—useful in both the collection side as well as the protection side. We call it the *Intelligence Assessment.* Others might prefer intelligence audit, yet sometimes that sounds a little too ominous to a group whose worst nightmare is to get a call from the IRS, inviting them to attend an audit to be held in their honor on a certain date and time.

The Intelligence Assessment is a structural mechanism that we find especially useful when evaluating the Business Intelligence competency inside a firm. Initial interviews of the enterprise's leadership not only reveal what they would like the intelligence team to answer but also help to identify the sources of information they use now. Typically, such an interview lasts thirty minutes and involves a structured set of questions, which allows not only the development of intelligence questions but also the background issues associated with the conduct of corporate intelligence activities. Usually, we conduct the first couple of interviews in the start-up phase of a Business Intelligence team, then turn the process over to one of the members of the team who accompanied us on the first interviews.*

Whether done in concert with someone outside the organization or doing it alone, intelligence begins with leadership. Ask potential consumers of the intelligence product about where and to whom they turn for information today, and who and what have they relied on in the past. In most cases, they'll tell you about print sources; some will refer to the on-line service that provides them delivery every fifteen minutes as a screen saver. But the real winner is when the decision maker or other senior member of the enterprise says, "Well, there's Tom Thomas over in engineering. He and I go back thirty years and he stays on top of every single technical development that ever comes around in this business. If I ever have a question that needs an answer, chances are good that Tom has it."

Most senior managers have developed relationships with the people throughout the organization who provide them with wisdom and advice as well as information. In several hundred interviews of senior leaders during our Intelligence Assessments, we have never had one tell us that they were unwilling to reveal who their sources were; in fact, they usually encourage the team members to contact their favorite sources, tell them that they're doing so with the leader's blessing, and ask for that source's cooperation.

Of course, there will be the odd manager who wants to keep all of his sources to himself. Sometimes it's because of the special relationship that

---

*Since we're in the business of getting as many things done as possible at a time, this set of interviews also allows the leadership of the organization to help identify those corporate cultural and ethical standards around which CI activities can be performed. We'll be talking more about legal, ethical, and cultural issues in Appendix B.

has developed between them; sometimes it's a bit more like a *Dilbert* cartoon, and the manager is looking for a sycophant; and sometimes, the manager wants to wait awhile and use that favorite source as a means of validating or challenging the information provided by the BI team. That's just life in the Big City.

The second basic mechanism is to gain an understanding of the number and type of *professional organizations and other groups* your employees belong to as a result of their careers. Gaining an appreciation of who belongs to what not only gets you far down the road toward maximizing your return on professional meetings, which we speak more about in chapter 12, but it also helps you learn a bit more about the breadth of your firm's activities. We've found that some of the most revealing information comes about as a result of understanding precisely what it is that different departments do—and how they relate to the outside world. In this way, the BI unit members reduce the number of times each month they say to one another, "I didn't know we did *that*!"

So, the question is, where do you start?

On the level of first principles, we simply follow the kind of advice made famous by Deep Throat's response to Bob Woodward during the Watergate years. When Woodward wanted to know where to go to validate the information he was getting, Deep Throat's advice was "Follow the money." That's what we set out to do as well, under our operating dictum that "Where money changes hands, so does information." So, look to the financial linkages that your firm has throughout the company.

Chances are, they have a separate reporting code in the accounting language that specifies what has been paid in membership fees to which organizations on behalf of which employees. Companies often have a central listing of all the organizations they support, locally, nationally, and professionally. It may be in human resources, public relations, investor relations, training, or any one of a dozen others. Maybe such a listing only exists at the approval-authority level, where the manager responsible for the expenditure keeps her own record. At bottom, it doesn't really make any difference where the information exists or whether it's somewhat difficult to extract.

Why? First, because the effort is always worth it in the number of potential sources you can identify. Second, the more you get out amongst the people in the company, the more you'll learn about it and the better intelligence collector and gatherer you'll be. This raises another of those old operational intelligence maxims: "No intelligence officer worth his salt spends more than 25 percent of his time behind his desk; otherwise, he's an analyst." Granted, in the Business Intelligence world, where we tend to do a great deal of work on the telephone and at the computer terminal, the percentages would have to be different, but the message is clear.

Of course, this automatically develops the thought in your mind about membership directories, doesn't it? Once you understand the numbers and locations of the people throughout your firm who belong to professional and other work-related groups, you can now begin to cover the waterfront. There is a considerable, and additional, advantage to pursuing this range of professional organizations, as you'll soon see in the following chapter on developing external sources.

The third approach, which may seem a little arcane in some companies, is nonetheless a valuable one in some industries. It's what we call *company alumni populations*. In some industries, there is so much migration from one company to another, or shakeouts deriving from mergers and acquisitions activity, that company alumni groups have sprung up. They have social meetings at industry events, providing excellent opportunities for many corporate requirements to be satisfied. For example, if your firm helps sponsor an alumni group, HR people can be at the hospitality suite to encourage former employees to come back—and share costs with the BI team that is interested in learning what the former employees are doing at their new company.

Even without a formal alumni association, identifying the whereabouts of former employees of your company has considerable merit. For example, how many of your retirees have gone into private practice as consultants? And for what firms do they consult? Do you have any way, at present, to track where people go when they leave the organization? Do you have a follow-through means of remaining in contact with any of them? Do you share in any of the information that your HR people gather from the departing employee's out-briefing? Will you be doing any of these things starting tomorrow?

The fourth and final of all those sources we might speak about is perhaps the most important. After all, if we're talking about people as sources, who knows more about people than the *human resources department*. And what can we expect to get from them? Legitimately, tons.

At the outset, think about the nature of just one of your projects or requirements in a large project. What are the technologies involved in this project, for example? Do you know already who in your company has those same kinds of skills, competencies, or education? Wouldn't it kill you to find out that the world's leading expert on fusillator technology is someone in a sister division of your own company? Wouldn't it even be worse if your technologist's best friend from grad school was the number two guy at your competitor and that they exchanged e-mail daily? Or, that he'd collaborated on two dozen technical papers with thirty or forty people at various other companies and universities?

Now wait a minute, aren't we getting into some gray areas here?

Areas like employee privacy and such? Hardly. After all, it's hard to imagine that it would be inappropriate to let you as the intelligence collector know the technical and professional backgrounds of your firm's employees—especially when the firm is using the same kind of information in all manner of competitive situations such as the management of volumes of technical proposals. Is the information going to be used against the employee? Hardly. Is learning about where someone worked previously a legitimate intelligence practice? It certainly is, if you consider the fact that you're conducting Business Intelligence operations in the first place in accordance with what your firm and industry define as legitimate business practices.

Well, you might say, "There are other areas, too." Isn't there something bad about the intelligence-unit people making contact with a new employee within a week or two of starting work? Isn't there something wrong about being debriefed about their role at their previous companies? About people they've worked with? Or, how about even the intelligence collection activities of the previous employer, as we'll talk about when doing an assessment of our vulnerabilities to other companies in part III? The only response we can ever hope to have about these questions is that universal "It depends."

It depends on the degree of cooperation you'll get from your HR leadership. If they're not on board with your mission and objectives by now, it's time for some fence mending.

It depends on how you actually make the approach to the employee. If you're thinking about some kind of "We know where your mother lives" approach, you've missed the point of everything that's gone before.

Further, *it depends* on the point in the hiring process where the approach is made. This can sometimes be a fairly sticky point. While virtually every company we've ever worked with considered it well beyond the scope of proper business ethics to have a BI team member as part of the pre-employment interview process, there is a great deal of diversity of thought about what to do with people once they've been hired.

The box, *Well, Isn't There an Ethical Problem Here?* is drawn directly from an Intelligence Assessment interview with a chief operating officer who, interestingly enough, had come up through the ranks via the legal department. Knowing about his background before the interview took place, we thought we could anticipate what his responses were going to be like, since many in-house counsel are, well, defensive and protective. After all, that's their job.

Well, Isn't There an Ethical Problem Here?

We approached the final set of questions in the Assessment Interview with a little more trepidation than usual because of the COO's legal training and background. We asked: "How long will an employee work at your firm before you think it's appropriate for him to be interviewed by your intelligence staff about what he's done in his last job?"

"Are you kidding me?"

"No, sir. We're also interested in making sure that everybody knows what's right and proper in your organization from a legal and ethical point of view. We'll be helping your BI team—along with your legal team—formulate your CI guidelines, and we want to make certain that those guidelines reflect the views of the leadership. In some companies, the answer is that they don't think it's appropriate to interview a new employee until he's been on board for six months, some say it's a year, some say three years, and some say never."

"Well, I'll tell you. I don't know about those others, but they sure don't work here. As far as I'm concerned, the day I'm starting to sign some SOB's paycheck is the day that I start owning every bit of what he's got in his head about anything. We won't do anything before he actually starts working for us because that just breeds problems. But after that, it's a different story."

And finally, *it depends* on whether you're hiring a full-time, permanent employee. Some firms see absolutely no problem with hiring a temp in the age of temporary workers, or a contract employee for a specific project, with the intelligence interview being one of the first ones they experience on the new job. And, they'll often hire them and pay a bounty for contract or temporary employees who've been most recently employed in certain areas of projects by their nearest and fiercest competitor. Why? To get the cheapest and fastest insight into how the other firm is operating right now. This is merely a variant on the seemingly age-old approach of hiring away your rival's best workers. The downside in both approaches is the same: It's one of the sharpest double-edged swords around.

Since this kind of employee can help a company cut down on both short-term and long-term overhead expenses, the trend certainly seems to rising. The downside is that they are also the most seriously disgruntled population who know about a company's secrets. In fact, the first conviction under the new Economic Espionage Act, of which we'll hear more in Appendix B, was of a manager of contract employees.

Please understand that we're not trying to be the ethics police and say that any of these approaches are correct or incorrect. We're just attempting to show that "good men, honest and true" can have wholly different responses under identical circumstances. Like you, that's what they get paid the Big Bucks for: making leadership decisions that set the tone and operation for the enterprise. And, that's why it's wise to raise such issues form time to time. Courtesy of Mr. Lincoln, you don't have to stay if you disagree with the leaders decision.

The lack of loyalty that seems to pervade the modern workplace is no more acutely felt than in the highly connected, technically skilled, disgruntled, and transient contract worker who can be employed by your competitor today and by you tomorrow. Which brings us to external sources of information and how to find them.

Have You Looked at These Groups Lately?

Which functional elements of your organization can provide you access to additional sources? Perhaps there are just duty assignments instead of separate departments in your firm. No matter, the principle remains the same—finding people who know, or finding the people who know the people who know.

Purchasing	Customer Relations	Environmental Safety
Engineering	Corporate Travel	Production
Operations	Legal Security	Speaker's Bureau
Investor Relations		

And, by the way. Keep these same people in mind for when you want to protect your own information. You'll see why when we enter part III.

CHAPTER 11

The World Can Be Your Oyster: External Sources—Who They Are and How to Find Them

When these types of agents are all working simultaneously and none knows their method of operation, they are called "The Divine Skein" and are the treasure of a sovereign.

—Sun-tzu, *The Art of War*, XIII:6

EXTERNAL SOURCES

Just like the internal sources you met in the preceding chapter, we categorize external sources into three general classes as well. These include sources who are *internal to the target company, connected with the target company,* or *unconnected and uncontrollable sources of information about the target company.*

- *Target internal sources* are those who are full-time employees of the target company, each of whom has his or her own reasons for cooperating with an outside contact about information of competitive value, *whether they recognize it as such or not.* The ways in which they are approached to provide information of intelligence interest are as varied as there are researchers— ranging from the highly ethical Society of Competitive Intelligence Professionals to those who use a variety of ruses and other means.

- *Sources connected with the target company* are those people who are employed by companies that regularly and routinely do business with the target company, such as vendors, union leadership, subcontractors, distributors, and on-site contract or service workers who may or may not be constrained by confidentiality and nondisclosure agreements.

- *Unconnected and uncontrollable sources of information about the target company* include those people who have an interest in what the company does but who have no direct, formal relationship with it. These can range from analysts, business writers, and public-policy groups that follow companies and industries on behalf of a social cause to government monitors, community groups such as chambers of commerce, and government-agency representatives at all levels from local to national.

Widget, Widget, Who's Got the Widget?

If we're looking at Tom's Widget Company, where he's been manufacturing 10×10×10 widgets that weigh ten pounds each, we may well call his box and packing provider, Joe.

Talking with Joe about how well his business is doing may reveal that he's looking at a banner year because of the work he's doing for Tom. Since we know about the 10×10×10, we make some purposefully inaccurate statement about production figures to support Tom.

Not only does Joe like to correct us, he's proud of his little company. He gives us the first inkling that Tom is going to be building a 5×5×5, five-pound widget, because Joe needs to deliver ten million boxes in six months.

This gives us not only the basic fact of a new product, but it tells us when to expect it and in what numbers, starting us off on a skein of sources all along the line such as truckers, railroads, and others in the distribution channel.

Operating here are two fundamental principles that drive intelligence collection, and they're not rocket science.

First, remember that we can always start off with the "follow the money" dictum. You're bound only by your imagination, but here are two examples:

- *Suppliers.* In this group are perhaps the most complete sources of information, and most companies who engage suppliers don't recognize the value of the information the supplier has well enough to try and protect it.

- *Customers.* It's often in the best interest of a customer of Tom's Widgets to be open to alternatives to his products. The buyer may be dissatisfied and looking for another provider; the buyer may be interested in playing one off against the other; the buyer may simply be one of those folks who talks too much anyway.

The second principle is what the military refers to as "force multipliers"—using the resources of others who collect information for their own purposes, which are not necessarily congruent with your own, who are willing to share it with you. These are people who don't have any financial linkage with your target company but who still have access to the kind of information you're collecting and bringing together into a coherent picture. Often, they're not just individuals but organizations with multiple sources of information of their own who collect and aggregate the information for wholly different reasons from yours. As a few examples, there are:

- *Public-interest groups,* each of which has an agenda of sorts. Their memberships include people from all walks of life, including, quite often, employees of firms that might be considered your competitors. We've seen contacts with such organizations pay off in large ways in industries ranging from defense and aerospace contracting to manufacturers to meat producers. Public-interest groups actively collect information so as to ultimately influence public policy—and the best way to do that is to know what is happening and tell as many people about it as possible. Making yourself one of those recipients saves much time, effort, and money.

- *Media people of various stripes.* Call the writer who did the great story on the new facility of your rival, Ferndock Furniture, and compliment her; then later in the conversation wish out loud that she'd had a chance to write about X, Y, or Z. Her reply? "Well, I covered that in detail, but the editor cut the six thousand words down to two thousand." It's not a long step from there to learning far more from the reporter than what merely appeared in the article—and it may even be some of the information she wasn't intending to write about in the first place. Again, the journalist's sources become your force multiplier. Since almost everyone can read these days, it should be obvious that your other competitors may be looking at the same company you are, and for the same reasons. If one of your purposes in using competitive intelligence is to gain marketplace advantage (not just over one rival, but many), then reading the same things the other guy is reading doesn't provide you much of an edge, does it? Getting what they haven't gotten, on the other hand, clearly does. This is especially true with local papers that really do follow the major fish in their small ponds. While national media sources may never hear of Backwater Electronics in Horned Toad, Montana, you can bet that the *Horned Toad Beacon and Tattler* knows almost everything worth knowing.

- *A circle of competitors.* Touching this set of sources means relying on the principle that many people know what's happening inside a company but also tend to undervalue the information because they have no stake in protecting it. For example, if the target company is Company A, we wouldn't necessarily call Company A's people. Instead, we'll talk with people at Company B, and C, and D. This gives us access to people who used to work at Company A and who maintain contacts there; people who are married to people at Company A (what is often referred to a Pillownet) or who play softball with them; or who have some other kind of relationship with Company A or its people.

- *Government and quasi-government sources:* There are two distinct and separate ways to go about dealing with the B&B crowd, or bureaucrats and boosters. As bureaucrats, government people will always respond—although not with any special alacrity, despite what the law says—under the Freedom of Information Act (FOIA). Those inside the government who want to protect information and retard its flow into the marketplace viewed the FOIA with growing concern as it flowed through the federal government in the late 1970s. I remember it well, because it seemed to me that there were some things that clearly needed more protection than was being provided under the conditions of the act. Be that as it may, I now realize the error of my ways. The FOIA is without a doubt the very best piece of legislation ever conceived by mankind—for Business Intelligence purposes, at least. In many cases, the overreporting to government agencies of all kinds allows FOIA requesters to obtain much more about rival companies and organizations than could've ever been intended. We've even gotten the names of the people occupying all the positions supporting particular government contracts, an added bonus to what we were after in the first place. We'll have more to say about FOIA from a protection perspective in chapter 15. Suffice it to say at this point that the FOIA is also alive and well in many states and local governments as they've attempted to follow the federal lead—that is, you have lots of places to go where local and state FOIA laws dictate the release of information you might not otherwise expect to get.

And, as far as boosters are concerned, local chambers of commerce, economic development committee members, and local media follow business issues at a community rather than industry level. Local elected officials often know great amounts about what a company is doing in their backyard—and also know the potential sources that are inside those companies you are interested in learning more about.

Now that we've got a starting point about the kinds of people who might serve as external sources of information for your firm, we need to develop ways to find them. Of course, we could go to those many services that sell specially screened and updated lists of business professionals—lists that help those people who kill half a gazillion trees a year just to make sure that you get all those magazines and brochures you can't live without. But that would be tacky—and fairly expensive, as you know if you've ever bought an updated and quality mailing list by name, position, company, phone number, et cetera.

We believe that finding external sources is just like charity: It begins at home. Using those resources that you already have in place but probably aren't yet using to their fullest.

INTERNAL STARTING POINTS

Remember, we're still looking for sources who are outside your firm and who know about what's happening at your competitor. Yet the first one on this short list is your own human resources department. Does that make sense? Absolutely.

Human Resources

Your own HR department has been receiving résumés from prospective employees for years. Many have been scanned and stored in modern

HRMIS for ease of retrieval. Résumés that have been unsolicited, those that have been in response to advertising or other recruitment means (e.g., job fairs and campus visits—where you may well find someone who was a summer intern for your target company), or referrals from contingency and retained search firms, to name just a few. Instead of those résumés lying there gathering literal or electronic dust, make them a routine part of your internal database of potential sources.*

Finance and Accounting

This department is one that allows you to rely on the "follow the money" principle described earlier. Your firm probably shares common suppliers and vendors, customers, and distributors—as well as many other groups—with your competitors. These potential outside sources of information are listed, if not by name at least by firm, as a starting point for sources who know what's going on inside your rival firms.

Operations

People throughout the operations side of your firm have gone to school with, been previously employed at other firms with, or have friends who have left your firm for other companies, some of which may be the companies in which you are interested. Of course, if your rival is located in the same town, people at various levels of the firm interact with their opposite numbers in their neighborhoods and at soccer games, country clubs, swim teams, church, or political groups.

Membership Lists

Remember that in the last chapter we talked about how we look for internal sources by looking through the professional organizations to which your employees belong? Not only does it help to find those poten-

---

*You'll need to make a decision at some point as to whether or not you'll contact the individual résumé sender as soon as you've received it, or if you want to wait a few months or so—particularly if the résumé came in as a result of your advertising for position vacancies. By way of explanation, some companies share our concern that actual or apparent false advertising of vacant positions, followed by interviews by their CI people rather than HR people, is a step toward or over the ethical line.

tial correspondents inside your own firm, but it also provides you great access to outside sources. And there is a synergy between the two, as you can imagine: either get them to tell you a little about the other person before you contact them or, better still, encourage them to become one of your correspondents, train that correspondent in what you're trying to do and in some of the ways to do it, and have them build or continue a relationship.

Just like anything else worth doing, however, there is sometimes a stumbling block or two. Since in most cases there is not a central repository of such directories, this requires a little bit more work than some other ways of developing a database of leads and sources. Moreover, many people inside the company prefer to husband their membership directories for their own use. Getting a directory to copy—and getting it back to the employee/member quickly—can pay real dividends. In those cases where employee/members object to sharing their material, they can often be encouraged to share it, based on the high probability that their annual membership dues in professional societies are paid for by the company in the first place.

Sales Force

Obviously, your sales force can help you learn about a lot of things in this business. Perhaps more than anyone in a company, they're the kind of correspondents who keep track of, and really strive to maintain relationships with, other people. People across the range: present employees who used to be employed by the target company; other former employees of the target firm who may be with another firm now; employees of common customers, some of whom may have come from the target company. We see this as an especially common characteristic in consulting and telecommunications firms where an employee of a vendor of products or research services joins the customer after a certain period of quality performance.

Obviously, many other departments and groups in your organization have their own peculiar character and set of contacts who are in positions to provide information or leads to other external sources. With a better appreciation of how those departments listed above can be used to identify sources, look around your organization through a different set of eyes. Maybe you'll view other groups of people and other resources and activities inside the firm in a different light.

EXTERNAL STARTING POINTS

Hundreds, if not thousands, of resources are available in libraries throughout the land. Increasingly, there are businesses that do little more than provide information services; indeed, some private and public libraries and institutions are providing quick access to the names, locations, and contact information for external sources. Yet you can do much for yourself quickly and economically on the Internet.

Of all the hyped benefits and promises for the future that the Internet has for mankind, the intelligence bonanza is by far the one that has had the most immediate payoff. Even as recently as 1995, most people would've been astounded at the amount of information that it's now possible to collect on the 'Net in just a few focused and well-spent minutes.

But that sells the 'Net short when it comes to finding and evaluating potential external sources of information. For any intelligence professional who slaved away in the days before the Internet and its associated toys such as e-mail, the ability to locate and connect with potential sources is simply wonderful to behold. Overall, the Internet is perhaps the single fastest, most economical and wide-ranging source-identification and development means available. Included here are some of the less apparent ways to identify people through the 'Net, based on the presumption that anyone who has done any modern research work at all has developed a familiarity with the more popular search engines.

THE INTERNET'S CONTRIBUTION TO SOURCE IDENTIFICATION AND DEVELOPMENT

Electronic Libraries

The articles, papers, research projects, and monographs that are available on the Internet are just terrific. In many cases the information that the 'Net can provide represents a significant chunk of what you're after in the first place. Yet the greatest value of a site such as The Electric Library (www.elibrary.com) and a host of others is that the articles were written by, written about, refer to, and quote people. People who can be turned into sources of the information you seek.

News Groups/User Groups

In these parts of the Web it's very profitable to go through a site such as "Dejanews.com" where you can simply enter the name of a company, for example. You'll find references that are individual based as opposed to company based: people who are responding to interest-group conversation and "threads" of conversations.

Frequently, searching under a specific company name will yield an e-mailer who is writing from his or her company's office and using their company e-mail address for the communication. They might be writing about something altogether unrelated to the company, for example, ocean kayaking or mountain climbing. Another person—you, for instance—with an interest in mountain climbing enters into on-line conversation that quickly gets to what you both as individuals do for a living. The relationship with a new source develops from there.

The same conditions and characteristics that apply to face-to-face elicitation apply in this highly informal, nonconfrontational environment. It's especially effective when dealing with technology types who are much more comfortable at a computer than in person.

Think about this for about a nanosecond. Don't you know some Internet addicts who sit up all night—and half the day at the office—chasing neat things on the 'Net? People who write into the electronic abyss in the hopes that someone will care enough to answer them? To share their little corner of the world? Their *real* reward is when someone originates an e-mail exchange with them. A message from a person they don't know. Just a person, seemingly from out of the blue, who found our Internet junkie and wants to open a dialogue. Maybe just an Oblique Reference to what that person is really interested in. Something that can wait for the next e-mail exchange, which is certainly going to occur within twenty-four hours.

After all, in many cases, we're talking about an Internet addict on one side of the dialogue who sits there much of the nonworking day and night munching on peanut butter crackers, granola bars, and double caffeine beverages. This is the sort of person who puts one of those baby sleep monitors near his computer. When he hears the little bong that announces "You have mail," he scurries to the computer no matter what time it is. Why? Because that piece of mail validates his claim that he really does have a life. This is the kind of person who is probably very much the object of attention by the clinical psychologists at the Center for On-Line Addiction (Bradford, PA). This is not a joke. There really is such a place. And, I expect that they have a pretty good sense of humor, too, if they actually use the acronym COLA.

But they're not the only ones who will find this person interesting. Ponder for another nanosecond what this means as an opportunity source for a trained elicitor. Why? The kinds of information that people exchange is sometimes just awe-inspiring when they're communing with fellow spirits on a common interest site.

For example, you want to find out what kind of working conditions contract employees enjoy at Microsoft? Visit <cbp@lists.studiob.com>. That's the site where you can sign on to the Computer Book Writers forum and get all the e-mail that is roaring back and forth among writers. Often, these writers are contract technical writers—people who know the characteristics of software that's going to be coming out six or nine months from now, while it's of potential competitive importance. Rarely are these people treated very well. An example of a two-day exchange is included in the box *Life in the Microsoft Woods*.

Life in the Microsoft Woods

Initial Comment—November 19, 1998

A friend of mine sent me this from the Washington Alliance of Technology Workers' listserv. This may be of interest to people on the list. I'm not sure what the effect will be on the local writing industry, but I do know that Microsoft has been having trouble finding the contract writers (and possibly developers) that they've wanted to hire on a contract basis, so I can't see that this will help their ability to get products out the door.

November 18, 1998

MICROSOFT's 31-DAY FORCED LAYOFFS MAY BE 'JUST A START'

Nearly five months after Microsoft rolled out its 31-day "break-in-service" policy, company managers report that they have been told by representatives of Microsoft's Contingent Staffing Group (CSG) that the company intends to increase the length of the mandated break and expand the categories of workers that the break will affect.

Nationwide, Microsoft employs more than 6,000 workers through employment agencies. More than 5,000 of these, or approximately 35 percent of the company's total Puget Sound workforce, work in or around Redmond and Seattle.

"They [CSG] have acknowledged that the 31-day break is just a Band-aid. It's just a start," said one Microsoft manager. "CSG doesn't want any contractors working at Microsoft for more than 12 months without them working somewhere else in between. That's their stated objective. They've said that at a couple of meetings I've been at." According to this manager, Microsoft is contemplating upping the length of the forced layoffs to three or more months.

One Volt contractor recently told WashTech that he had "confirmed" with a full-time Microsoft employee that the company intends to increase the forced layoff to 90 days or more by July 1999.

A written summary of a meeting that took place this summer between CSG Director Sharon Decker and Microsoft managers reported that Decker said "it is logical to assume that the length of the break in service will increase in the future."

To read this complete report, including more information on the pending expansion of Microsoft's permatemp layoff policies, see http://www.washtech.org/roundup/break2.html

To read the story of one of the first contractors affected by the 31-day break policy, see http://www.washtech.org/roundup/affected.html

To read how one agency challenged the unemployment claim of a Microsoft contractor affected by the forced layoff policy, see http://www.washtech.org/roundup/claim.html

---

Second Comment—November 19, 1998

I'm doing some contract work over at Microsoft right now, and this mentality is becoming pervasive to the point of silliness. The other day, an edict came down from on high saying that contingency staff (i.e., contractors) could not have dinner provided for them if they were forced to work late to complete a project—in other words, if a manager sprang for a pizza out of company funds, according to new contingency rules a contract employee couldn't eat a slice.

This position HAS hurt them. They can't find the people to fill the slots they need in Seattle's already tight labor market, and one reason has been that many contractors won't accept jobs from them anymore. This has the added impact that the people that they do get are more frequently younger and less experienced, which has an additional adverse effect on getting product to market.

Websites

Most companies spend so much time and effort building wonderful and informative Websites that they have no idea how much easier it makes a source identifier's job. You want to know the name and division of various people. The company wants you to feel comfortable contacting their employees to do business with them. After a while, in many companies, everyone wants their e-mail address on-line as a status symbol. This adds to the "target-rich environment" that the Web provides.

Résumés

A highly effective way of finding people who work for a company, or who used to work for a company, is to visit one of the many open sites that cater to those who are openly looking for jobs, for example, <www.headhunters. com>. Not only is this an excellent opportunity to evaluate whether somebody knows what you need to know, but it also tells you what they're doing right now. They're clearly out in the job market and the only thing they have to sell is their experience—and that experience derives from their employment at a company of interest to you.

On one hand, if they're former employees whose information isn't quite up to date, they represent a means of referring you to others who still work there. On the other hand, it would appear at first blush that no one with a current job and the ability to walk upright without a wheelbarrow would not be placing his or her résumé on the open Internet. After all, anyone—including their present employer—can see the résumé. Yet, quite the opposite is true.

Third Comment—November 19, 1998

Yes, I've had various recruiters tell me that their experience ranges from 33–50% of the contract writers in town won't work for Microsoft, with weighting toward the senior people. This can't be good for Microsoft but policies like this just drive the wedge in further IMO. Oh, well . . .

There really are people who are not especially clever and who still post themselves as searching, in spite of the clear potential problem from their employer learning about their job search. In speaking with colleagues in the recruiting business, this is not an uncommon event at all. They're no longer astounded when a potential candidate, whom they found while surfing, is almost paranoid that somehow his company will find out that he's in the job market when the recruiter starts to do the reference checking.

Fourth Comment—November 20, 1998

I imagine that the reason that Microsoft forces contractors to take layoffs is that otherwise the IRS will rule that they are really employees. The whole contractor bit is probably mainly a way to get around employment taxes and benefits.
Or else I'm wrong.

Government Websites

This is an obvious treasure trove of people and organizations who want to justify their existence and prove how important they are to the future of democracy and the human race. Some of the government organizations that have previously been especially good sources of information—and afford access to their people—are now starting to remove such information from their sites. But not because their people are saying anything more than what they're supposed to be saying; they're scrubbing the e-mail addresses and organization charts because of privacy issues. Nonetheless, these are people who have prodigious amounts of information and little real reason to safeguard something that is reported to them by a commercial firm. It's not classified government information, after all.

Guest Books

Looking at a guest book reveals all those others who have visited that site. The operating premise here is that these visitors obviously have an interest in the topic of the site. In almost every case, the visitor's e-mail address is part of the register, along with an area of interest or concern, a question, or a comment. Not only will the e-mail address give you the name in most cases, but the extension also gives you an inkling of their relationship with an organization and perhaps some insight into how to plan and develop your approach. For example, the extenders .gov and .mil would suggest one approach, while .org or .edu would suggest another, as would .com.

Electronic Dating Is Different from Carbon Dating

In a relatively recent vulnerability assessment project on behalf of a military program that was supposed to have large chunks kept under wraps, someone still felt it important that the project have a Website. Although the Website had lots of eye candy, it was fairly short on information. That seemed good from a protection point of view.

Yet it was the guest book that provided some of the greatest joy. Of the ninety people chosen from the guest book, seventy responded to e-mails concerning performance characteristics. Only a very small percentage of these contacts were government people; the bulk were either university researchers or employees of contractor organizations that were doing work on behalf of the project.

Each provided their own piece of the pie; each was interested enough to share how important their piece of the pie was. And, about 50 percent of them provided the names and e-mail addresses of their friends or associates who knew more about a particular aspect of the project than they did.

And, with the inevitability of the Law of Unintended Consequences, an electronic relationship grew rather rapidly—and one-sidedly— between our female researcher and one of her new electronic friends. We cannot report any of the other detail.

Now that you've got all this information about these sources, what are you going to do with it? You're going to keep records of it, manage it, reuse it and the sources. But bogging you down in administrivia when you're still interested in operational Business Intelligence matters would get me shot. Yet we want to make sure that you get the most bang for the buck over time, so we've included quite a bit on the administrative side of managing an intelligence operation at Appendix F. Indeed, others have paid a lot larger bucks than you have for what's contained in that appendix, so please don't just write it off as boring stuff you'll get around to later. It's really not that bad.

Besides, I need to make certain that you did not think to violate one of the most basic precepts in the Business Intelligence world: The day of the paperless intelligence office will arrive on the very same day as the paperless bathroom.

CHAPTER 12

Trade Show/Conference Intelligence Operations: Getting the Most for Your Already Heavy Investment

People are more violently opposed to fur than leather because it's easier to harass rich women then motorcycle gangs.

—Counter-demonstrator's sign opposing animal rights activists at a fashion industry exhibition

If there's a more "target-rich environment" for the collection of competitive information, I've never seen one. The floor of a trade show or the halls and presentation rooms of a professional conference represent the most potentially fruitful of all venues. And just because your organization hasn't looked at things this way doesn't mean that the other folks in your industry aren't taking fullest advantage of the opportunities.

Organizations spend millions of dollars on trade shows each year—some client companies spend up to $20 million at *individual* trade shows. Yet most organizations never maximize their intelligence return on these investments at all. By the time you finish this chapter, you'll never view a conference or trade show the same way again—either from a collection perspective or from a protection perspective.

This "target-rich environment" is really just that for intelligence collectors—and the organization that employs them to the fullest. It's rich with sources of information from across the spectrum, yet most people just think along one or two lines.

Maybe they expect to return with a couple of bags full of brochures, product samples, and baubles. They'll plan on sorting through it all when they get back to the office. In most cases, they know they'll have to justify their travel to somebody. In order to get their travel voucher paid, they'll have to write a trip report. In order to write their trip report, they'll make a couple of contacts, visit the exhibit hall for a while, and hope that some booth maven is indiscreet about a new product or price.

It's the professional version of hanging out at the mall.

Most conference attendees have little idea of what else they can accomplish while there. Nobody tells them what the company would like to know that's of competitive value. Nobody sensitizes them to what's actually going to be happening. Nobody challenges them to think ahead and plan what they're going to do once they get there—who they'll talk to about what, where, and when. That's where you come in.

Even if you've only got a few weeks remaining before your next trade show, there are plenty of things you can put into place; with more time, there are a terrific number of things you can do to maximize the payoff.

RIDING THE CYCLE

One of your first jobs is to find out what you need—and about whom. Just like starting the intelligence cycle all over again.

1. Tasking

Determine from—or for—the leadership what is needed. What kinds of information do you need to make the right kinds of decisions? The questions will be either standing intelligence questions (SIQs) or essential intelligence questions (EIQs). We'll talk later about how to manage these for greatest effect in the TS/CIO environment. For the moment, though, we'll keep these in the back of our mind as we ask a few questions to start the discussion.

Just a few of the starter questions. Clearly, this helps with the initial definition of the requirements in the same way that we went through planning in earlier chapters. But there are more questions that also have to be answered as we go along the cycle, particularly the matter of The Who.

2. Your Correspondent Network—Collector Selection and Preparation

The seemingly simple questions are sometimes the most difficult to answer. How do we find out who's going in the first place? This may not seem like the challenge of landing a man on the moon, but for some organizations it's just as daunting. Especially when there are dozens or even hundreds of people attending conferences or trade shows from the company. It's our experience that many companies provide really very little organizational direction or control—and certainly little real planning for maximizing the intelligence efforts.

Who's been there before? Who did they deal with previously? What, if anything, of intelligence value did we get from that person in the past? Who is willing to serve as a collector of information while they're there? What can we do to encourage them to collect information while there? These are just a few of the operational issues associated with trade shows and conferences.

In virtually every organization there are gatekeepers. Choke points. People who are central to all the various business issues confronting a firm. Putting up a notice on the bulletin board won't get you very many responses—any more than the responses you got when you were looking for a cheap ride home from college during semester break. Companywide e-mails hardly fare any better.

If you're really looking for the people in your firm who are working the conference circuit, contact the people at your firm's travel office and tell them what you need to support the company's intelligence program. Develop them as intelligence correspondents just as several chapters back you were capitalized on the contacts that your accountants, security managers, HR people, facilities managers, and others have in the course of their normal work.

Or, if you need to find those who have an interest in specific categories of conferences and trade shows, there may be money to be made in the travel finance section—those lists of who has been paid how much for attending which activity in which city. A variation on this theme is to identify those organizations that the company belongs to as a corporate member, or those professional organizations that receive company checks for employee memberships dues. Of course, one of the best parts about the company paying for the employee's membership dues and such is that certainly no employee privacy issues are at stake; the company is certainly able to track where and how it spends its money.

Tricks of the Trade Show—Number One

One company has used an interesting part-time employee to great advantage for several years. An older, obsequious gentleman with a decidedly European mien and accent is one of their best collectors. And he doesn't go anywhere near the conference sessions or the exhibits floor.

His position is in the men's room. Most of the meetings he attends are held at larger, nicer hotels. Instead of going into a stall, closing and locking the door, and putting his feet up so that anyone coming won't know he's there—which might not be playing by the rules—he takes a different tack.

Wearing a white shirt, black trousers, and a black vest, sans name tag, he walks into the men's room with a stack of paper towels. As the gentlemen come to the sinks to wash their hands, he simply hands them a towel or two rather than them having to pull the towels from the rack themselves.

Ladies are not the only ones who go two by two to the loo. And the really interesting thing is that this older fellow remains essentially as invisible as the maintenance and service workers in other venues. There are even times when the two talkers walk into the rest room, stop their conversation for a moment while they make certain that no one's feet are showing under the closed stall doors, and then freely continue their briefly interrupted conversation as if the towel man wasn't there.

"Can this really be worth it?" you might ask. After all, what kinds of things can a washroom attendant learn that would be of any value? On one level, the response to my same question to the BI manager at the company was "Absolutely terrific! Two guys at one meeting came in and didn't even break stride in their conversation about what good things a joint venture would do for their two companies. They happened to be our two most aggressive competitors and this was a real early warning that helped us to forecast, anticipate and act pre-emptively."

On another level, it just simply reinforces my view that just like the "Disappeared" in Chile, there are "Invisibles" all throughout professional life: janitors, window-washers, guards, receptionists, and so forth who are all treated like furniture.

If you have no central travel office or finance/travel office, try the training department, which probably has had a bit of experience sending people out for the educational advantages that some conferences provide. The smaller your firm, perhaps the easier to find out who's traveling where. It may be that all corporate travel, as a policy, has to be approved by the president, divisional GM, or someone close to her. That's the choke point where you find the source of all the potential sources.

Tricks of the Trade Show—Number Two

Another company has taken its approach to information collection to dizzying heights.

Three employees rotate on a thirty-minute basis through the elevator bank, taking elevator A to the top, taking elevator B to the lobby, C to the top, and D to lobby or the first parking-garage level. Since they're not really attending the trade show, they're not wearing name tags at all. After all, every hotel has nonconference guests during shows, right? And who could be less threatening than someone without a badge?

Wouldn't people just naturally shut up when they see that someone else is on the elevator with them? Absolutely—but only if they get on at the same time. It's an interesting phenomenon; try to observe it yourself. Simply, people tend not to discontinue the conversation they were having in the hallway if there's someone already on board. They'll stop talking if someone gets on after them, but they don't seem to have the same suspicion level when someone is already there.

It may be that they feel they're invading someone else's space. I don't know. All I do know is that this company has found people will continue especially revealing conversations when there is absolutely no question that someone is within clear earshot.

And, of course, these kinds of interesting conversations are continued as the participants step out onto their floor. The easy rider has the latitude to get off too and walk as far as she needs to, or feels it appropriate. Perhaps even to the point of the discreet knock on a randomly selected door, which may be all that's needed to defray any potential, momentary suspicions that might have arisen.

Of course, the key to finding potential sources from among your employees is understanding your company's structure, relationships, and patterns and then going out to contact those who know what's happening. Once again, business intelligence collection is not a spectator sport.

THE COLLECTORS—PREPARING THEM

Certainly, such groups have preconference meetings. Contact books get put together that assign a booth maven (or booth bunny, depending on your company's nickname for the people who work trade-show floors) time to certain people. They include listings of those who will visit all the other booths and on what schedule; a page or two on which customers are likely to be there and who is in the best position to deal with a particular customer; and handouts that remind attendees about which company clothes are going to be the uniform of the day.

But we're talking about much more preparation than the logistical side of things. Such preparation includes matching the collector to prospective sources; making that internal collector aware of exactly what you think she'd be able to collect from those certain people she already expects to meet at this conference; making certain that she knows how to collect information from people without making them nervous or crazy or suspicious—what we've already spent considerable time describing as elicitation; making certain that she knows what time she's supposed to be in which room of an adjoining hotel for her daily debriefing; making certain that she's been prepared with the means necessary to keep a record of what she's learned during the interim between her regularly scheduled debriefings.

Preparation also includes making certain that record keeping does not include the Linda Tripp signature-model, voice-activated microcassette recorder; making certain that it also doesn't include pulling out a notebook during a conversation; making certain that notes about sources, or deriving from conversation with sources, are not lying on the counter next to the booth sign-in sheet. Seemingly obvious certainties that have to be checklisted, because if they're not, there'll be some fallout—fallout that companies have recounted in great detail—and sometimes chagrin—as we have helped build a trade-show and conference intelligence competency and learned what had happened in previous conferences.

More Than a One-Shot Deal

So far, this may have appeared as preparations to attend just one trade show or conference. Yet in fact it's been about establishing a culture of intelligence within the organization and installing processes and plans to continue to capitalize on your investment in conferences and trade shows. Haven't your people been attending conferences and professional symposia for years? Do you think they've never heard anything of any competitive value? Is it somehow possible that they just didn't know where to go with the information they collected without thinking or trying—the most telling variant that's summed up in the "Nobody ever asked" principle?

Let's look at the structure of most professional conferences for a moment. We see that they're almost always supported by their membership for the papers and presentations that dot the landscape. And rarely do the professional association executives or employees make the decisions about whose paper is accepted for publication in the proceedings and for presentation.

Instead, the volunteer members of the society or association do the brunt of the grunt work. Members who are, by day, mild-mannered employees of your very own firm. Is someone in your company serving as a conference chair at this moment, exerting all manner of influence on who does what to whom? Is someone serving as the chair—or even a member—of the abstract evaluation committee? Is someone in your organization willing to serve, if asked and supported by the company to a certain degree?

And now, you'll ask, why? What good does any of this do the company aside from the arguable benefit of getting the firm's name out in front of the rest of industry? A few answers.

PAPER, TOPIC, AND THEME SELECTION

Having one of your employees who wants to work within the society's volunteer structure has significant, although not necessarily immediately apparent, benefits. Think about how influential a member of the conference organizing committee can be in developing the theme for the program next year. Think about how useful this can be if it's an area your firm is vitally interested in developing.

Most companies, if they think about it at all, encourage their employee membership on such a committee so that they can possibly get free company advertising by having one of their employees present something that the firm is doing. This is what's called the 45–5 rule: attend a fifty-minute presentation at many professional meetings and you'll get five minutes of substance and forty-five minutes of advertising. Yet there can be other, substantial benefits.

From an intelligence perspective, as opposed to a strictly marketing and cheap advertising perspective, being able to influence the conference theme can allow you to set the stage for invitations to be sent to specially skilled or respected people at other companies. People who are working in technologies or disciplines that are of particular interest to you competitively. People whose papers might well provide the kinds of insights that you need to understand where their firm is headed in the years to come. The nearby box entitled *Call for Papers* illustrates this process a little further.

Call for Papers

Setting the theme for an electro-optics conference can be very valuable from an intelligence collection perspective, especially if your employee is able to suggest and have approved a section on X-ray pulsed lasers. He may know full well that there may only be twelve people in the world who are working in that discipline—and two of them work for a competitor. If one or the other of those two—or both—respond to the personally addressed call for papers announcement, what chance will they have of getting their paper approved without reservation? I'd say they have a good chance, wouldn't you? The "Congratulations, Your Abstract Has Been Accepted" letter should have been written a long time ago.

It doesn't have to be the conference chair or cochair who does the setup for this; it can be someone down in the bowels of the committees where much of the rest of the work is done.

For example, at this level, consider that the person who is going to be named as the moderator or introducer for a paper presentation has certain roles and responsibilities. Her duties can be as simple as making sure that the lavalier microphone is in place three minutes before the presentation to those wonderful folks who offer. Or, she offers to help the presenter all the way through the development of a paper—providing an outside set of eyes, if you will. This may not be one of your employees at all; instead, it may be one of your trusted consultants, for example.

Other aspects immediately suggest themselves to the intelligence professional who applies a little imagination to the setting. Is there someone who can be assigned to attend the presentation—other than the moderator—who has certain specific questions to ask from the floor? As often as not, the presenter will honor the question, even if it's a little on the margins of sensitivity, rather than appear to be someone who declines to answer something in front of his peers.

On another level, your moderator has the opportunity to wait until after all the questions have been asked from the floor and the session is over. He can stand on the edge of the group of those who come up and ask questions after the presentation, listening to the answers the speaker provides—and noting for future reference the names and companies of those who ask interesting questions that can indicate the direction in which their companies are headed.

Remembering the principle of the continually raising bar helps here, too. Now that the presenter has finished his paper and answered the questions from the floor and from the assembled multitudes afterward, the sensitivity bar is just about at its highest possible point. Here's where your kindly and caring moderator, mindful of the needs of the presenter, invites him for a drink or a cup of coffee, depending on the hour—and the speaker.

Bear in mind that the bar is fairly high, and the moderator's conversation starts at that level, not down at the basics of the paper. It's the logical thing to do, after all, to say thanks; to point out the things that seemed to be the most well received by the audience; the brilliance of the paper or concepts. Your moderator already has the picture. He read the elicitation chapters before the conference as part of his preparation.

THE TARGET POPULATION

By now, you've come to know that there are more people out in the world who know things about your competition. You've learned to follow the money in search of sources of information that can be turned into useful and timely intelligence. The trade-show and conference environment even helps to broaden this population, broadening it not only for the immediate collection objectives but also for setting up those longer-term relationships that have excellent payoffs because you're more than just a disembodied voice on the phone: You've actually had some face time with these sources that pays large dividends in later contacts.

And since many times the environment is so much like that elusive "comfortable setting" where elicitation can be very well employed, the relationship can be based on a nonconfrontational, comfortable, and collegial contact, one in which people are preconditioned to expect an exchange of information. Information of all kinds. After all, isn't that what conferences and trade shows are designed to do? To bring together as many people into one environment as possible and get them to say things to others about their business, their companies, themselves?

Who's going to be exhibiting at this trade show? Who's going to be presenting at this conference? What is the focus of this upcoming symposium? Who's been there before? Who's not going to be there this time? What kinds of things have we seen at shows like this before? And then, a whole other population can be found at meetings who are part of this information-rich activity. Just a few of the many include:

- *Vendors:* Not only the competitors you know who will be there, but the vendors who serve your industry; just because they seem to be somewhat lower in the food chain doesn't mean that they're any less valuable as sources. And besides, they're actively pursuing their customers—your competitors—for their own reasons. Of course, this means that as they collect "customer intelligence" for themselves, they come into possession of "competitor intelligence" from your perspective. Often, that information is almost one and the same. Some vendors are not just willing to talk about what they have learned from a competitor, they are so interested in your continued business that they are willing to actively seek out information they know you're interested in having. Need we remind ourselves, however, of the two-edged nature of this sword?

- *Consultants* are a wonderful group of people, and not just because I run a management consulting firm. Consultants can be excellent sources of information as well as collectors. As collectors, they always have a custom-made reason for wanting to know everything they can get their hands on, and no one really questions it. Very often, they have sources of information that date back to when they were employed by the companies they now serve. The force multiplier effect is very clear, obviously. One look at your name tag, with company name on it, immediately raises the hair on the back of your rivals' necks when you walk into their booths or hospitality suites. Consultants, who either don't have their firm's name on the tag or whose consultancy is so established and well regarded that they certainly can't possibly pose a threat, get in where your employees can't— even if they may be there at your behest. Think about it. When was the last time you heard someone ask a consultant for his or her client list as they entered a trade-show booth, or engaged someone in conversation after a paper presentation? When was the last time a booth maven asked a consultant who was paying for the consultant's trip to the conference? On the flip side, the consultant population can be seen as sources themselves. Sources who have those same traits that we as collectors find so endearing in the professorial type: always ready to teach, perhaps more ready to preach, and certainly always ready to proselytize on their own behalf. Just *try* to keep a consultant from talking about his most interesting assignment, which just may have some application in your firm. Or, it might not; but it's certainly worth hearing about how it worked at your competitor's facility.

- *Trade publications:* Subscriptions hardly pay for the postage on trade magazines anymore. Advertising is clearly the name of the game, and the publishers and their advertising-sales types are constantly on the lookout for that increase in space that just might accompany a new product. Surprisingly, few people at the company level pay much attention to how many insights their advertising budget plans and expenditures reveal about their intentions. The box below gives an example of this from an industry where one might have thought they'd know a little better than most; and it illustrates the kinds of insights that can be obtained in this kind of an environment. While the example deals with the indiscreet conversation of a company executive on the trade-show floor, there are other aspects of dealing with the publishing community. The kind of conversation described in the box is really quite common, spurred by the publisher's need to know what's going on in the industry so that his editorial calendar is relevant. Relevant not only in terms of content but also as a reflection of what kinds of advertising he can sell. Clearly, the publisher falls into exactly the same category as the journalist, but without the need—necessarily—for there to be a quid pro quo for the publisher.

Even Good Families Have These Sorts of Problems

Two years ago, I was attending an international security conference and trade show. I had just finished presenting a paper on competitive intelligence collection and analysis activities; a fairly large portion of the 6,000 plus attendees heard the presentation, one of whom I was about to meet.

While visiting the booth of a publisher for whom I've written about a dozen articles on competitive intelligence and countermeasures, one of the senior leaders of a security hardware company came into the booth. The publisher with whom I had been speaking immediately recognized this fellow as one of the key people he'd wanted to see about increasing his advertising budget.

The publisher introduced me to the executive, identifying me as one of the people who wrote fairly regularly for his journal. In response, the visitor talked about how many of my articles he had read and applied in his business, and that those articles were the reason he'd attended my just completed presentation. I was grateful, but that gratitude turned almost immediately to surprise when he responded to what that publisher had to say next.

The publisher asked him why his advertising buys had been fairly flat for the previous year, and what he could do to encourage the company to spend more with his journal. Knowing full well what I do for a living, and having no clue as to who our clients were, this executive nonetheless launched into a wonderful description of the new family of security products that his firm was going to be launching nine months in the future: specific characteristics, the target customer population, the price point he was going to be able to hit between his new product and those of competitors, the reasons why he'd be able to kill the others on price and maintain quality, and a number of other things.

The executive offered all this as background to the reasons that he was going to be raising his space requirements from half a page to two full pages a month beginning the month of the launch. All offered without the slightest apparent clue about how much he was saying; all offered without any kind of hesitancy whatever; all offered without any apparent concern for how I—as a clear witness to this discussion— might use this information to his firm's disadvantage had I been so inclined.

- *Media* in all its forms have people they develop at conferences— people they develop as industry sources, people they develop as experts whom they can call on for high-level comment when the occasion demands, people who influence the course of an industry and who, by their mere presence, can suggest new industry directions. And as the earlier description of uses of the media suggested, many other aspects apply that are only aided and extended by the sociability that attends conferences and trade shows. The amount of preparation that goes into developing sources for yourself from among the media is directly proportional to your success. The preconference planning that goes into preparations for dealing with media types is well worth the effort: plans to meet the writer at his favorite watering hole or near the pressroom; plans that include reviewing articles the writer has had published recently—and especially not so recently—before actually arriving at the conference, allowing you to truly appear to be knowledgeable about the writer and his work, and more importantly, a potential source for him. Remembering that this will be a two-way street, the planning includes what you're prepared to say so that he doesn't get more out of it than you do.

- *Poster Children:* Who among us has not seen those poor and forlorn creatures whose papers were simply not judged worthy of inclusion in the conference proceedings or of a place at the podium? Who among us has not felt some pity for the lack of sizzle the paper might represent, or the lack of personality that the researcher exhibited on his previous (and only) presentation to the same conference on a different topic? When members of our own conference teams encounter these folks, they always stop and chat. Why? Because the forever lonely, the forever personality-challenged, the forever hopeful that someone will stop by their poster paper to prove that life is worth living after all always, *always,* know far more than just what their paper is about. And no one to tell. No one, that is, except for the person with the interest and time to spend in conversation, the person who has been tasked with learning as much about this particular topic as possible. No one except for that person with the skills that allow her to know when—and how—to end a conversation with a source of information.

Tricks of the Trade Show—Number Three

Talk about expecting the worst and the best.

One company's Business Intelligence manager was screening a number of people to send to a trade show. Two of the potential correspondents were women, clearly friends as well as co-workers who wanted to go. One of the women, however, was in her seventh month of pregnancy, and the BI manager was concerned that it might not be best for her to attend this particular event.

She and her friend prevailed, and the expectant mother became one of the most prolific collectors at the entire meeting. Why? Simply because the people manning a booth couldn't help but ask the first question that would come to anyone's mind when an obviously pregnant and footsore lady entered their booth: "Would you like to sit down for a minute?"

Minutes stretching into tens of minutes, while the booth mavens continued meeting customers and all manner of other visitors to the booth. And this was despite the fact that she was wearing her conference badge, complete with her company's name on it. Clearly, mothership has its advantages.

3. Collection Operations at Trade Shows and Conferences

Of course, there are often significant differences between trade shows and pure conferences/symposia. Your up-front work will be just as different as the selection and preparation of sources will be. Yet many elements will be similar. In this section, we'll identify some of the ways that clients have capitalized on the opportunities such meetings provide for the intelligence collector. We'll also discuss some of the ways that we've seen our clients' *rivals* perform as we've sought to assist clients in protecting themselves in this information-rich environment.

In actuality, we distinguish between these twin perspectives with some football vocabulary. The actual on-site operations, where there is a central control element to provide direction, coordination, on-the-ground initial analysis, and several other things, are called *quarterback operations.* Conversely, operations where the focus is more on protection and defense than on collection and offense are called *linebacker operations.* And, naturally, we see companies that take an integrated approach that encompasses both sides of the line.

QUARTERBACK OPERATIONS

Clearly, there is a requirement for planning and practice before the game actually gets under way. There are myriad details that are associated with trade shows in the first place in order to get the most out of them, even without intelligence operations: Is the equipment going to get there and is it going to work? Why aren't we getting the power, telephones, food, chairs to where they're supposed to be? Who's going to fill in for Barney at the last minute?

Maybe you thought that the planning that went into collector and source identification that we just went through was enough. Hardly. There's a logistical tail for just about everything.

LOCATION

Choosing the best location for the quarterback is critical to the success of the operation. Choosing a hotel that's on the other side of town caters to the whims and fantasies of those who think this is all about James Bond, Aston Martins, and "shaken, not stirred." In the real world, however, it's practicality that wins out. While it may not be best to have the operational site at the conference hotel itself, choosing an adjacent hotel allows your correspondents to have easy access to it when they need it. This also cuts down on some of the excuses they might have for missing a scheduled meeting. At the same time, we most strongly advise against trying to save money by using the exhibit booth or public break areas where your people are being met for meetings to discuss their activities.

COMMUNICATIONS

Pagers and cell phones are more and more the order of the day, especially at larger shows and conferences, exacerbated of course by the number of people you've brought to the meeting. Nothing is any less fulfilling than not being able to track someone down at a meeting when you have something quite important—either to task or to warn about—to pass along. And sometimes, even though we're not talking about human life or world peace, there is some value in being able to reach out and touch someone. Please consider, however, bringing your regular cell phones and pagers from home. The kind that are available for rental are not usually recommended, especially if your firm is using the same communications equipment supplier in the same city.

But please, stop short of the chalk marks on the wall, the rose in the lapel, secret code words, and trying to elude the surveillance that's very rarely there. That is, unless you're at a trade show or conference in a fairly monolithic police state where virtually all the rules are different. In fact, in the lexicon of my old world, "Moscow rules" have even entered the commercial arena. Moscow rules relate to the practices that are necessary for intelligence contacts under certain hostile conditions. For the most part, however, those who insist on such things are still too much caught up in their own sense of the mysterious.

PLAYBOOKS

Now that you're on the field, you can look back and begin to think about the things that will make life so much easier for you and for those you meet. Looking back, you can see that you spent a fair amount of time in planning and preparation: identifying the specific questions that need to be answered, both the standing intelligence questions (SIQs) and the essential intelligence questions (EIQs) that pertain to the meeting at hand. In case after case, we have had clients tell us that perhaps one of the most important lessons they gleaned from the first efforts at trade-show and conference intelligence operations was the way that developing SIQs and EIQs helped them focus on what they knew and what their informational gaps were. Quite often, as they have gone through the process, they've found that more information about a particular question was already inside the company than they thought. In turn, this allowed them to refine better and more precise questions.

We've found it especially useful for there to be a playbook for each of the correspondents you'll be employing at a particular meeting. Construction of the playbook begins at the outset of the planning, with whatever background information that will help the individual correspondent understand her mission better:

- Background information on the conference.

- Background on prospective contacts.

- Background on the companies that are targeted by the collection team, broken down by the individuals who have primary and secondary collection responsibilities for those rivals, customers, vendors, publishers, consultants, media mavens, conference organizers, association leaders and executives, et cetera.

- Lists of hotels, restaurants of note, meeting sites, and room numbers, along with telephone contact information.

Additionally, the playbook can be a very useful means of helping your correspondents keep up on a daily basis, if your playbook contains

- Sanitized or abbreviated reporting from other sources at the conference.

- On-the-ground or home-office analysis of materials that have surfaced during the conference thus far.

- Additional EIQs that are the result of other correspondents' collection and reporting.

- Warnings about what others have been attempting to collect about your firm, as reported by your correspondents and other sources.

- Warnings about people your correspondents should avoid, or at least how to deal with those who might otherwise be problematic.

And, before we leave the playbook, a word of caution. Keep the playbooks in the office. Carry the playbooks with you to the meeting site (meaning, don't put them into the checked baggage) and keep them there throughout the conference. Don't give them to your correspondents to keep in their offices, because they'll surely want to take them to places where they can be lost. Don't let the correspondents carry them on the plane so that they can get up to speed while en route to the conference—they won't pay attention to the person in the seat next to them or across the aisle behind them, even though more than likely that other person will have an interest in the very same things. Don't let them carry them to their rooms to study—they'll inevitably be found somewhere else, such as lying about in your booth, by decidedly the wrong people. Keep them in the meeting site, and control them when you leave for the airport. See the nearby boxes for the list of things that we've found—and where—associated with conferences and trade shows by doing little more than following Yogi Berra's observation that "a fella can see a lot of things just by looking around."

OTHER GEAR

Obviously, this means that there has to be some organizational support. This may mean at least one laptop, but who leaves home without one these days? And a portable printer. You're not going to be developing client-ready proposals with it, so you can afford to err on the side of production versus pretty. Your modem will link you—through your reporting—to anyone back at the office who has a support role, either analytical, logistical, or research to support the project. Since you'll have your modem, and presumably an on-board fax, please consider very carefully whether or not you'll use the hotel's business service for incoming fax traffic. It's surprising how many of us will simply give the number that's on the phone card for the hotel fax and let the hotel people handle our fax traffic. And all that entails. Think about how many bellmen you've tipped for one thing or another. Have you ever given any thought to just how securely your hotel keeps your incoming faxes until they're delivered to your room? Have you ever thought about how much it would take for someone to ensure that every one of the faxes intended for you got photocopied and routed to someone else first? Do you think that just because it happens in France and other countries it doesn't happen here in the United States? Or worse, do you think it would never happen in a friendly country? Or worse yet, do you believe that no one would ever do anything like this to you because, after all, *you* play by all the rules, don't you?

Of course, you'll remember the paper, the flip chart to substitute as portable white boards, the reference materials, file folders, stick pins, and masking tape for the things you'll want to put up on the wall, and notebooks that you'll need for the debriefings of the correspondents as they arrive in the room. And certainly, you'll want to make sure—if you're the intelligence team leader—to have those important things like snacks and beverages. Not just for the correspondents who come by for their debriefings, but for you too. Because you probably won't be leaving the room until the conference is over.

MEETINGS AND DEBRIEFINGS

You arrived a day before almost everyone else. You've gotten the debriefing site organized. It'll probably be a suite, because you'll want to be close to the debriefing materials and all the ancillary materials without leaving them for such mundane matters as eating and sleeping. If you don't get a suite the first time you run a quarterback operation, no big deal. With the words "Never again" on your breath, you'll make reservations for a suite somehow, anyhow, for the next conference. And if anyone questions the slightly additional cost, invite them to attend as a debriefer the next time around.

Long before ever leaving for the conference, you've arranged for the side meeting room at the out-of-the-way restaurant that's some distance from the conference hotel. Each of your correspondents will have been asked to arrive in time to make the final group meeting the night before the trade show or conference begins. Here is where the final organizational items will be presented and ironed out, where final tasking and requirements will be reviewed, and where the debriefing schedules for each individual correspondent will be worked out.

Of course, each correspondent will know the communications plan: when they have their individual appointments and their fallback appointments, just in case the old adage of "Life is what happens when you have other plans" comes into play; the telephone and pager numbers for the other people they have to contact, including you; the hotel and room number for the debriefings.

THE QUARTERBACK'S ROLE

How involved or outvolved should a quarterback be in actual collection at a trade show or conference? The box *Tricks of the Trade—Number Four* gives one idea of the possible pros and cons. Beyond that the answer may be: If you're not known at all to your competition, then work it; if you're known to your competition because of professional duties, exposure, or similar histories at the same companies, then you might reconsider whether you can be the collector *par excellence,* or the orchestra leader from afar.

Tricks of the Trade Show—Number Four

Speaking of you, what kinds of things are you doing in your intelligence quarterback role? Are you out on the conference floor, the exhibits hall floor? You have to weigh the pluses and minuses. In some cases, if you're a SCIP member who's been seen at county fairs and goat ropings, you might consider the experience of one of our clients.

Known reasonably well across the industry, he walked into his primary competitor's booth only to be immediately met by his counterpart. After an exchange of greetings, the counterpart from the rival firm escorted him to a corner of the large booth area. The counterpart waxed eloquent for forty-five minutes about everything from kids' soccer teams to hang gliding—and absolutely nothing in between that pertained to the business in which they are engaged. With his face showing his discouragement at being shunted off and away from the

---

booth dwellers, the client congratulated his counterpart on having kept him from collecting anything at all. The rival was clearly pleased with himself for having kept his opposition away. He might have been even happier had it not been for the fact that while he was gone, four others from the client firm had enjoyed considerable, and rewarding, experiences in the booth.

4. Processing the Information

The processing portion of the cycle involves getting the information from the person who actually collected it and into the hands of the people who can begin to organize it for analysis later.

A real basic has existed for centuries in the intelligence business. Your first question should always be "How much time do we have?" The second thing you do after that is set up the next meeting arrangements: the time and location if they're going to be on a variable schedule. Why? Because inevitably, there's a pager that goes off, or a call that comes in and the meeting gets put off for a while. It's not only possible, it's likely that your correspondent will wind up running out of the meeting site and it'll be three days before you can establish contact again because of all the things he's doing at the trade show. If it hasn't happened to you yet, you've been lucky.

As far as the debriefings themselves, you're going to have people who come in the morning because of a late-night assignment. Perhaps they'll be the types who respond well to suggestions that they make some notes before going to bed. Some will come in directly from their contacts with their sources. It really doesn't matter what time they come in. Their notes will always be better than their memory of a conversation three hours and thirty people later. Encourage them to make notes; more importantly, encourage them to safeguard the notes.

These kinds of notes will greatly aid—and shorten—the debriefing. After all, this is the reason you're at the conference in the first place: It guards against someone forgetting what they learned if they have a space between collection and reporting. Perhaps they'll even use the electronics the company provided them as laptops or palm pilots or the like. Downloading will be much easier than you writing it out in notes by hand during the debriefing. But in reality, that's a perfect world. If we know anything, this is not a perfect world. So, the brunt of the processing will fall to you. Debriefing will be easier and easier as you become accustomed to it. The first couple of times will be the learning experience you crave.

And how do you do the debriefing? Not much differently than we've already talked about: get them to start with a running chronology, hopefully supported by their notes, of what they've done and whom they've seen since your last meeting; let them go in a stream of consciousness, or guide them along according to the established list of questions you've already developed.

You ask, isn't there a general rule? The answer is yes. Absolutely, yes. Introverted correspondents prefer to operate off a script, and in that order; the extroverted source typically wants to do stream of consciousness. But the reality is, do what's worked best with this correspondent already; if this is a first, test the introvert/extrovert approach and see which is the best.

But bear in mind that organization is the key; especially if you're dealing with a particularly excited and pleased-with-himself extrovert, the greater your organization, the more on target you'll be able to be. Make your marginal notes and don't interrupt. Come back to the notations before the debriefing is over. In most cases, the correspondent will really appreciate your interruption-free style and will especially appreciate your coming back to something they spoke about fifteen minutes earlier. It shows them that you're more than just an order taker; you're really paying attention and thinking about what they've been telling you.

And, at the end, you have the opportunity to give the correspondent that additional tasking you've developed through other correspondents— or that tasking you'd given to others who didn't get what they set out to get.

Before we leave the processing stage, please remember that storage and transmission are just as much part of processing as anything else. How are you going to ensure the integrity of the materials if maids and room service have unfettered access to the room? How well do you know the people who pay a lot of attention to your comings and goings? And does your knowledge of them automatically confer trust? I suspect not.

5. Analyzing the Information

Who's going to be doing the analysis? If you'd like to take a page out of the intelligence-community book, where there is a clear division of responsibilities, you'll be certain to avoid having the collectors do the analysis and evaluation of the information. Why? Simply because the closer you are to the collection, the more elegantly you've pursued the sources, developed them, and then gotten the information from them, the greater the validity, accuracy, and completeness you naturally attach to the information. In fact, if you're the collector, all the more reason that a different set of eyes looks at the reporting.

Sometimes, it can get to be a little on the confrontational side, but that's ultimately for the good of the product. At least that's the experience of most intelligence services worth their salt.

Rather than being a section on intelligence analysis—and falling short since there are several entire and good books dedicated to this matter—we'll only talk about where and at what level it'll be done in the context of trade shows and conferences.

On the Ground

First-order analysis while at the meeting can pay off in large ways, based on the simple principle of "nearer my source to thee." With this orientation, you're doing a bit more capitalization on the real reason you're here in the first place, instead of waiting for your correspondents to get back to the barn for debriefings. Once they've told you something they did not recognize as being of importance, but you do because of what someone *else* in your correspondent cadre has just told you, you can respond with additional tasking, not only to them, but to those others you have been debriefing according to the regular schedule.

While this may not sound like especially detailed or high-level analysis, it's at least more than what had gone on before. Bear in mind that your detachment by not being the correspondent who collected it in the first place takes away the "too close to the forest to see the trees" problem.

Back at the Ranch

You can add to the quality of the process even further by having an on-line relationship with one of the people back at the headquarters whom you would have engaged in the analytical process anyway. These are the people who—hopefully—helped in the original development of those SIQs and EIQs on which your correspondents have been reporting. For one reason or another, usually financial, the analysts stay at the office and get periodic updates from those in the field, at a trade show or conference.

Very often, they're the ones who've been following the competitor or the customer or the other folks in whom you have an interest—perhaps regulators, for example. Often, getting their read on what a particular source had to offer can be quite timely in getting additional collection objectives fulfilled while people are still in contact during the trade show.

And the kind of reporting that you're getting from the correspondents? It'll range all the way from product and service kinds of information to the sort of things that'll be useful later on as your intelligence organization begins to grow in competency and holdings. In this latter case, we're talking about the source data sheets that were discussed earlier. Remember the old intelligence axiom: An intelligence service is only as good as the sources it develops and keeps. Your organization should be no different.

Of course, this discussion about "analysts back at the ranch" is for those Large-Time Charlies with big budgets and organizations. If you're part of that growing population of medium and small businesses that are beginning to avail themselves of a Business Intelligence *function* versus a full-blown organization, you can see that the orchestration, collection, analysis, and reporting may all fall on your broad shoulders. Reporting to the boss, if he's there, has considerable value. And, while you've been granted your audience, don't forget to debrief him too—after all, you gave him some collection of objectives before *he* came to the program, right? Who can tell how much he's learned from his opposite numbers— or how much more tasking he'll give to you on-site so that you and your correspondents can still make the most of the conference environment?

6. Disseminating the Intelligence Product

While this should be really one of the simplest parts, it often becomes a bit more complex as you get into the distribution of the intelligence product. And just as we did earlier, we'll continue to emphasize the need to keep raw information and processed and analyzed intelligence apart and distinct. Raw information stays with you; the intelligence, with its validity established, gets sent to those who need it.

This is not, of course, always and only the decision maker who asked for it in the first place. In many instances, it's useful for many other people as well. Yet that's not necessarily a decision you should make. Wait until after you've had a chance to brief your findings to the leadership before you decide on your own to whom it should be sent. In fact, many wise intelligence officers wait until the very end of their presentation to the leadership and ask, as their final question, "Who else do you want on distribution for this, Boss?" Those wise intelligence officers became wise, after having been unwise in making distribution according to their own lights.

Of course, opportunities will be presented at the end-brief as well. For instance, you may not have had an opportunity to speak with the leadership about the people they met—at their level—during the time they may have spent at the trade show. Very often, no one else in an organization can enjoy the level of access to the rival leadership as your seniors can. If you happen to be in the process of building a remote psychological profile, wouldn't it be helpful to have a peer review—from inside your own firm—contribute to the profile scoring?

LINEBACKER OPERATIONS

Rather than waiting until the countermeasures part of this book, we'll slip in a little at this point about the protection side of trade shows and conferences. After all, you're not the only people who are attending the conference, you know.

Just as we have run an offensive collection operation up to this point, a variety of things can and ought to be done from a defensive perspective, too.

Some are pretty straightforward; some are not.

Among the fairly obvious—and forgotten—are the boxing up of all the extraneous papers and notes and sending them back to the office with the rest of your materials. We have encountered far too many people poking in and out of Dumpsters around hotels to think they are simply homeless or unable to get a hotel room for the conference; far too many people whose seemingly sole purpose in life is to pick up whatever appears to have been left, discarded, or simply unguarded. Spend a few minutes in Appendix B, where we discuss legal and ethical issues, both here and around the world. You'll soon see that not everyone plays by the same rules—and some play by no rules at all.

Some of the less obvious defensive strategies, ones that should be included in virtually every debriefing, include questions about what the competition is doing by way of intelligence activities during this event.

The first of these topics is asking, "Who's asking what of whom?" If you have any clue about the people who are working this conference for your competition, you're off to a good start. Yet most of the time, companies that are interested in making as much intelligence hay from the meeting as possible aren't getting everything that is of value. Consider for a moment that one of the major things that intelligence agencies around the world are constantly attempting to find out is "What do they want from us?" and "What are they after?" And, they rely on their counterintelligence services to help them learn about these things. The reason is quite simple. They wouldn't be asking if one of two circumstances were not present: They are going in that direction themselves and want to know how far along you are and, based on your progress, what they can do to preempt you in the marketplace. In fact, the counterintelligence function can frequently be one of the first indicators that another company is heading in a particular direction. Once they get their initial indications of a rival's interest, the message goes directly to the collection side of the firm. The collectors then have a place to start where one hadn't existed; a new area of interest where they had not had any previous intention or reason to look.

On another level, this also begs the question set "How are they collecting, how well, or how poorly?" This is often the set of questions that begins to provide some insights into the competencies of the other company to collect against you. It begins to suggest how well organized, trained, funded, or sponsored they are within their own firm. It's fundamental to assisting in one of the tasks in the protection business that you'll be hearing more about in a few chapters: assessing your rival's ability to collect against you.

Even more fundamentally, it sets the groundwork for you to continuously prepare and defend your own people and information. Identifying who's collecting what, and how well, and how poorly, allows you to prepare your people—during your debriefings as well as in getting your correspondents ready for future shows and conferences.

At the other end of the spectrum are those activities that you can undertake in the wonderful environment of the trade-show or professional conference. Activities that we'll talk more about in the section on countermeasures.

Lastly, what do you do if you can't be everywhere? What if you don't have an organized approach like quarterback or linebacker? The next best thing is prebriefings prior to the departure for the event by as many cooperating internal assets as possible. Some clients have had wonderful success developing groups of correspondents by having pizza brought in and setting up an "Eating Your Competitor's Lunch" session. It's here that they give the general and specific questions and organize their correspondents by topic and by individuals or companies on whom the correspondents will focus once at the conference.

It becomes part of the company's intelligence culture that correspondents begin to anticipate, to await their prebriefings that occur in either group settings or individually if the event is small—or the company's attendance is. And, it's even more of a cultural thing when the intelligence collectors have an appointment with the correspondent on the first morning of the day he gets back from the meeting. Correspondents who get "taught" to expect a visit on the first day back are always prepared and ready, willing, and able to talk about their experiences. Some of them have been so successful that they're bursting at the seams for the chance to tell someone about their great success; waiting to collect some of those strokes that you as the intelligence collector are so good at giving out. All of them are overjoyed that the debriefing that you're going to do absolves them of the need to write that damnable trip report that you, as the willing laborer in the vineyard, so graciously agree to do for them.

A Day In The Life of the Trade Show Collector

Start out with breakfast in the restaurant or breakfast room of the competitor's hotel. Most people don't leave their hotel for breakfast meals and of course, they're planning their day: who they'll be seeing, what they'll be talking about, what approach they'll be taking on this or that. You get the idea.

By mid-morning, when most of the early visitors have gone off to the conference sessions and the exhibits floor is nearly vacant, the nearby break area is a good congregating space for a lot of organized whining and sniveling. Since most of that is done in louder than normal voices, it can often be heard several tables away. If someone cared to be there.

By lunch, if it's a trade show or exhibits environment, the break area where the barely edible sandwiches are provided is a useful place to visit. People with sore feet from hours of standing don't want to wander very far. Whining and sniveling continues, as does a review of the things that have gone well and things that have gone poorly.

And, in those cases where the lunch for the booth bunnies is later than when the attendees have eaten, the volume and sincerity of the whining is greater.

Mid-afternoon, low visitor times have the same—or marginally better—opportunities in the break areas.

By dinner time, the exhibits floor is closed. Depending on the conference size, location and even the pocket depth of some of the exhibitors, there may be crowds moving in varying directions from the hotels. Some are going to hospitality suites and steamship round. Others are going to dinner at someone's aunt's recommended restaurant a few miles from the hotel. No matter. Groups are going to meet in the lobby at 6:30. Say your competitor's booth maven crew numbers eight people. The first five or six show up on time. One comes down at 6:40 with apologies; the last one comes down complaining about how much e-mail he had to answer—and explains the problems he's had to deal with in making his case of forgiveness. What have they been talking about while waiting to hear this tale of woe? Right again.

And after dinner, does anyone want to find a bar and then try to find their way back to the hotel? Hardly, everyone who left for dinner together comes back together. Most will plead the great e-mail excuse and go to their rooms. The others, the more gregarious and extroverted who gain energy from the exchanges, are still ready for more. The hotel bar is the logical place to cap off the day and talk about what's on the horizon for the next day.

CHAPTER 13

Developing Personality and Psychological Profiles of Business Rivals

I have studied the enemy all my life. I have read the memoirs of his generals and his leaders. I have even read his philosophers and listened to his music. I have studied in detail the account of every damned one of his battles. I know exactly how he will react under any set of circumstances. And he hasn't the slightest idea of when I'm going to whip the hell out of him.

—**General George S. Patton, Jr.**

The ability to avoid surprise in the marketplace is one of the primary reasons that we do competitive intelligence. Fundamental to avoiding surprise is our ability to anticipate what our business rivals are going to do.

We sometimes try to hallucinate what our opposite numbers are going to do. Sometimes, we even think we know the other guy based on having met him a few times. But that's hardly the kind of knowledge about the opposition that Patton was talking about. It certainly falls short of what Napoleon referred to as the kind of success on the battlefield that comes from being "inside my enemy's decision-making process."

Over the course of the past thirty years, a variety of psychological profiling instruments have come into greater use as predictive instruments; instruments that can help to predict behavior, as opposed to those that are useful in a therapeutic or institutional way; instruments that don't require advanced degrees to administer, assess, or understand; instruments that are constructed in such a way as to allow a certain amount of flexibility in the ways they are used.

The Myers-Briggs Type Indicator (MBTI) is the instrument that we've found to be the most easily and effectively used in intelligence applications. It's perhaps the most universally applied of all instruments, in use around the world in over two dozen languages and administered to over two million people annually. Initially developed in the early 1940s for use as a screening and selection instrument, it's been continuously refined, improved, and validated.

REMOTE PSYCHOLOGICAL ASSESSMENT

By the early part of the 1980s, we had been using the MBTI as a means of screening and selection for intelligence officers. Some "types" were well suited for analytical tasks; others were more suited to operational assignments in the field. Most of us can see the parallel between the intelligence and business communities by comparing accountants with sales and marketing people; there is no "one size fits all" type for every assignment in a business setting.

Many organizations—businesses as well as the intelligence community—use the MBTI rather extensively for everything from team building to assigning different people to different tasks. Other organizations use it extensively in helping employees know each other better as a means of enhancing organizational performance. And, of course, there are always the curmudgeons who discount anything new as being irrelevant, unnecessary, or just plain old witchcraft.

Professionals from outside the intelligence community had tried without much success to expand the potential for various "emerging human technologies" in the intelligence community. Instead of finding open and immediate acceptance for things that worked well in business or academia, these "outsiders" found resistance, superstition, and xenophobia. Part of the problem was that the intelligence community as a whole had been under the gun for a few years at that point and there was always a suspicion about the people who came to help us do our jobs better. Of course, this only happens in the intelligence community, right? After all, whenever an outside consultant of any sort comes into your business, you embrace that consultant with open arms; you accept unconditionally every suggestion he makes.

In any event, our leadership was certain that some of these emerging technologies really might have some potential for improving the way we went about our work. The leadership decided on a slightly different tack. They asked a few of us to consider ways to expand the edges of the envelope. We were mostly intelligence officers who had been around for a while and whose reputations were reasonably well established—both as operational officers and as skeptics.

Over the years, those of us who were skeptical of outsiders who knew virtually nothing about our work had a tendency to dismiss these new and wonderful solutions. If *we* became convinced that these emerging technologies had operational utility, the issue of acceptance would become moot—largely because of the credibility we brought from our operational backgrounds. If we could become convinced that one technique or another was indeed useful in an operational setting, we could then be agents of influence with our colleagues; we could be at the point of the spear in getting our fellow skeptics to accept new ways of delivering better intelligence operations and products.

Since the community had been using psychological testing and profiling for a couple of years already—and since most of our officers were familiar with the MBTI—we decided to look at the potential for operational use of this instrument.

Of course, the normal means of employing the MBTI is to instruct the person who'll be answering the questions about the instrument, give him the questionnaire form and answer sheet, and then score it upon completion. But, you can see just how problematic this could become if you wanted to profile a foreign leader or a business rival who would probably be uncooperative to say the least. Yet, something in my personal life occurred that ultimately opened our minds to a new way of viewing the MBTI and its additional applications for intelligence practitioners.

To the Untrained Eye

At roughly this same time, my wife and I were in the process of adding another child to our family through adoption. While going through the screening as adoptive parents, our adoption agency administered several psychological tests and instruments to us—including the MBTI. Yet, there was a wrinkle.

Not only were we to do the self-reporting that is central to the MBTI, we were also supposed to do it again. Except that the second time we were to answer for the other: I was to answer as I thought my wife would answer, and she would answer as she thought I would answer.

Not surprisingly, she and I came out as the two completely different people we are. When the psychologist conducting the evaluations came back with these results, we were concerned that we would not qualify based on how much emphasis he placed on just how different we are.

Yet he went on to assure us that while our personality type differences were indeed great, our reporting on each other's responses showed that we knew each other perhaps better than any other couple he had ever met. Indeed, the scores for our self-reports matched almost exactly the other-party reporting.

This little episode got me to thinking about ways that we could use the instrument without any contact with the target personality.

Each of the members of our little task force still had operational assignments around the country and the world, so it was a month or two before we convened again to consider applying the various technologies we'd been talking about. By that time, it occurred to me that this "remote" kind of assessment of psychological type might be useful for us in the intelligence community. The group thought that it was worth a look, and with the help of the staff psychologist, we picked out one of our leaders to profile. Each of us knew this individual reasonably well. We answered the MBTI questions as we thought he would answer himself.

The answers were very revealing. Each one of us came up with the same profile, and indeed the individual scores on the four different continuums were quite close to each other. More significantly, though, was what the staff psychologist told us about the comparison between the scores we reported and the actual score of the "target" leader. Our individual and thus our collective scoring was almost exactly the same profile as had emerged from his self-reporting. We repeated the process with ten other people of common acquaintance with the same results.

This suggested the possibility of doing what we eventually began calling "remote psychological assessments" as an additional intelligence product. Within the next few months, we were asked to do some real-world testing of this possible approach. There were a number of foreign leaders whom the national leadership wanted to better understand. We sought out several people who had known these foreign leaders at different times and places and made them familiar with the MBTI, taking them through the process of self-reporting, and then second-party reporting as my wife and I had done. This gave them a reasonably good appreciation of the workings of the instrument. Then they were ready to answer as the foreign leader might answer about himself.

Not surprisingly, the results were as consistent as they had been in our other experience—with the exception that we did not have any record of what the target individual's actual scoring was. After all, we had no way of handing him the forms and asking him to be so kind as to fill them out.

Nonetheless, the predictive nature of the MBTI came into play. With the national leadership about to have dealings with several of these target leaders—whether in conflict or in negotiation—we were able to provide them insights into how the target personality would probably respond given a particular set of circumstances and stimuli.

THE ACTUAL APPROACH

Clearly, we couldn't could send the forms packet to a foreign leader and ask him to oblige us by filling out the MBTI form. We can't do that in business either. Furthermore, we can't go out and recruit some long-term reliable sources to cooperate in the process as we did in government operations. Neither can we be as direct as handing the forms to prospective sources and asking them to complete the instrument. The solution set is somewhat different.

Over the past decade, our profiling team has completed a few hundred remote assessments each year for businesses using an approach that works quite well. At least this seems to be the judgment of those clients who keep asking for more of them to be performed. After all else is said and done, this is really the only means of testing a product or service's efficacy in the marketplace.

Yet it doesn't take a graduate psychology degree to follow the process we've developed. Perhaps that's the real beauty of the MBTI. It serves as a very useful organizing and analytical framework, it's been validated in study after study, and it's simple enough to be used by people with a modicum of interest and competency. You're about to get your modicum.

HOW DO YOU GET SOMEBODY TO SIT STILL FOR 126 QUESTIONS?

The answer is really quite simple. You don't. You've already learned elicitation. You already know how to reformulate questions into statements and get responses that can be significant and informative. Responses that come from multiple informed sources who know the target personality. Multiple sources that may range up to 100 to 125 people who know the target personality. Sources whose collective insights ultimately come to answer most of the 126 questions found in the MBTI Form G.*

---

*We don't use all of the questions simply because some questions are undergoing testing of their own before being included in a subsequent edition of the instrument.

We've been at this awhile and I'll be the first to admit that it required some considerable tweaking before we considered it a reliable approach. It certainly involved an understanding of which questions related to which characteristics. An understanding that came from having done much reading and study over the years, to include the one-week certification program at the Center for Application of Psychological Type at Gainesville, Florida.

Yet this is an understanding that you can marginally—and inexpensively—achieve by a combination of independent readings and on-line exercises. Indeed, the on-line version of the MBTI was developed by Michael Kiersey and Marilyn Bates and it can be found at www.kiersey.com. Download it and self-administer their version of the MBTI. Then start developing your own understanding and protocols that work for you. If a group of broken-down old intelligence officers in Alabama can do it fairly well, then certainly you smart folks in the rest of the country and the world can do it too.

SURE, AND JUST WHERE DO WE FIND 120 SOURCES?

Come on now. You've been at this for a couple of hours. Maybe even days. Surely you've thought and learned about where to find all manner of sources for all manner of information.

- Maybe there are people right there in your own organization who used to work with or for the target individual. These would certainly represent a great starting point. If you can get them to sit down and familiarize themselves with the instrument, it'll save you a great deal of other work.

- If the target individual came from another industry, that still means that there are people in his past who have gained some insights into the way he deals with the world; ways that will be revealed as the MBTI serves as the framework for the conversation you may have with them.

- Clearly, the target individual lives somewhere and has neighbors, coaches soccer, or plays golf with many other people, and has old fraternity brothers or sorority sisters, former professors, and colleagues in professional associations, to name just a few.

Once you've gotten responses from these first sets of associates, friends, and colleagues, now is the time for you to ask for some additional people who know the target. It's not long before you have a good solid picture of the person and what makes him or her tick.

The best part of this is that by way of having conversation with the various sources, they provide the effective elicitor with the background and anecdotal data that puts meat on the bones of the profile. People will almost naturally offer explanatory examples of your target in action—examples of how he reacted in a variety of situations and circumstances, how he overcame challenges, or who his close confidants are.

Your final picture—your report—should then have not only the fairly generic profile of whatever type emerges from the research, but it should also include the anecdotal history of the target's personal and professional life. On a fairly good day, your report can also include—in fact should include—suggestions about how to deal with the target personality in that upcoming acquisition negotiation or other business activity.

Let's be clear about something right up front. This is an approach that might offend a purist who uses the MBTI according to the precise standards established by the developers. The purist might insist on an uncorrupted, straightforward question where every word has been carefully written, tested, and refined. Of course, that would be the optimum condition.

But just as the perfect is often the greatest enemy of the good, we rarely encounter optimums and perfection in the real world. The result may not be a laboratory acceptable, scientifically valid, sampling. But, we're not into science and validity, necessarily. We're into what works. A method, an effectively predictive instrument, that helps our clients anticipate how a rival will act or react in the marketplace. That's what's important for us.

In dealing with these multiple sources, we focus on the various elements of the four scales associated with the MBTI: Extraversion—Introversion; Sensing—iNtuitive; Thinking—Feeling; and Perceiving—Judging. And no, Virginia, there aren't any misspellings. Carl Jung chose to spell Extraversion and not Extroversion; iNtuition allows us to use N as the shorthand for intuition without confusion since the letter I already stands for Introversion. An MBTI profile results in a four-letter designation for one of sixteen personality types, which are depicted in the table below.*

The Sixteen Types			
ISTJ	ISFJ	INFJ	INTJ
ISTP	ISFP	INFP	INTP
ESTP	ESFP	ENFP	ENTP
ESTJ	ESFJ	ENFJ	ENTJ

In formal MBTI scoring, these four-letter designations derive from a numerical value—on whichever side of the midpoint—on each one of the scales as shown on the accompanying box. These numerical points tell us about the preference that the person has (e.g., for extraversion or introversion); the strength of that preference is indicated by the numerical distance from the midpoint. In the example shown below, the individual shows relatively strong preferences for Introversion, Sensing, Thinking, and Judging: an ISTJ.

```
E _____ x ___ I
S ___ x _____ N
T ___ x _____ F
P _____ x ___ J
```

There are pages if not reams of discussion and description in the literature that tell us what the primary characteristics of an ISTJ are, covering a

*Full descriptions of each of the sixteen types can be found in a variety of locations, ranging from the on-line reference mentioned earlier to any one of numerous books on this instrument available at your local bookseller or through the Center for Application of Psychological Type in Gainesville, Florida.

wide range of issues. For example, in the area of making decisions, this type prefers to deal with few people and relies upon his own counsel to a large extent; when taking in the data that gets him to his decision, he will focus intently upon, and be able to manage well, the details that are involved, often losing sight of the so-called big picture in favor of the minutiae; is someone who values logic over emotion; and has a strong desire for closure and completion, as opposed to always wanting more information and waiting until the last minute to make a decision.

As you might expect, certain characteristics are shared by several of the types across the spectrum of MBTI profiles. Yet when the focus is intensified and clearly depicts an individual within the framework of one of the sixteen types, there are characteristics that emerge clearly, consistently, and, from a predictive perspective, reliably.

To place the application of psychological types, complete with an anecdotal history, into the ways in which business can begin to appreciate its usefulness, the short version of a much, much longer executive profile is repeated in the box *A Typical Remote Assessment and Results*. Obviously, we're not in a position to identify the participants or the actual extent of what was ultimately a forty-plus-page report, but it should provide you an understanding sufficient to decide whether you want to develop the internal capability to at least understand your business rivals in the way that George Patton tried to do. Successfully.

A Typical Remote Assessment and Results

Junipero Corp, a fairly well-established and profitable manufacturer in the electronics components industry, had just hired a new president, Jack Jones. Brought in from outside the industry, Jones's arrival was announced as the event that would put the company on a wholly new course. That had actually been one of the search criteria the board had insisted on. The outgoing president was too caught up in day-to-day operations and had no real long-range, strategic vision. The client in this case, Hildegaard Industries, wanted to be able to understand how Jones was going to run Junipero and what—if anything—they might be able to do competitively to gain share at Junipero's expense.

In fairly short order, Jones's profile began to emerge. Historically, he'd had only one other senior leadership position—one in which he had been moderately successful, albeit on a fairly short assignment.

Nothing seemed to have been out of the ordinary about the apparently friendly departure. And he'd been brought into the other position for his visionary and imaginative orientation.

He was highly intelligent, articulate, personable, and well-liked, engendered great feelings of loyalty and dedication, and had a prodigious capacity for hard work. Energized by intellectual discussions, he actively encouraged diverse opinions—especially those that took into consideration new ways of dealing with old problems. He seemed to never grow tired of additional information, frequently reserving judgment until all the available information was in—and even then, only making decisions or completing actions when forced to do so by events. His "employee first" attitude had come through in each of his previous assignments, and he was highly compassionate toward the needs of the rank and file.

The personality profile that emerged, together with the anecdotal data that fleshed out the profile, showed a man who was long on imagination, short on attention, who bored easily with details, projects and programs that did not excite his imagination, and who rarely took full responsibility for projects that went awry. In fact, his carefully cultivated reputation for people issues fell away upon examination of those situations where he either had to accept responsibility for his actions or inattention or deflect the focus away from himself.

Interestingly, Jones exhibited exceptionally strong control needs, particularly in the area of decision making. Several of his former subordinates independently provided anecdotal comments about his lack of trust in the judgment of others. They explained that when many of the decisions he had personally made turned out badly, it was quickly apparent that there would be a concerted effort to distance him from the problem. In fact, clear efforts were made to place the blame on people who had been among the most loyal to him and had shared his initial enthusiasm for the projects that had gone badly. In effect, loyalty was, for Jones, a one-way street. Yet where there was credit to be taken for something, he was the first to arrive at the press conference. The higher the visibility, the more people applauding his efforts, the better for Jones.

The profile also suggested that employee matters would represent the lion's share of Jones's attention. In the event, on-premises child care, expanding maternity/paternity leave programs, environmental issues, and community relations gradually began to occupy more and more of his time. The industry, however, was exceptionally fast paced and technology driven, and first-to-market was nearly the only criterion for success. Decisions had to be made on the basis of the best available information in the shortest possible time.

These elements, together with a comparison of the organizational profile—energetic, fast-closing on targets of business or product opportunity, short on people interests and long on technology leadership—suggested to us that he might not be the ideal fit for the company. The profile suggested a practical as well as a philosophical conflict with Junipero's established senior management—one that could also possibly be used to Hildegaard's advantage.

Hildegaard was able to use the knowledge of how the new president would perform in a variety of ways. Their expectations started coming true quite early in Jones's tenure and they were prepared to exploit their foreknowledge of his preferred style. With their foreknowledge, they were able to anticipate that he would become preoccupied with non-revenue-producing aspects of the business, and that the new president's decision process would slow Junipero's cycle times to market.

His preoccupation with grand schemes and projects also caused much consternation among those of the leadership who had remained from the previous administration because resource reallocations and projects languished for weeks without decisions. For his part, he clearly increased his distrust of them and blamed them for quarterly performance targets being missed. This allowed Hildegaard to conduct some well-timed, focused, and carefully orchestrated recruiting efforts that helped to contribute to the downward spiral at Junipero.

Jones temporized over hard decisions and had little real talent for organizing and energizing the company's very talented technology population in a systematic way. In fact, his ad hoc style of reacting to events as they occurred showed that he had no real grand vision in the first place. Absent any real indications of leadership, important initiatives became mired down in the bureaucratic infighting that developed as his subordinates sought to protect themselves from the firestorm that was sure to come.

Hildegaard was also able, indirectly, to encourage some of the state's political leadership to call upon him to undertake the catalyst role in several high-profile social programs. Jones's ready acceptance of these opportunities meant that an already full plate became overloaded and his in-box filled even more rapidly. As it did, so did the disaffection of the production and engineering management on whom most of the company's previous success had been based.

In this brief example, which omits much other detail, Jones's Myers-Briggs personality type as an ENFP provided ample insights into his potential behavior in the marketplace; the anecdotal reporting that served as the examples of Jones's behavior in the workplace and the predictions that were based on the profile and the anecdotal data allowed Hildegaard to capitalize on what they now knew about him.

And, to follow the Patton model to its conclusion, and to complete the military metaphor, let's turn to an increasingly frequently used concept in business these days—one in which we have the privilege of participating often as a contributor: the War Game.

Business war-gaming is nothing new, but the increasing use of the intelligence process in war-gaming to give some vestiges of reality is another testimonial to its efficacy. While there are many pieces of the puzzle that should be apparent by now, the application of psychological type—and the remote assessments that we've been talking about here—become even more interesting.

Let's try another approach. In your firm, you've already been using the MBTI for a couple of years—and many of you have already anyway, so that's not a stretch. You take your top management team and you know how they function together; you know how they've complemented each other for a couple of years because you spent bongo bucks on the industrial psychologist who told you how to get along together in the sandbox.

The other team has to be led by somebody. Why not select from your staff those who are most like the other guys whom you've now profiled and can be expected to process things the same ways; people from your own staff who are most like them, most of the time? Whether they happen to be heroes or dregs of humanity, it makes little difference. You may just find that your war games are played with much greater realism and that the outcomes on the sandtables are closer to the ultimate reality than they've been in the past. What do you have to lose?

Once you've developed these type descriptions and thought about their applications, the how and how well you actually use them is up to you. Perhaps you'll think it's all smoke and mirrors. Perhaps not. It may be that you decide to investigate using such a process later, as you become more comfortable with using the insights that come from the intelligence process. That won't keep your rivals from looking at you. Perhaps the least you can do is find out a little more about yourself and your own organization.

In fact, that's fundamental to the last part of this book: looking at yourself and protecting your own piece of the planet.

Part 3

Protection

Denial is more than a river in Egypt.

—Joan Didion

In part II we've learned a bit about how Business Intelligence professionals collect information and how a well-informed leadership can make better decisions that affect the life of the enterprise. Most of what we've spoken about thus far has been restricted to the legal and ethical, the moral and the nonfattening.

Now, when we turn to the protection side of the equation, we're going to get a slightly darker view of the world. We'll have to look at all the actors—some of whom may not play by the same rules you do. On one level, we're going talk about those active measures necessary to safeguard your proprietary or sensitive business information from those who would use the kinds of approaches to collection that we've called competitive intelligence—approaches that follow the SCIP Code of Ethics.

Yet, on another level, it's simply foolhardy to think that your responsibility to protect your information stops where the SCIP code ends. Looking at life this way is like putting your head in the sand. Deep in the sand. There are far more people out there collecting information than just the SCIP membership, and they play by wholly different rules. In fact, the Economic Espionage Act of 1996 wasn't intended to refer to competitive intelligence practitioners at all. It was written for those who are not afraid to fly their aircraft into the legal trees.

Some people who like to call themselves Business Intelligence professionals think that protecting information is not their job. They're wrong. Frankly, the ones that I've heard complain most loudly that BI practitioners have no role in protecting information are mainly consultants whose skills are only marginal in the first place. Almost inevitably, they have no actual real-world, practical intelligence experience. Maybe it's just a matter of being afraid that they'll have to work a bit harder or smarter. In fact, because true intelligence practitioners have such a profound experience base, they're far better positioned then almost anyone else in the enterprise to provide that particular protection function. Moreover, there's always the popular cost-effectiveness of what my engineering friends referred to earlier as multiplexing: getting several things done simultaneously, using the fewest resources.

Look at professional intelligence organizations the world over. They have to be focused on protecting their sources, methods, and intelligence products. They also understand that they're uniquely qualified to lead the protection of the information that a rival is trying to obtain. Let's take a look at the ways that governments conduct intelligence operations. The message will be immediately clear.

Governments perform counterintelligence functions to provide the best possible defense against intelligence collectors. Counterintelligence agents are specially trained and assigned to identify and neutralize the intelligence-collection operations of an adversary. An adversary who uses all the tricks of his trade that have been distilled from centuries of intelligence operations. Counterintelligence is done on an active, anticipatory level. The greatest amount of counterintelligence work is done in advance of an information loss, although from time to time counterintelligence agents participate in an investigation after the fact that leads to the arrest of a miscreant. Very often, the best counterintelligence agent is one who has a background on the collection side. She knows how the process works and can identify patterns, vulnerabilities, and countermeasures that will work.

Compare that to a police force. While there are some aspects of police work that are considered proactive, the greatest amount of police work is done after a crime has been committed. Police officers are accustomed to finding people who have done something and arresting them. Police officers are specially trained to deal with muggers and murderers, rapists and drunks, kidnappers and bank robbers—the entire spectrum of criminals. I know many terrific police officers, but I've never met a single one who was an accomplished criminal before he turned to a life of crime fighting. Moreover, I've never met one who could tell an international spy from Adam's house cat—or one who says he can either. Of course not. It's not their job.

Let's extend this police force out a little further into business. Out to the place where many police officers spend their second careers: in a corporate security role. They have great credentials to protect life and property. Physical property, personal property, and even to a certain extent, intellectual property—at least from a document-control and accountability point of view. Yet the gates and guards, guns and dogs that are the security practitioner's stock in trade are simply not impediments to intelligence collectors. We don't break into buildings or hotel rooms. We don't lurk and skulk at midnight, waiting to grab someone's briefcase or laptop.

If you want to protect yourself and your company from those actors who range from competitive intelligence professionals to industrial and economic espionage actors, you're going to have to rely on far more than those gates and guards, those guns and dogs.

And if you think this is going to be too hard—whether you're a business leader or an intelligence grunt working for the decision maker—you've got the same choice you have when you go to the doctor. Stay well or get well. Change your lifestyle away from that of a remote-clicking, high-cholesterol couch potato to that of a more active, exercising, and nutritionally balanced person who wants to live long and prosper. Veggies and fruits now, or pills and surgery later. Your choice.

And, a final note to any competitive intelligence practitioners who may be tempted to dismiss the way that counterintelligence professionals practice their craft. Confusing counterintelligence with security can wreck your whole afternoon.

CHAPTER 14

Operational Counterintelligence: Keeping Score and Keeping Them Out

If you're constantly putting out fires, chances are that you're working with a bunch of arsonists.

We're not in the Land of Cuff 'Em and Stuff 'Em anymore, Toto. And we're not going into the world of Aston Martins, "shaken, not stirred," rumpled trench coats, or secret decoder rings either. Just another straightforward business practice that is necessary and effective.

Instead of hooking some miscreant up with handcuffs and stuffing him into the back of a patrol car, counterintelligence is completely different. A counterintelligence approach to protection in a corporate environment is as different from a security approach as intelligence collection is from market research.

You've already seen our definition of Corporate Counterintelligence. Yet, it's important enough to deserve a short reprise in the box below. Like most things that appear simple, this definition can use a little explanation.

Corporate Counterintelligence

Active measures—sometimes taken in conjunction with federal agencies—undertaken to identify and neutralize the intelligence-collection activities of a business rival.

First, "active measures." Some of you may have read about active measures, especially those practiced by the intelligence services of the former Soviet Union. Active measures that ranged from disinformation to assassination and everywhere in between, according to some. Active measures from our point of view is much simpler: active as opposed to passive; active as opposed to reactive; forward looking and anticipatory rather than backward chaining and investigative, for the most part.

Second, "sometimes in conjunction with federal agencies." You've already heard that Appendix B is where legal and ethical issues associated with Business Intelligence practices will be discussed. That's also where you'll learn about the role that federal agencies can have as effective partners in the investigation and prosecution of evildoers under the Economic Espionage Act of 1996. But they have to operate under a variety of manpower and other constraints in the real world. And you'll also learn that there are often quite clear and important reasons why a business leader might be less than willing to go public with, and involve a federal agency in, an open investigation of a loss of business secrets.

Third, "to identify." Nothing unusual here, since everyone wants to know whom to blame for something that doesn't turn out well. And that's just the point. In doing counterintelligence, the emphasis is always on the identification taking place before—not after—the loss or event.

Fourth, in order to "neutralize" the adversary. That may also sound somewhat sinister. After all, many have used the word "neutralize" to mean something altogether different from what you would normally consider appropriate in a business context. But it's really simple. It means to disable, or prevent, someone's ability to injure you and your organization before they get a chance to do so. It goes hand in glove with early, pre-event identification.

Fundamental to this concept of corporate counterintelligence are three basic issues:

- What to protect.
- How to protect it.
- How long to protect it.

It's amazing to me sometimes that even the most sophisticated and talented corporate and government leaders miss these simple points. The box *Copy, Copy, Who's Got the Copy?* shows how even an important government program, without any planning or organization at the outset, put itself in a nearly unfixable position.

WHAT TO PROTECT

In their quest to keep everything under wraps, some organizations—both government as well as business—often miss these simple truths and expend precious resources in a wasted effort. They fail to follow Bismarck's admonition, "He who seeks to protect all, protects nothing."

While it could be argued that there really are some things in a government-program environment that demand complete protection, it's rare that a business can afford to keep absolutely everything about their activities secret. For example, the Coca-Cola formula story. They know what to protect, and they've taken virtually every step known to man to keep it secret, and it seems pretty clear that they want to protect it forever. Yet they don't go so far as to keep their product off the shelves lest someone break down a sample into its precise ingredients, quantities, and process and be able to replicate it. No company can stay in business if it keeps its products or services under lock and key so that a rival can't see them—and at the same time keeps them away from customers too.

Copy, Copy, Who's Got the Copy

In the mid-1980s a senior government official realized that he needed to provide some protection for a major project that he'd been involved in for some time. He called for some assistance in protecting his project from disclosure, especially to the Soviets.

The planning meeting started poorly and went downhill rapidly. He started off by saying that the program was well enough along that it looked like the technology would work, and that it would be another eighteen months before it could be fielded. In the meantime, it absolutely needed to be kept under wraps.

A few well-pointed questions got some awkward answers. "How many people know about this project." When the answer was "over three hundred," eyes began to roll, especially after hearing that there was no "knowledgeability list" of those who had been made aware of the project. But at least it was a place to begin fixing the problem.

The next answers were even worse. The project had been going on for over three years at that point, and one room held nearly fifty safes, all filled with the written materials and technical drawings related to the technology. Virtually no other measures had been taken to protect the project, its open contracting for research assistance, or any of the other, myriad elements that should have been in place for years.

The recommendation: get twenty-five junior people with appropriate security clearances, get twenty-five photocopy machines, fifty more safes, and an eighteen-wheeler. Photocopy everything in all the safes, and put the copies into the new safes. Put the new safes on the tractor trailer and drive it into Washington. Drive it through the front gates of the Soviet embassy and leave it. Abandon it. In their suspicious, paranoid, and xenophobic way, the Soviets will look at every single document and every element as if it was all part of a massive deception operation. They'd spend far more than the eighteen months needed to safeguard the new technology in trying to figure out what was true and what was not, and they'd be paralyzed. In the meantime, the project could go forward with new protections built in.

Needless to say, the out-of-the-box solution set was not what the humorless bureaucrat was looking for as an answer. But you get the point.

Let's stay with the Coca-Cola formula for a little while longer as we try to figure out this problem of knowing what to protect. Clearly, anybody who has ever heard from Coca-Cola's lawyers has learned that trying to get the formula would be a long and very costly process. That goes for anyone who has spent—and is making—billions on a product that is worth protecting through all means possible. Are you going to try and gain some competitive advantage from Coca-Cola—or any of your competitors—by attacking their strongest and most vigorously defended asset? Hardly. Instead, you're going to attack other aspects of their business base. You're going to go after their distribution channel, for example. New packing approaches. New cobranding and strategic relationships. New line extensions and where they're headed. Information about these kinds of things is what a competitor would be after. Information that the rival can use either tactically or strategically. That's the information that Coca-Cola, you, or anybody else is going to have to protect.

THE VALUE OF CUES AND SIGNALS

And that's not the only level where you have to protect it.

You have to look for all those cues that, when aggregated and analyzed, tell the tale. Cues and signals that are those small pieces of information we learned about in part I. Cues and signals that can be elicited from the person who has them. The person who doesn't attach any particular significance to the cues and signals because he doesn't understand the piecing together of the jigsaw puzzle that is the hallmark of the intelligence process. Cues and signals that tell a competitor where your firm is headed and which horse you're going to ride to get there. Cues that are sometimes individual items themselves. Cues that are sometimes patterns that can reveal how and when something is going to happen. Cues and signals like the pattern that one of your competitors likes to make new product launch announcements with a great deal of fanfare at a particular resort—and because they made the travel and hotel reservations six months early, that provided their main competitor an early warning sufficient to counter the product. Cues and signals that get intercepted on the football field, as described in the box *The Eyes Have It.* Or, cues like those described in the box *I've Got a Headache* for a purely business example.

The Eyes Have It

Back in the days when the Oilers played in Houston, they had several terrible seasons. Bum Phillips, their head coach, talked about their offense being the reason they were so bad, and in particular, the offensive line. He said that on virtually every play, his team would tell the opponents which back was going to get the ball and where he was probably going.

Several people challenged him on this point, so he went on to explain.

He said that the offensive line was so ineffectual and porous that all the defense had to do was look at the faces of the running backs. The one whose number had been called—the one who was going to get the ball—was the one whose face was as white as a sheet. And, he began looking, staring sometimes, at the hole he was supposed to hit almost as if he was praying it would open like the Red Sea before Moses. And of course, the defense would know exactly how to respond.

There's another set of cues that are indications of what's happening in the marketplace that affect you. Cues that tell you the range of a competitor's use of the Business Intelligence process. It may be good at this point to review some things we touched on in the introduction. Bill DeGenaro, my colleague at The Centre for Operational Business Intelligence, suggests that we look at these cues from at least three different perspectives. Look at your competitor's situation: Is your competitor growing faster and becoming more profitable, or perhaps more innovative, in spite of other information that seems to suggest almost irrational actions? Look at what your competitors anticipate: Do they seem to be able to anticipate, and respond before you can, to legislative or regulatory changes, technology shifts, or customer requirements? Look at your competitor's actions: Does your competitor counter your new products rapidly and reduce your first-to-market advantage, preempt your new products or strategies, successfully attack your high-margin products and territories, identify your other vulnerabilities, and cost you money, or recruit away your best and brightest people at precisely the wrong times?

I've Got a Headache

Johnson & Johnson was making a gazillion with America's Number One Pain Reliever *Tylenol*. Bristol-Myers really thought that there was a place in America's bloodstream for another painkiller and developed *Datril*. They test-marketed it in Peoria, Illinois, and Albany, New York, two bastions of headache-suffering Middle America. Two cities that they'd used many times for test marketing in the past. Two cities that helped Johnson & Johnson identify when and what new products Bristol-Myers was planning on launching. Two cities that were part of Bristol-Myers's pattern of cues.

Johnson & Johnson's monitoring of these patterns revealed the Datril test marketing. Cues that revealed that Bristol-Myers was going to attempt a price penetration for Datril at $1.89 a bottle, compared with Johnson & Johnson's $2.89 a bottle for Tylenol. Cues that revealed Datril's entry on April 15. Cues that led Johnson & Johnson to tell Mr. and Mrs. America and all the ships at sea that in making Tylenol America's number one pain reliever, J&J had recovered their developmental costs years earlier than projected. Cues that let J&J tell the folks at home that J&J wanted to pass along savings to them in the form of an immediate price reduction to $1.89 a bottle, complete with rebate coupons for anyone who'd bought a bottle in the last month. Cues that let J&J do this on the first of April. Cues that let J&J completely disrupt the entire Datril advertising campaign, to include the media blitz that would have to be put on hold until the new Datril strategy could be developed. Cues that let J&J take the offensive in a campaign that eventually made the media refuse to take any Datril ad space until they had their act together.

Cues that kept Datril from gaining anything more than a 1 percent share a year later, when Tylenol was able to withstand the Tylenol-cyanide murders. Imagine. Something that is supposed to help people overcome pain winds up killing them instead. Certainly, not through any fault of Johnson & Johnson's. But what would've happened to Tylenol if there'd been a strong number two at the time of the murders? Anybody's guess. But it wasn't Datril.

Remember that most basic of all intelligence axioms: There's no such thing as a coincidence. If you see these kinds of things happening in your market-place, and that it's your competitor who's winning out more than you ever thought he might, there is a reason, not a coincidence. Or, after what you've learned so far, do you think there's a possibility that it's your rival's use of the intelligence process that's contributing to his success? A possibility that your rival is responsible for that dulling of your competitive edge?

HOW TO PROTECT IT

We'll just be doing a short overview of this point, and later we'll see a variety of things that can be done to protect the information—those cues and those whole chunks of information that say more about your enterprise than you want to have out there in the world. But first, we'll need to think a bit about *how* we're going to protect ourselves—and that's not as easy a question as it might appear.

The question of how to protect your most important information raises any number of other, potentially sticky questions: How is our company culture, so long used to openness and freely given information, going to be affected by new rules and procedures for protecting information? Does this mean that the company doesn't trust the employees any-more? How draconian can the protection measures be and still let us do our jobs? How liberal can the protection measures be and still keep what we need to keep? How much is this countermeasure going to cost in dollars and cents, new people or equipment, compared with alternative countermeasures?

These are a few of the many issues that need to be considered before you get truly serious about protecting your information. Yet, they all fit into a process. And that's the beauty of the way that corporate counterintelligence operates as a process—a process just like the collection process we described and followed in part II. We'll get into that process right after we talk about just how long you need to protect something.

HOW LONG TO PROTECT IT

Put your most valuable eggs—and their component parts—into the most protective basket possible, and keep them there as long as you need to. Don't spend a minute or a dime more than you have to beyond the time necessary. But at the same time, don't be crazy about making the walls tumble without thinking. For example, we've seen literally hundreds of situations where companies have protected their competitive bids to federal, state, local governments—as well as to major companies—with everything they could find. Then, when the competition is over and the winner is announced, they simply throw away their bid because it was a loser. They remain completely oblivious to the ways that a previous bid— in the hands of a smart competitor—can be used to anticipate pricing, technical, or management approaches in future competitions.

In this kind of situation, companies thought they knew what they needed to protect—the proposed bid—but neglected to think about the component parts of the proposal, all the notes and associated papers, even the copies of the large sheets of paper that went into the storyboarding. Of course, what we're talking about here is what could be exploited through what we call "waste archeology." That's because it's tacky to call it Dumpster diving, although garbageology is making a strong run at it.

Why are we talking about such a nefarious, not to mention dirty and smelly, approach to collecting information? Isn't that in violation of the SCIP standards? Well, actually, no, if you're speaking strictly. We don't advocate it, since we can usually get the information we need without stooping to this level, so to speak. But, you see, waste archeology has resulted in the jailing of only one person in U.S. history. That was a California executive who, while acknowledging in a trade-secret case that his firm had gone through its rival's garbage, denied that it had used the products of the diving expedition. When the plaintiff proved that the defendant had actually used them, the judge put the executive in jail for perjury, not for Dumpster diving.

Yet, more importantly, we're talking about such a thing as waste archeology because there are many others collecting information who have never heard of SCIP, let alone been guided by its code of ethics. Remember, we're on the protection side of the equation now. It means that we've got to become a little schizophrenic—thinking about collecting information at the same time we're thinking about protecting it. In this instance, schizophrenia is not only okay, it may be the best way to approach the problem.

The rules are different—and our focus has to be as well. For many of these people and companies, while distasteful, it's also highly profitable—for them as well as their clients. If you want to deny that such things are happening and leave yourself vulnerable to them, then you have a far different view of the diligence that your board of directors expects from you in the way you run your operations.

It doesn't stop there, though. If you want to look at how an SCIP member in good standing might approach this without getting his hands dirty doing Waste Archeology, consider that he still has whole panoply of human sources to pursue.

Consider how many people know many of the technical, management, or cost details of this proposal. Are they aware enough of the value—even after the loss of the competition—to keep the details to themselves? Perhaps in an ideal world they would be. In the real, practical world, our experience says just the opposite. And when is the time for an aggressive and competent information collector to strike? Only while the proposals are being developed? Hardly.

We teach that the collection cycle in such competitive environments never really ends. It certainly doesn't end at contract-award time. Yet far too many knowledgeable employees think it does. People who'll say things a month after a contract loss such as "I don't know how XYZ Company could get their rates down so low. I've heard that their bid rate was an average of $37.65 an hour. We couldn't get any closer than $46.25, and that was with building a whole new cost center, cutting benefits for the people who were going to be on the project, and moving to cheaper facilities."

Hopefully, this discussion will bring to mind some things that are peculiar to your industry, your company, or your division.

THE CORPORATE COUNTERINTELLIGENCE PROCESS

Before we go much farther about corporate counterintelligence, there is something important that I should mention. No matter how many times we describe the elements of a typical project as replicating the approaches of business rivals, who often do nefarious things, we still get people who ask—halfway through such a presentation—if we really do such things. If we advocate doing those things. If we aren't violating legal and ethical standards.

We've gotten to the point where we find it useful to take a page out of our old, government playbooks: the pages that referred to Warning Notices on sensitive documents. Alerts such as WARNING NOTICE: SENSITIVE METHODS AND SOURCES INVOLVED and WARNING NOTICE: REALLY SENSITIVE STUFF—BURN BEFORE READING, and so on.

In presentations about Corporate Counterintelligence, we often have to remind people that we're doing things against the client, *for* the client. We have to restate that we as a firm do not practice, follow, or advocate such collection practices. Expecting that some readers may have such thoughts occur to them from time to time, we've developed a warning notice for this book, which we'll use periodically. It's

---

WARNING NOTICE: TRY THIS ONLY AT HOME

Please don't take the reminders throughout the rest of the book personally. They're intended to help keep this point in mind for *other* readers. Thank you.

In our firm, we have developed the Business Intelligence Protection Model, which serves as our process that complements the collection process described earlier. Just like the collection process, the protection process is a cyclical one. The cycle begins again at the top—at the top of the cycle and at the top of the organization. It operates in a counterclockwise direction, beginning with the tasking from your leadership. Tasking starts with a question that's similar to the one that got the collection process started. Instead of asking "What keeps you awake at night about your rival's plans?" the question becomes "What keeps you awake at night for fear that your rival is going to find out about what your firm is about to do?"

The Business Intelligence Protection Model, when viewed counterclockwise from the top, starts with the *Requirements Definition*. It depends upon getting specific *tasking* from your leadership about those elements of critical concern from the perspective of continuity of business operations. This helps to narrow your focus to the point where your orientation is only on those things that truly need protection, not all those other things that ultimately become the sound of a boy crying wolf. Examples of such requirements definition might include:

1. What investments is your firm making in new product development?

2. What new products/services will your firm be introducing within the next year?

3. What is the reliability of your product X?

4. What are the quality measures for your product Y?

5. Who are your strategic partners and what is the nature of the relationship between you and each of the partners?

6. Who are your primary and most important customers and what is the true nature of your relationship with them?

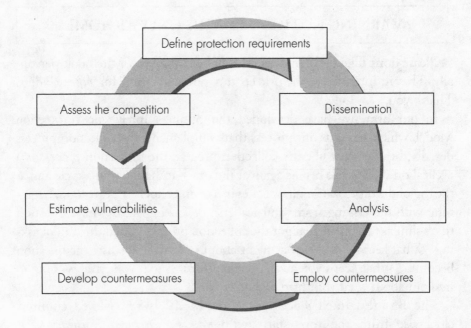

Once you've gotten that tasking, it is then refined into the particular subcomponents that represent—in their totality—the principal *Protection Requirements*. What we've already started calling cues. It's at this point that you identify where the critical information can be found by anybody peering in from the outside. These cues are then catalogued and matrixed as you identify the people who have access to the disparate elements and pieces of information. Then, you have the opportunity to look realistically at how information that falls into these categories is actually handled and stored and treated by those who have access to it.

The next step in the process is to *Assess the Competition*. But this is not a typical competitive assessment. It doesn't look at the entire enterprise that is your rival. You're only interested at this point in assessing the capabilities and competencies of your rival to collect information about your firm and how they use it to their advantage, that is, their internal resources or processes. There are a variety of ways to look at this assessment, ranging from the typical four-corners analysis model to the traditional SWOT (Strengths, Weaknesses, Opportunities, and Threats) analysis. In fact, this part of the process and most of those to follow are worthy of enough discussion that they get treated in their own chapters. Once we briefly touch on each of the rest of the points in this process, we'll start with more on assessing the competition.

Following that assessment, you should undertake an assessment of the *vulnerabilities* of your critical information to the collection activities of your rival. In essence, we'd suggest that you include in your active and aggressive approach to this assessment what we call a Red Team Analysis. Attack *yourself*. Use the same techniques and approaches that you now know your rival and its associated firms have been seen using in the past, or that you can reasonably assume are being used now. It's important to approach this using a rigidly outside-in set of approaches. Cheating by using what and who you already know about your company to shorten the time or make your job easier corrupts the process and doesn't give you a real appreciation of your vulnerabilities. If you don't have the time, energy, resources, or inclination to attack yourself, go outside to a trusted resource. Bear in mind that if there was ever a time for a nondisclosure agreement with a consultant, this is it. After all, exposing your weaknesses as well as potentially allowing access to your most important information could be just as injurious to your long-term corporate health as anything a rival might do.

At the same time, it's also useful to point out that when you take such measures as these, you're really putting quite a bit of money in the bank. Remember that the Economic Espionage Act requires that your company be able to demonstrate that you've taken countermeasures that are consistent with the environment and that you've appreciated the sophistication and level of threats to your information and that you've done default testing against those vulnerabilities. Records of your self-testing go a long way to convincing a judge that you've taken all reasonable steps necessary to protect yourself. In fact, it sometimes can inferentially show that if you've replicated everything that someone might do to you legally, the only alternative explanation for them having your information is an illegal activity.

Once you've established a clear understanding of your vulnerabilities, the next step is developing and implementing those *countermeasures* that would be appropriate for your firm to undertake. These countermeasures should be designed to be consistent with your vulnerability profile, the competitive environment, and your internal corporate cultural issues and daily operational considerations. There's rarely a one-size-fits-all solution set, although you may find some of those listed in chapter 18 to be useful guides.

The next step in the process is the *analysis* of how these countermeasures are actually working. Sometimes this can be done as simply as testing yourself several times to ensure that the processes and countermeasures you've taken are preventing your own Red Team from getting the kinds and amount of information they'd gotten before. In other cases, where the countermeasures are a little more sophisticated and complicated—depending on which outcomes you and your leadership have chosen—you may well want to see how the competition is reacting to your countermeasures and adjust accordingly.

Outcomes? Outcomes that are more than just something like "protect our stuff"? In fact, lots of outcomes of various shapes and sizes. Yes, Virginia, this may even be one of those situations where the terrible word *deception* may be used as a countermeasure. But, rather than you having to wait a couple more chapters to find out that deception as a countermeasure may not be as malignant a term or process as you might think, the box *Who's Afraid of Virginia Lobo* might help you place this all into perspective.

Who's Afraid of Virginia Lobo

Johnson Controls, a manufacturer of building-control systems for commercial and other large buildings, decided to capitalize on a trend in the United States and Europe toward smaller buildings. They had invested about $20 million over three years in a new digitized technology that would allow them to capture most of this market. One of the many things they did to keep their main competitor, Honeywell, in the dark about their efforts was to code name the project Loba, short for the nineteenth-century Russian mathematician Nikolai Lobachevsky.

Things were pretty much on schedule during the beta testing for a February 1990 release date when Johnson found out that Honeywell had learned of their efforts to develop this new product—except that they misheard the title just a bit. Their sales force had heard about Loba—albeit by the name of Lob*o*—and were out all over the map asking for additional detail.

The problem was that Johnson Controls was still ten months away from product launch—a considerable amount of time to allow Honeywell to close the first-to-market gap if they could learn more about the product. One of the suggestions was simply that Johnson Controls launch early. Management said no. Launch when ready with a good product, not something that might be an embarrassment in the marketplace. Find some other way to keep Honeywell out of the game.

Johnson Controls had a relatively minor upgrade of an existing control system ready for release at about this same time. They decided to manage Honeywell's misperceptions, particularly about Lobo. They spent about $500,000 on a splashy and loud advertising campaign on Lobo, which Honeywell quite properly dismissed out of hand as the minor upgrade that it was. Honeywell bit even further, since they were confident they could deal pretty well with this minor upgrade. They even slowed down their own efforts to do what they'd heard this Lobo was going to do.

Honeywell lost millions in market opportunities starting in February 1990 when Johnson Controls rolled out the Operating System Formerly Known as Loba, the nearly flawless *Metasys,* to rave reviews from customers, analysts, consultants, and architects, on time and on budget.

Think about this for one more millisecond, please. If you were reading about this in a book about regular business practices, and not something called intelligence, wouldn't your impression of this event be called just "smart business"? Does the fact that it is characteristic of intelligence and counterintelligence practices change your mind at all about whether this was an appropriate business response to a business situation? Didn't think so.

And finally, let's not forget the people who started all this sun and fun. *Dissemination* means getting the results of that analysis back to the people who can use it. There are often more consumers of this product than just the leader who asked for the process to kick off in the first place. Some of the other candidate recipients might be people in other divisions, groups, or units of the company; perhaps they include joint-venture or strategic partners so that they can shore up their own defenses, lest they negatively affect your organization; and sometimes, it's even important to ensure that those who are doing competitive intelligence work in your own company know what the results are. This is especially true when you can find out what the other firm is asking about, what they're interested in. Why? Because usually, there's a clear linkage between what they're asking about today and where they're headed tomorrow. By giving the results of this countermeasures and analysis effort to the active collectors within your own organization, you can perhaps more quickly identify some of the marketplace intentions of your rivals than through any other means.

CHAPTER 15

Who Are Those Guys and Why Are They Doing Such Terrible Things to Us?

The two most common reasons for losing are: not knowing you're competing in the first place, and not knowing with whom you're competing.

—John W. Conway

Chapter 14 showed us how the leadership of your enterprise is actively involved in and essential to the process of deciding what to protect and for how long it should be protected. Once we had a pretty good picture of the key protection topics, writ large, we worked downward to identify those individual cues—those subelements of the Key Protection Topics (KPTs) that we know are the focus of the professional intelligence collector. When aggregated and analyzed those subelements provide those insights into your company's operations that you'd prefer he did not have. Now that we know the what, it's time to turn to the who.

ASSESSING THE COMPETITION'S ABILITY AND ORIENTATION

In times past, there was a very simple formula for identifying who represented a threat to a country or to an organization. For far too many years, this formula was used to identify, fund, and develop countermeasures against military, economic, political, even cultural threats. This applied to intelligence threats as well.

If somebody was your enemy, your adversary, they were a threat. End of discussion. Time for action. Build a newer, bigger, faster, more powerful weapon. Destabilize the currency or national industrial base of someone who was looming on the economic horizon. Infiltrate and neutralize the hostile political action group that could threaten a friendly country's stability before it can get rolling.

Granted, most of the time the formula for assessing a threat bordered on the paranoid and the simplistic. This was especially true of those who were doing evil themselves. The problem of mirror-imaging, long discussed in international relations literature, ascribed the same kind of evil intent and malevolent capabilities to your opposite numbers on the other side of the fence.

Wearing the Union Label—The Background

At 6:00 A.M., Monday, November 21, just before the heaviest travel holiday of the year, the relatively small* Association of Professional Flight Attendants (APFA) struck American Airlines. The APFA leadership had announced the impending strike over several issues approximately two weeks earlier, indicating that it could come at any time after the 14th. Accordingly, American had taken some measures designed to blunt the effects of the strike.

CEO Bob Crandall saw the upcoming strike as a management-labor problem between American and APFA. APFA saw it differently: They saw it as a competition for the hearts and minds of the traveling public, which would probably and ultimately translate into pressure on national politicians, and then on Crandall.

Key to APFA's preparation was the use of intelligence prior to and during the strike. Intelligence that needed to be comprehensive, timely, and accurate. Intelligence that was based on numerous and reliable sources. Intelligence that would allow APFA to prevail. APFA knew from previous airline strikes that American's probable strategy would be two-pronged: first, downplay the breadth and depth of the strike's impact on its operations while giving the appearance of business as usual; and second, lay the blame for any traveler inconveniences on a few malcontents within the APFA. American needed to accentuate the number of flights that were continuing to operate, the number of passenger miles that were continuing to be flown, the small number of actual flight attendants involved in the strike, and the overall reliability of the American system.

On the other side, American had little apparent clue about what APFA was going to do or how they were going to do it. Two aspects of American's approach were soon to prove fateful in the outcome: poor

---

*Slightly under 22,000 members.

intelligence about the union's strategies for the strike, and understanding how well the APFA had prepared itself to collect and use intelligence against American's strategy.

Once APFA developed a fairly clear vision of what American's strategy would be, they were able to plan their intelligence collection, analysis, and dissemination activities—essentially, to integrate intelligence into its overall strategic plan for the strike, as we'll see in the next box.

This formula was a very simple one: capability equals threat. Almost automatically, if someone was your adversary, your enemy, they had capability—real or postulated. Often, it made little difference. If they had the capability, they represented a threat. Just because they were out there—and there were many of *them* out there—they represented a reason for expending bodacious dollars and rubles to protect your national assets, resources, boundaries, and systems from all potential adversaries.

It was never a particularly useful formula. When dollars and rubles became scarcer, people began questioning some of the longer living sacred cows. Smart people started off asking questions like: "Well, can they really hurt us?" and "Do they *really* have the capability?" and rapidly got onto another level of questions. Questions that drove a wholly new set of analytical approaches to find the answers to these questions. And the answers to questions that hadn't been asked before, such as: "If they have the capability, do they also have the *intent?*" and "What indications do we have that they really mean business?"

Thus, a new formula became capability plus indicators equals threat, or $C + I = T$. It's these three elements that bring us now to the issue of assessment. Threat assessment, if you will. Assessing your business rival's capability to collect valuable competitive information about your company and use it against your interests in the marketplace. Assessing your rival's indicators—indicators of actual intentions and actual collection activities. Activities against you and activities against others whom you know or need to know.

You should know by now that we're not just talking about those people who are your direct competitors in the marketplace. It extends out to those people who have an interest in what's going on in your firm and how it impacts them. The box *Wearing the Union Label,* may help to expand your view of what other kinds of organizations represent your business rivals and their resources. After reading this, you may never think in just competitor terms again.

Wearing the Union Label—The Actions

APFA developed relationships with a wide range of sources throughout the airline industry: sympathetic pilots, nonstriking flight attendants, baggage handlers, and reservationists. Pilots who were laying over in cities across the country would take up positions in rooms on the top floors of hotels so that they could get a good look at the tail numbers of every American flight taking off and landing. Every fifteen minutes they would report their observations to the APFA command center on the floor below. The local command centers around the country, equipped with PCs and fax machines, reported the pilots' observations to the APFA main command center in Dallas every hour. When Crandall attempted to claim that all flights were flying regular schedules to all cities and that Mr. and Mrs. American public should feel confident that they'd be able to travel over the holiday season without incident, APFA issued its own statement within an hour with amazingly accurate detail. Detail that Crandall wasn't able to challenge.

Crandall's fallback was to claim that the strike had forced a small reduction in the number of flights on purely economic grounds, that passengers were staying with American, and that the flights were carrying larger and larger numbers of people. This appeared to be true whenever television crews showed up to film people arriving in various cities. APFA's sources among the baggage handlers told them that even though there were apparently full flights, there was a significant reduction in the amount of baggage. The seeming contradiction was quickly resolved when APFA's colleagues among the reservationists showed that the bulk of the flyers who were making it appear that things remained normal were actually off-duty management and their families who were simply packing the aircraft, going back and forth from city to city as if they were regular passengers.

Runners who were positioned around the airports reported these and other statistics to the local command centers, and the reporting continued up the line to Dallas. The reporting, with highly accurate numbers that showed Crandall to be misleading the media again, made the outcome of the competition all but moot. Crandall was not believed, people flew less and less, and even when American did make accurate reporting, they were disbelieved by the media and the traveling public. Even though the White House had said that it was going to leave the dispute to the union and the airline, it was soon in the middle. In fairly short order, Crandall announced that he had no real choice but to accede to presidential influence and agree to certain terms to get the flight attendants back to work. Within hours, APFA sources helped APFA tell the world that Crandall had actually sought the presidential involvement to make it appear that American was responding to the White House and not a successful strike. More egg on American's corporate face. APFA emerged from the competition as the winner.

A winner who knew in advance from their preparations how the battle was likely to be fought. A winner who set out to answer very certain and specific kinds of questions. A winner who set out to develop the kinds of sources who could be counted on to provide those specific kinds of answers. A winner whose sources collected and then reported high-quality information through rapid and reliable processing to the people who could collate and analyze what was really going on. A winner who knew how, when, and to whom to disseminate the intelligence gleaned from their efforts. An unlikely winner in a David and Goliath battle, in a different kind of competition.

Who are your unlikely competitors?

ASSESSING CAPABILITIES

Intelligence collectors are as varied as any group can be. Naturally, we can begin to make gross distinctions pretty rapidly:

- Competitive intelligence collectors who obtain their information openly, legally, and within certain ethical standards—that is, the population that largely abides by the Code of Ethics of the Society of Competitive Intelligence Professionals.

- Other competitive intelligence collectors who abide by the law but whose ethical standards are not developed by a governing body as much as they are by the situational ethics of the moment—most often bounded by dollars and sense of doing whatever it takes to get the job done. They may use the intelligence process or they may not, depending on the extent of their background, such as whether they have been more of a private investigator or the like.

- Information collectors who come very close to, or who step over, the legal boundaries in obtaining information of a competitively valuable and sensitive nature. In the class are those who would pay bribes or place the holders of certain kinds of information in potentially compromising positions. These are the collectors who are the logical and quite potential defendants in prosecutions under the Economic Espionage Act of 1996. Some advertise themselves as information brokers, although this term is also used by an entire population of other, quite reputable, information brokers who ply their trade just as openly and as above board as SCIP members.

- And, finally, there are the professional intelligence officers who represent their countries and in so doing, obtain information of a competitively valuable nature on behalf of their own domestic companies, using tried-and-true national intelligence methods. Methods that include the exploitation of human weaknesses and foibles for some form of compensation or remuneration to betray one's country or company. Methods that include technical intelligence collection systems such as high-resolution overhead platforms (i.e., satellite imagery), clandestine listening devices in sensitive areas, or voice and data intercepts that rely on sophisticated and costly facilities.

Once we have these gross descriptions established, the next step is to determine the approach that you can expect your business rival to use. And since most companies these days have a variety of rivals, each with different approaches to business practices, deciding to protect yourself against the least threatening of your competitors makes little sense. Essentially, if you look at the weakest and least effective of the competitors who're collecting information about you and build your defenses against them, what's to stop the competitors who're playing hardball? On the other hand, if you have only the most nominal and feeble of adversaries, at least in terms of how they collect information about you, it makes no sense to build a system of defenses that cost far more money than the threat warrants.

Let's take a look first at those who adhere to the SCIP Code of Ethics. Even in this case, you can find different levels of aggressiveness.

Some combine both the secondary and the primary source approaches described in part II of this book. Others restrict their collection activities solely to the exploitation of publicly available, open, and printed material: documents, patent filings, technical journals and papers, media reporting. Still other companies restrict themselves to conducting primary and secondary source operations on only the most overt, noncontroversial—and some say Pollyanna-ish—level.

And yet, some of these same companies are among the first to reach out to independent firms whose approaches are much more aggressive—and who can provide services that touch the very edge of legality. Interestingly, these firms frequently avoid having their fingerprints on a project by hiring the independent collectors through a law firm so that whatever is provided by the outside firm is covered by attorney-client privilege.

Assessing what these different companies represent as threats to your information is often surprisingly easy. Let's just cover three of the many possible ways.

Approach Number One

In some cases, all it takes is to attend one of the many competitive intelligence seminars held annually around the country and the world. If you're not able to attend, chances are that the network you're building includes someone who has.

Speakers at these conferences and symposia are invited, quite often at their own expense, to tell others how they do their work, how their department is set up, and how much of a budget they've been blessed with by the leadership to whom they report. They each and all have their own reasons for making such public presentations.

Remember the section on susceptibility to elicitation and the popular belief that somehow intelligence practitioners are among the least susceptible to elicitation? Like most popular wisdom, this is quite unfounded. Attend a SCIP meeting and you'll hear many people sharing professional experiences with their peers in the interest of recognition, acceptance, self-aggrandizement—the lot. Questions from the floor to a presenter are always encouraged, and the responses are quite revealing themselves, and often more responsive than the presenter had intended his paper to be.

In other cases, a call to an intelligence practitioner inside a firm is all that it takes to start an assessment of your competitor's competencies and company's orientation toward information collection. At other times, as you're engaged in the assessment process, you'll see direct opportunities—

or maybe even leadership-mandated requirements—to do something about your competitor's attacks against your firm. The closing part of this chapter, which deals with FUD—Fear, Uncertainty, and Doubt—will depict how one company moved from assessment to protection in ways that the ongoing security program had never attempted.

At the other end of the spectrum, you may encounter situations where corporate intelligence needs are satisfied by the national intelligence services of the firms' home countries, as we'll discuss further in Appendix B. Determine the answers to questions such as "What have they done in the past?" and "What have their leaders, such as Marion and de Marenche of France, had to say in their memoirs and in published interviews about their support to national business interests?" You'll also find people—generally, fairly few in number—who play so close to the margins that their firm has already been the subject of actions under the EEA or some state statutes. A review of whether or not a criminal or civil complaint has been lodged against a rival for inappropriate business practices, or the findings of a court in a matter already settled, can prove to be very insightful when it comes to taking the steps necessary to defend yourself against a firm. One of the more interesting aspects of this is that even when a company has been charged—and even when found liable or guilty—it doesn't always follow that they'll change their ways of doing business. In the Hitachi-IBM Adirondack Cookbooks matter also discussed in Appendix B, Hitachi apparently decided that it would use the information it obtained through various means and was prepared to take whatever penalties were assessed against it in the civil courts, because the risk-versus-gain equation always showed that the company would make more money in the long run, even if it did have to pay some hefty fines at the end of the trail.

APPROACH NUMBER TWO

A few chapters back we asked some rhetorical questions about how long would you wait before debriefing a newly hired employee who had most recently been working for your competitor. We shaped that in the context of competitively sensitive or otherwise important information. Would you have any difficulty in asking your new employee how the previous firm conducted its research into your company and the rest of the competitive field? Would you be interested in learning who, how many, and to whom they report, the approximate number of correspondents they have, the kinds of sources they use, the kinds of companies they use—and maybe even their names and approaches to collecting information—from among the consulting companies in the competitive intelligence field? Would you be interested in identifying the kinds of successes they've enjoyed, the kinds of failures they may have had, the kinds of training that was afforded the Business Intelligence people, or that which was provided to the correspondent population? Would you be interested in the people inside your firm, or among your vendors or subcontractor population, on whom your competitor routinely relied for information? Would you be interested in knowing what kinds of information the other company has gotten about you in the past and how they've used it? Would you be interested in knowing whether the other firm restricted its CI collection activities to solely open sources such as magazines, newspapers, newsletters, industry reporting, and even government filings?

At bottom, are the rules of engagement as far as debriefing new employees different when you're in the protection mode than in the collection mode? They certainly should be.

APPROACH NUMBER THREE

Since we just mentioned government filings, perhaps you might be interested in helping yourself through the use of the Freedom of Information Act. Wait, don't we use the FOIA for collection information and not for protection information? Another nanosecond please.

Think about the process that is associated with FOIA requests. An FOIA request is submitted to one of the agencies that you make certain filings to in the normal course of business. For example, you have to make filings every month to the Environmental Protection Agency about how much waste you discharge into the rivers around one of your plants. The process is pretty much the same across all agencies, whether federal or state. The request comes in, and it's recorded on the agency's FOIA log. This helps the bureaucrats do CYA just in case somebody gripes later on about responsiveness or a lack of responsiveness. The FOIA log will reveal who has asked for information about your firm, when they asked, and what they asked for. It'll also indicate what was sent back out in response to the request, and what was withheld and for what reasons. Guess what value this has for you? You're right. As an official government document, the log itself can be requested under the FOIA. Ask for it and review it routinely. It'll tell you who your competitors are who are interested in you enough to do FOIAs. It'll tell you how frequently they've looked and in which areas they're interested. Does that help you identify and assess those who are collecting against you? You bet. We'll have more to say on the defensive nature of the FOIA in chapter 17.

Of course, there are a few other ways besides simply looking at court records or newspaper accounts of the legal cases made against your competitors, since not all of them will have actually gone to trial. This is where networking in a professional community comes in handy. For example, industry security managers can often get together to speak of issues of common concern and to share information about the practices of the less-than-honorable players on the street. You know your industry and your company well enough; now with a little prodding, you can begin to let your imagination and wisdom take over.

ASSESSING INDICATORS

Just because another company has the capability to collect against you doesn't mean that they intend to use it. After all, they may not be a competitor. Yet the entire calculus changes once they have demonstrated an intention to enter your market.

For example, in this era of unprecedented mergers, acquisitions, joint ventures, and other strategic relationships, there are companies that suddenly and synergistically possess the competency and the intent. Alfatah Products, which had always been a relatively small but imaginative fish in your pond, and which has never given you any indications that it was especially interested in your product lines, is suddenly acquired by Behemoth Industries. You've never really thought about Behemoth Industries in the past.

Does their new arrangement change things? Maybe. Look a little closer.

Does the fact that Behemoth Industries has one of the largest and most frequently benchmarked Business Intelligence units in the world make any difference? Does your leadership know anything at all about this? Does it help your leadership sleep any better at night? Does anyone else in your firm care enough to make inquiries about this? If you're interested, you may be the first and only one who has ever really thought about it.

I'll pretty much guarantee you—after over twenty years of association with security professionals across many industries—that your security management team has never even paid any attention to the merger and acquisition activities of your present or upcoming major rivals. They're certainly not looking at the support functions such as the size, strength, competency, or organizational sponsorship of Behemoth Industries' intelligence apparatus.

That's not what they get paid to look after. They're not interested, in most companies, in what's happening on the business side of an industry; they're far more attuned to the myriad problems of personnel safety and security and guarding against physical threats to plant, people, materials, and documents.

Other indicators of Business Intelligence interest by a competitor come to you through many sources. How often have you spoken to your booth mavens who regularly attend trade shows and conferences about those who ask questions, make repetitive visits to your company's display, or otherwise give evidence of a rival firm's actual attempts to obtain information about your firm, its products, processes, prices, or people?

What mechanisms do you have in place that allow you to keep track of where the calls that are received by your employees each day are coming from—not listening in on the conversation, mind you, just getting the report of which outside numbers have dialed into your system? And who, in which departments, are receiving those calls? Has anyone in your organization ever contacted the people in your firm to discuss the nature of incoming calls from competitors, for "researchers" of a thousand different stripes, from anyone who seems especially interested in what's happening inside your firm? Didn't think so.

Maybe after reading the box *Indicating Our Intent* you'll view the process of determining indications and intent a little differently. In fact, it shows the reverse of the Behemoth Industries example; in fact, it shows the weaknesses of some kinds of Behemoths. The names have been changed to protect the innocent—and others.

Indicating Our Intent

Imagine a relatively small but high-tech city. Highly entrepreneurial environment, a real incubator for new millionaires and cutting-edge technologies. It gets the attention of people around the world, especially Large-Time Charlies who want to add to their portfolio of companies that they think will allow them to grow even larger.

One well-known and aggressive Large-Time Charles comes in and identifies an especially attractive, privately held local firm that is really doing cutting-edge stuff. Large-Time Charles begins to woo Little Guy and makes the leadership/ownership a wonderful offer, including a three- year noncompete clause. After all, Large-Time Charles can walk upright without a wheelbarrow—and has a brigade of lawyers to make sure he does things correctly. Large-Time Charles adds Little Guy to the mix of products and begins to run Little Guy like all the other companies they own. Large-Time Charles has a well-known and well-respected Business Intelligence unit that is highly placed within earshot of Mahogany Row. They support grand strategy. Perhaps they help out a little in the acquisition, but that's about the extent of their involvement with, or support to, Little Guy.

Fast-forward to three years later. Little Guy's original owner has been contemplating his return to the market. He wants to start another firm and repeat what he did before, except he wants to grow the New Company in such a way that nobody will catch him. He's got more than a couple of million of his own, and there are a few other millionaires from the sale of Little Guy. They, along with some friendly bankers, kick off New Company. Soon, they've not only got the facilities locked in, but they're aggressively recruiting the best and brightest engineers who're working at Little Guy.

Once the best and the brightest sign on at New Company, they start calling their old buddies at Little Guy. Regularly. Just to keep in touch. See how things are going. Maybe there's a chance that the guys at Little Guy might be interested in coming to work at New Company when New Company gets bigger. Great ideas for products, some maybe even hitting production in the next eighteen months. Sorry, can't quite talk about it, especially in case the new bosses at Little Guy should find out. After all, they could kill off New Company. But, speaking of Little Guy, how're you doing with that thing you were coming out with at the end of the year?

Fast-forward another five years. The real heart of Little Guy is gone, having all moved over to New Company in the course of regular business. During those literally thousands of telephone calls from New Company, and during those hundreds of visits to the "old plant" for a quick lunch in the cafeteria—followed by a short walk out to the production line or into engineering to see some of the old boys—Little Guy's technological edge dies off. And, not surprisingly, the leadership at New Company that's always been known as really smart and agile folks are bursting out all over.

The same year that New Company goes public and trebles its opening price on the first day, Large-Time Charles brings in a new management team to try and reverse its falling fortunes. Eighteen months later, Large-Time Charles puts Little Guy on the block. A couple of potential buyers came sniffing around. Nobody really needs a place that has no real quality people or product. No offers. Large-Time Charles closes the doors and says that Little Guy was in a declining market segment that wasn't worth their time anymore.

And the amazing part is the sheer volume of calls from New Company, and the sheer number of visits by New Company people, and the ever increasing number of New Company employees who'd been employed by Little Guy just a short while ago. Volumes and numbers that earned New Company the nickname "Little Guy East," because it was located three miles away, on the eastern edge of the industrial park. Well-stated intentions to operate in the same industry as Little Guy; clear indications of brain-drain away from Little Guy to New Company; clear indications that New Company was looking over Little Guy's shoulder in everyday engineering and production. Amazing that everyone knew but dismissed these intentions and indicators as unimportant because, after all, Large-Time Charles had really deep pockets, a world-class Business Intelligence organization, and more smarts than the above-average bear.

Dismissed by everyone, that is, except for the happy stockholders in New Company.

And finally, as a bit of a preview of things to come, you have to ask the question, "What do you do once you've done your assessment?" We'll take a short run at answering that in this closing business anecdote from a project that took place in late 1997 through mid-1998.

FUD—FEAR, UNCERTAINTY, AND DOUBT

Fear, Uncertainty, and Doubt. We've spoken about them before. How they've actually been used is another story altogether in the Business Intelligence world.

It's the process of introducing wedges between your competition and his important relationship partners. While it comes closer and closer to "dirty tricks" when it's used to disrupt a competitor's product introduction, such as you'll learn about in the French case of *Mirror, Mirror on the Wall* in chapter 18, it's about setting up your competitor for a fall with some long-lasting consequences.

FUD can be practiced either offensively or defensively, and since we're in the midst of protection issues right now, this is the place to talk about it in a case where a client firm we'll call Ramparts Plastics sought to protect itself by introducing FUD into the relationship between its major competitor, Holt Manufacturing Industries (HMI), and Rubie-Jones LLC, a fairly well-known Business Intelligence consultancy. In this case, Rubie-Jones researchers had been reported on a number of occasions as having made especially aggressive—and unwanted—overtures to some of Ramparts' middle management's secretarial staff.

An assessment of recent competitive events told Ramparts' president, Chuck Ferris, that HMI and Rubie-Jones were seriously affecting his business. Ferris decided that enough was enough; just calling his rival over at HMI to complain would do no good whatsoever. He told his protection staff to find a way to defang Rubie-Jones without alerting HMI.

Within a month, the plan was placed before Ferris, he'd approved it, and it began to disrupt the relationship.

The first step was to begin to "poison the well" with pieces of preapproved and deliberately leaked information of a competitive value. Carefully orchestrated to allow HMI to get some information on its own, some that was placed into "flow channels" where it was sure to be picked up by Rubie-Jones's monitoring activities, and some that was given to specifically chosen Ramparts employees whose allegiance to the company was questionable at best—without them being made privy to their role in the project. The interim objective here was to provide sufficient enough corroboration, through multiple sources and channels, that Rubie-Jones's somewhat superficial source- and information-validation process would actually serve as a transmission channel: a channel that would carry enough incorrect and erroneous information that HMI's decision process would become more and more flawed, and ultimately result in HMI's distrust of Rubie-Jones and its own BI department. A final objective of this step was to reduce HMI's use of Rubie-Jones and perhaps degrade the internal reputation of the BI unit to the extent that HMI would no longer find them useful or necessary In other words, those *outcomes* we spoke about a couple of pages age.

The second part of the FUD project was to actually provide other elements as seeds of distrust between HMI and Rubie-Jones. For this purpose, Ramparts asked Rubie-Jones—ostensibly as one of four consulting firms—to submit a proposal for a prospective BI project. The project was large enough to attract a bid from Rubie-Jones. It also included HMI among the list of target companies. In designing the bogus RFP, Ramparts was careful to not reveal any actual business intentions. The interim objective of this part was to determine whether or not Rubie-Jones would decline to respond (which would have been consistent with their long-term, supposedly exclusive arrangement with HMI) or whether they would opt for the money. Once they responded with the bid, any questions about their professional integrity were answered. The final objective of this effort was to portray Rubie-Jones as an unreliable supplier of BI services, not only to HMI, but to anyone they might tell about it.

The third part of the FUD project was to capitalize on the seeds of doubt sown by the first two elements. At a professional meeting some six months later, Ramparts' BI manager asked another practitioner from another firm in an unrelated industry if he'd ever used Rubie-Jones. The Ramparts manager made certain that he asked the question within earshot of the HMI BI manager, knowing that it would attract his attention. Without acknowledging that he was aware of the HMI manager's presence, he then began discussing several aspects of recent Rubie-Jones proposals that had appeared to be either overly boastful about what they could provide or were overly expensive for what they were proposing to charge. In his finest acting moment, the Ramparts manager turned and developed a surprised expression followed by an immediate change of subject when he "realized" that the HMI manager was nearby.

The end result was that HMI stopped using Rubie-Jones. Indeed, when tied to the declining performance that resulted from parts one and two of the plan, Rubie-Jones was seen as having decided to play both ends against the middle.

In the eyes of the HMI leadership, Rubie-Jones had played fast and loose with the relationship. The way they saw it, when Rubie-Jones realized that their recent track record wasn't as good as it'd previously been and that their days with HMI were numbered, they began to shop elsewhere for clients in the same industry. To HMI, it was clear that Rubie-Jones was trying to market to others—notably Ramparts—for whom they could undertake projects against HMI based on their considerable knowledge of HMI's business plans. HMI's leadership decided against any outsourcing of BI services, and their own internal BI unit was hard-pressed to satisfy many of the objectives that had previously been sent out. Ultimately, HMI's own BI department was downsized, under the "what have you done for me lately" principle that seems so prevalent in today's marketplace.

And, with the careful employment of FUD, Ramparts had effectively blinded the HMI leadership—an outcome that is the effective goal of virtually any counterintelligence function. Remember the definition? The part where we refer to "Active measures to identify and neutralize the intelligence collection activities of a business rival."

CHAPTER 16

Just How Vulnerable Are You to Your Rival's Collection Activities? Test Yourself, Attack Yourself

No matter how many times the mule kicks you, the first time is the one that teaches you the most.

—**Will Rogers**

In the two preceding chapters, we have followed the Business Intelligence Protection Model. You now know how to involve your leadership in identifying those key protection topics. You have worked to define and refine the actual protection objectives and questions that need to be answered. You have assessed your competition's ability to collect sensitive information about your firm. In this chapter, the focus will be on testing your vulnerabilities against the collection capabilities of the business rivals who are trying to figure out where you are going as a company.

A good thought to keep in mind is that the two most common reasons for losing are not knowing you're competing in the first place and not knowing with whom you're competing.

REPLICATING THE COMPETITOR AND OTHER COLLECTORS

Central to this process is knowing that you have to replicate the ways your business rivals are attempting to gather information about you. In military operations, it does you absolutely no good to fight the wrong enemy on the wrong battlefield; in intelligence operations the same principle applies. If you want to know what your real vulnerabilities are, you have to "attack" yourself using the same methods and sources your rival is using. Otherwise, you are left with a false sense of security, or you protect the wrong things from the wrong people.

Just because your organization follows the SCIP Code of Ethics for intelligence collection does not mean that everyone else does. In international relations, "mirror-imaging" refers to the way that some countries make bad decisions by imputing their own motives, mores, and capabilities to their adversary. In war, the result has always been disastrous. The same problem faces the business community; nowhere else is it more potentially problematic than in protecting your own competitive information.

The assessment process in chapter 15 emphasized that it is not enough to be concerned with the in-house resources that a competitor can use to gather information about your firm. You also have to know what kinds of information they ask others to obtain for them. It may be a consulting firm that allows the competitor to leave no fingerprints on the project; it may be an investigative firm that works under the protection of work product for a law firm that represents your rival; then again, it may be a different division of a primary competitor, which is very often the case in situations where foreign firms are interested in your organization.

TESTING FOR VULNERABILITIES

In the last chapter, you learned how assessing the competition's ability to collect against your firm is a step beyond the standard "gates, guards, guns, and dogs" approach that describes most corporate security organizations. Active and aggressive testing of a company's vulnerabilities is also a rarity in corporate America, at least in our experience. This is especially true when the issue is information protection. The reasons are many and varied. They range from management simply not really wanting to know to the inability of a security department to go beyond the reactive/passive approach and achieve an active, anticipatory approach to safeguarding its information.

Actively testing your organization's ability to protect itself not only makes good business sense, it has also become recognized in the law. If you have no clue about your vulnerabilities, you certainly cannot make a case to any judge that you have taken the measures necessary, consistent with the threat environment, to protect yourself. No judge in the country will grant you relief in a trade-secrets misappropriation case, for example, if you cannot show that you valued the information highly enough to protect it in the first place.

THE CEO TAKES CHARGE—A CASE EXAMPLE

Remember how we "rode the cycle" in chapter 13 to show how collection all comes together in a trade-show environment? We're going to take the same tack here, except that we'll take a ride on the protection cycle, where we'll look at the parts of the process that lead up to, and then demonstrate, vulnerability testing. And, we'll use an example from an actual project rather than dealing in abstractions and maybes. This project probably encompasses more elements than we've seen in any other case, although the separate elements and others like them have been seen in protection project after project. Granted, there'll be parts of this case that don't directly and immediately apply to your situation, but perhaps you'll look at your firm in a different light from now on. And I'm sure that the lessons you draw from this example will be relatively easy to implement in your own enterprise.

This example involved a firm that we'll call SouthTech, a leader in a world-class technology, where the stakes were as high as those in many industries and higher than most. Here the Business Intelligence Protection Model operates to provide a coherent and rational approach to information protection.

First, the *tasking* came directly from SouthTech's chief executive officer, Tim French. SouthTech was about to make a considerable investment in a set of technologies that could alter the future of their industry, and he wanted to make certain that the investment was protected. French had directed that extraordinary security precautions be taken to safeguard the project. When told that their security was already as tight as it needed to be, he asked how many of his subordinates would be willing to risk their careers on that assessment. When there were no takers, he considered that to be an eloquent statement about a need to reexamine the project's security. The *key protection topic*, then, emerged as "We must protect this project from now until the product launch date from each of our domestic and international competitors."

Defining the protection requirements was distilled down to five *key protection questions*. French felt that if a rival was to learn the answer to any of those five questions, the firm had a serious problem. What technology or technologies are involved in the project? How much investment is the company making in the project? How much of a market value is the new product expected to yield? What are the project time lines, to include the product rollout? Who are the primary strategic partners in the project and what are their technical contributions?

Assessing the competitor-collection capabilities meant evaluating the collection approaches and capabilities of five different rivals. Two were domestic, companies we'll call Alabaster Technologies and PrimeFusion; two were Asian firms, whom we'll call NucoMan Industries and Kimchi Electronic Products, Inc.; and one was European, a firm we'll call Schlitzohr. Alabaster, PrimeFusion, NucoMan, and Schlitzohr had all been encountered in previous protection projects, and a considerable amount was already known about their approaches. Kimchi Electronics, though, was relatively new on the scene and it required some additional work to identify their approaches.

Alabaster had a Business Intelligence staff that had originated in the firm's library function and was still led by a librarian. The bulk of their collection efforts were focused on publicly available, open source documents. The staff was known to be exceptionally good at technical-intelligence collection and analysis, although relying on virtually no human-source collection activity.

PrimeFusion had a very small competitive intelligence staff that provided essentially project-management oversight for consulting firms they hired to exploit both primary and secondary sources. They were known to use three separate consulting firms, each of which was very aggressive in its own specialty: public sources, primary sources, and technical intelligence analysis.

NucoMan, a Japanese multinational, had a large Business Intelligence staff at its U.S. headquarters that was considered a significant strategic asset by the company's leadership. They were augmented by the twelve-person Japanese detachment of researchers who rented space at the U.S. Patent Office, from which they provided trademark and patent tracking information through the Japanese Ministry of Industry and International Trade. Furthermore, it was known that they also relied on a Washington, D.C., law firm to provide access to U.S. government records under the Freedom of Information Act, since as a Japanese firm, they did not have status as a "U.S. person." Court records previously obtained showed that the Japanese firm had been accused of trade-secrets misappropriation on three separate occasions. Documents related to those cases revealed a number of highly aggressive intelligence-collection tactics, most of which went well beyond the SCIP Code of Ethics, including ruse interviews, false employment applications, misrepresentation of interests, and violations of confidentiality agreements in joint projects.

Schlitzohr also made considerable use of American consulting firms, including private investigative firms, to conduct their intelligence-collection activities. Having been asked by that firm on several occasions to conduct collection projects that would have involved some questionable or outright inappropriate activities, we knew that they would be most aggressive. The firm had also been linked with the DGSE, the French intelligence service, in providing support assets overseas in exchange for being able to call on the DGSE in their times of need.

Kimchi, a Korean organization, was soon determined to have a significant history of very aggressive intelligence collection throughout the Pacific Rim and was the target of numerous trade-secret misappropriations complaints. Their small but highly aggressive U.S.-based Business Intelligence unit was led by a former Korean intelligence service officer and had grown from one to nine people in less than a year. Research revealed that they also relied on several firms that specifically eschewed the SCIP Code of Ethics as being too Pollyanna-ish and did "whatever it takes to get the job done." In fairly short order, we had established a fairly accurate profile of the kinds of things that Kimchi had done in the United States and abroad—and had an idea of the kinds of things that they would attempt against SouthTech.

Thus, overall, the so-called threat environment required for us to *replicate* some of the most aggressive collection measures in order to give the client an accurate assessment of their vulnerabilities. We were bound by two caveats at the outset of the project. First, we would not identify, by name, any of the people employed by the company who served as sources of information—unless of course we uncovered an attempt at any illegal activity. Second, we would not replicate any illegal activities, such as breaking and entering of the company's physical or electronic barriers, theft, bribery, or illicit eavesdropping. Naturally, as would be the case with any internal or external vulnerability test, the most rigid secrecy agreements were signed, since the results could be most compromising and injurious to the firm.

Clearly, we needed a starting point, since in order to maintain the integrity of our penetration attempt, the client could tell us nothing at all about the project. Just like a hostile competitor, we would be out in the cold and completely on our own.

In approaching the problem, it was clear that there were going to be some results from open and public—secondary—sources, although we doubted that the company would have written much about such a new topic. More importantly, however, we needed to start with human targets who could provide us current intelligence, as opposed to history lessons—and that was the major focus of the secondary research that precedes almost every project.

WARNING NOTICE: TRY THIS ONLY AT HOME

Leadership Tracking

We proceeded on the initial assumption that Tim French would not have brought us in to penetrate a small or unimportant project. By extension, such a large and significant project would require the direct leadership of one of a handful of people in the upper management of the client firm. We needed to know who that leader was and follow the trail from there. Ten telephone calls later we had identified our first lead, Jack Isaacson. Isaacson was the only executive who was unaccounted for among the normal executive-suite crowd. After a few more calls, we learned that he was on a project outside the main headquarters and had only rarely been seen for the previous two months. An early-morning visit to Isaacson's neighborhood allowed one of our researchers to follow him to the other side of the city, where he pulled into the parking lot of a nondescript building, with no company signage or other apparent connection with the firm. From a distance, our researcher could see through the double-glass doors that a pair of security guards were stationed inside the foyer. Isaacson had fulfilled his function as far as we were concerned: He had led us to the "skunk works," a covert research facility.

Throughout the morning, a total of about seventy other cars parked in front of the building. The license numbers for all the vehicles in the parking lot were recorded and traced that night through a cooperating private investigator in that state. By the following morning, we had the names and addresses of almost sixty people.

Once we had Isaacson's name, we began rotating through the literature again. This time, we were looking specifically for any kind of writing or published research he'd been credited with, either individually or as a coauthor. In fairly short order, it was apparent that he had written about sixty articles and monographs, mostly coauthored with the same people over the course of the previous twenty-five years. Subsequent inquiries revealed that he and his coauthors had almost all been in college together before going off in various directions—business, government research, and academia.

Of the six outside the company, three were now living in the same metropolitan area where the company was located, having moved there within the previous year. One who remained in government was especially proud to talk about the very interesting work that several of his old colleagues were engaged in, work that could have profound changes on their branch of science. He was hoping it would have some spillover to government applications. Remember way back in Elicitation 101? The part about people who are more open than perhaps they should be simply because they don't have a stake in the end result? I thought you'd noticed. Good for you.

Then, armed with the names of some of the others who worked at the same facility, we ran the same kinds of literature searches. Not only did these searches give us a clear idea of what some of the technologies associated with the project might be, but it yielded a treasure trove of coauthors. Coauthors who, upon further examination, were ultimately found to be working for companies that were technology partners for the project.

Nontraditional Instruments

Within a week of ascertaining the names, home addresses, and telephone numbers of the employees from the cars in the parking lot, our researchers began to make telephone calls to their homes. The researchers operated under the guise of a survey on behalf of the State Department of Education. They claimed that they had been asked to help determine if the high school, junior college, and college curricula in the state were sufficiently preparing students for science and technology jobs in the future. We expected that the bulk of the people working on the project were technologists of one sort or another and might be more disposed toward a survey of this type. Of course, we had no real interest in their opinions. The survey was solely for the purpose of getting them to agree to talk with us.

Just as direct questions are used at the opening of the conversational hourglass, opening with the survey questions allowed us to employ elicitation techniques throughout the interviews that encouraged the respondents to talk about their responsibilities at work. The questionnaires ended with the obligatory "demographics-only" portion, which provided our researchers the data for the next round of contacts: personal levels of education and whether the respondents were working in the disciplines for which they were trained; salary ranges, but not specifics; and marital status and family size.

It made no real difference in some of the cases whether we spoke with the employee or the employee's spouse—the willingness of the spouse to speak about a husband's or wife's education, position, and compensation was often greater than that of the employee. This was another manifestation of the elicitation principle that people tend not to protect information that is of no direct concern to themselves.

Reaching Out and Touching Someone

Our next step involved a considerable number of telephone calls to the employees who'd been contacted during the surveys—and any others whom we'd picked up along the way. Yet, since the security organization was already alert to the telephone as the basic weapon of many competitive intelligence collectors, we wanted to mask our interest as much as possible. The company was clearly smart enough about its environment that it had probably alerted its operators to pay attention to any incoming calls from people asking to be connected with any of the people working on the project. In fact, we couldn't be sure whether the remote facility was even tied in to the company's regular telephone system or not—and attracting any additional attention to our inquiries would've simply been bad form.

One of our on-the-ground researchers visited the lobbies of all six principal buildings hoping to find an unattended company telephone book that might find its way into his briefcase. Once again, a departure from the standard SCIP Code of Ethics, but we were replicating the kind of harder ball that we knew several of the competitors were accustomed to playing. But, unfortunately, the company had gone to an all-electronic telephone book just for internal users, in the interest of enhancing security.

Instead of trying to hack into the company's intranet to get the information, we stumbled upon another option that took just a couple of hours and yielded great results. Oh, yes. That's to say we would've hacked into the system if we'd had to. Not all hackers are sixteen-year-old crazies. Many of the better, older, and more professional hackers who work on these kinds of projects with us have been doing it for defensive purposes only for years. But getting back to the other option, it turned out to be as simple as dialing a telephone number that was a likely and logical extension of the company's main, published number, for example, 555-5000. The box *See Jane Run* explains the approach that would've been taken by someone who had no remorse about the SCIP Code of Ethics—and because we were replicating that kind of person, we didn't play by the rules about truth, justice, and the American Way.

Within two hours, the five diggers had succeeded in replicating the entire company directory, not just the people we were initially interested in. This allowed us the opportunity to take some additional steps down the path: the following "Other Ruse Interviews" and e-mail elicitation, which we'll discuss later.

See Jane Run

We simply dialed 555-5718, 5719, and 5720 until we got a person rather than a voice mail. We started directly into the conversation by calling the person by name: "Hi, Diane, this is Bill Jenkins from Allied Highlighters. We've got this invoice that's been outstanding for almost seventy days and we're not a big company. Is there any way that we could get your help in clearing this up as quickly as we can?" This opening was used despite the fact that the person who answered the phone said, "Jane Doe." Of course, Jane Doe mentioned this small point immediately. Our researcher apologized immediately and said that he was just using a handwritten number on his copy of the purchase order for a contact person. He explained that he'd been getting a real runaround trying to find somebody who could help with the problem and was really sorry to bother her. Was there any way she could help him find Diane Jones? She was ever so obliging, giving him the employee dial-in number for the electronic telephone book. She even offered her opinion that it was a stupid thing to have it only for employees and not an option for regular callers from the outside. "Bill's" gratitude overflowed and a nice conversation ended a few minutes later.

The diggers then alphabetized their list of license-plate holders and dialed in, starting with the A's and copying down the names as they heard the first person say "Marie Able 5767," followed by the recorded operator voice saying "If this is not the person you want, please press 3 for the next name on the list," which yielded "Frank Albemarle, extension 6837."

Other Ruse Interviews

Beginning three days later, different researchers began calling the employees on whom we had developed demographic information during the survey phase. This time, the calls were made to them at their offices under the guise of executive recruitment, one of the more common approaches in the community that does not abide by the SCIP standard. The exception was that by this time, we knew enough about the employee's education and income levels—based on what had been elicited during the nocturnal surveys—to frame a very attractive "employment opportunity." Usually, the bogus job opportunity meant slightly increased responsibilities, a significant financial increase, and other sweeteners designed to maneuver the employees into the position where they began selling themselves to the "recruiter." And what would their selling points be? The projects on which they were most recently working.

Who's Hiring Whom?

The "headhunter" interviews yielded another interesting piece of information. While one of the employees was absolutely happy where she was, she was able to suggest someone who might be interested in the job—a normal thing for any headhunter to ask for in the course of any interview. In fact, it was someone who had recently interviewed for a job with their project, but with whom they'd been unable to come to an agreement. The candidate had come from another state and had been presented by one of the headhunter firms the company was using. She even gave the candidate's name and city. It was a small thing to find and contact the candidate.

We called him at his home, ostensibly representing one element of the company's human resources department. Our researcher told the candidate that he was not calling to see if the candidate was going to accept the position but only to make a quality-assurance check. We told him that this was one of the ways that the company liked to ensure that candidates had been treated well and been made to feel welcome, and we asked whether he had any suggestions about how the company's processing might be improved. Naturally, as in the case of the scholastic surveys done earlier, this contact had altogether different motives, including the name of the headhunter who had sent him in for the interviews, how the recruiter had treated him, how rigorously his personal and professional background had been checked, and how he felt about the process overall.

Armed with this information, we could replicate some of the known bogus candidate employee ploys that one of the company's more aggressive rivals employed. Knowing from the candidate that to his knowledge none of his professional or personal references had been checked prior to our telephone call, we concluded that reference checking was not done prior to sending the candidate in for a series of interviews. This allowed us to construct a completely bogus identity for one of our associates, providing her with an advanced technical degree and history consistent with her own background and competencies but with another name and university.

It was very easy for our associate to get herself included in the next round of interviews. She had no problem whatsoever signing a nondisclosure/secrecy agreement with the company when she arrived for the interview series—after all, she only existed on paper. The information that she was provided during the interview schedule more than made up for the extra work in putting together her résumé and bogus driver's license.

Waste Archeology

Some of the more junior members of our protection project team received specialized training as waste archeologists. It's almost always the junior members who are given such opportunities for personal growth and excellence—that's the natural order of things. While we had expected that such a high-profile, high-dollar-value project would have had an absolute requirement that all related documents had to be shredded, we nonetheless needed to test whether or not such policies were in effect—and more importantly, if they were being followed.

The first of the two Dumpsters visited on the first night was filled with bags that contained nothing but shredded materials. And, to the credit of the security managers, the shredders were of the best kind, using a cross-cut design that made it nearly impossible to piece the shreds together. The second Dumpster, however, was filled with plastic bags that contained unshredded waste, including copies of financial-planning documents that had obviously been discarded because they were not photocopied as clearly as a secretary wished. This demonstrated one of our longest standing rules: The trash can nearest the photocopy machine is the most dangerous piece of equipment in any company. Unclear copies, off-center copies, extra copies, badly stapled copies—they all go in there.

In protection projects such as this, we often come across similarly valuable documents that had been misfed into the copier so that the copies had come out crooked or only partially legible. Instead of being destroyed in accordance with the quality of information they contained, they were disposed of as regular trash. The assumption seemed to be that if it was not pretty and professional enough to give to the boss, then it obviously had no value. Of course, from time to time, the trashed copies will be torn in quarters or in halves in some semblance of an attempt at protecting it. All that really does is help make the waste archeologist's job easier. When you see something torn into pieces, it means that the person who did the tearing attached some value to it. Waste archeologists are drawn to these pieces of paper as magnets draw metal filings.

We began focusing on the second Dumpster during our regular nocturnal visits. In addition to the rather unsavory things that we will leave to the imagination, we gathered many additional and insightful documents. Among these documents was a spreadsheet of burn rates for the various employees presently employed on the project, as well as the number of employees per research team that still needed to be hired. There were various and sundry pieces of relatively innocuous e-mail from people in different parts of the company, as well as some from outside. And, the company code name for the project.

Included in the pure information that was found during the waste archeology project, four other points were especially noteworthy.

NDAs Aren't Worth the Paper They're Copied On

The first was a clump of nearly a dozen papers that had been torn into quarters and thrown into the regular trash. In this case, the pages were copies of nondisclosure agreements with eleven different companies in various parts of the country, signed by an official at each company. Clearly, there would be no reason to execute an NDA unless the two firms were involved in something of some significance and sensitivity. Research into the specialty areas in which the individual companies worked opened whole new avenues of inquiry, as well as whole new groups of people as prospective sources. It was a fairly small matter to link employees and their professional papers with individuals who were working at some of these technology partners.

Test Marketing

The second was a copy of the test-marketing plan contained in a proposal submitted to the company by a research firm in another state.

The schedule of cities where the prototype product was going to be test-marketed allowed us the opportunity to insinuate several of our associates into the pool of participants. From this series of events, our participants would report on the various characteristics of the prototype such as form, design and function, price, size, and desirability. The representatives of the test-marketing firm knew more than perhaps they should have known; they certainly said more to our "participants" than they should have—and more than they should have known in the first place.

Black Contracting

The third were some curious receipts. Some were receipts for payments to three consulting companies for their purchase of certain materials and equipment. Others showed some purchases from other suppliers, along with the suppliers' names and addresses.

Two of the consultancies had local addresses on the receipts, but there were no listings for them in the phone book. One of the addresses seemed familiar to one of the researchers. Indeed, it turned out to be the home address of one of the more senior members of the project, and the consultancy name bore the individual's initials. It was only a minute or two before she'd matched up the initials and addresses to two other project employees.

This gave all the appearances of what some government agencies do when they want to disguise that the government—and specifically a particular agency or group—is purchasing something that might compromise a project. When people in the intelligence business use this process, it's called a cutout; in the contracting world, it's called a black contracting office. The company had apparently chosen to mask or disguise some of its purchases by making them through the "consultants," who were trusted employees; then the suppliers would not be able to say the wrong things to the wrong people in the event that someone was "following the money."

The follow-on was to call each of the suppliers, representing ourselves as the "consultant" and saying that we'd lost our entire file of receipts from purchases we'd made from the supplier. Would the supplier be kind enough to fax a copy of each of the purchases to a certain number—a number that was the fax at a local photocopy store that had a fax service. Of course, nothing is ever as easy as it sounds. Three of the suppliers' receipts only showed the part numbers and quantity, not the things that were actually purchased. It took another day to call and ask for a catalog from the suppliers before we could learn what the ordered items were. Then, in the hands of our technology analysts, the ordered items plus the tested, wasted, and discarded pieces of parts that were being used in building the prototype—found in the unshredded materials Dumpster— the potential outcome rapidly became clearer, especially when combined with the other pieces of the puzzle that emerged shortly.

An Eye for an Eye

The final and perhaps most intriguing development from the waste archeology project was from observations of the Dumpsters. Our coverage of the Dumpsters began on a Wednesday night and was scheduled to be conducted every night. As a regular and routine part of the process, our divers always conduct a discreet surveillance of the Dumpsters to determine three things: the time of day that bags are deposited in the

Dumpsters (in this case, between 8:30 and 9:30 P.M. each workday), the time and day that the Dumpsters were serviced (between 2:30 and 3:00 A.M. Tuesday, Thursday, and Saturday), and whether or not they were part of a security patrol's building coverage (they weren't). Our divers recovered bags from both Dumpsters very early on Thursday and Friday mornings and had not noticed any security patrols to that point; on Friday night, as they were in position at around midnight and preparing to service the Dumpster, they noticed someone approaching the Dumpster that contained the shredded materials—a person who was not part of the guard force. As the person got into Dumpster # 1—which contained the shredded materials—one of our people decided to wreck his evening by driving to within fifty feet of the Dumpster and in plain sight of it. He sat there in the car for over an hour, just listening to the stereo, before driving off. His partner, meanwhile, watched as the intruder jumped out of the Dumpster with nothing in his hands following our first watcher's departure. He ran to a small pickup truck parked about seventy-five meters away. The second surveillant was able to close the distance to the pickup as it left the vicinity. Before breaking off the surveillance, he was able to follow it closely enough that he could make out the license-plate number and the fact that there were about eight trash bags in the bed of the pickup. Subsequent inquiries revealed that the pickup was owned by a registered private investigator in that state. As is the case with most PIs, this one never paid much attention to people following him, since he was so accustomed to being the hunter and not the hunted. He also was the type of person who talked too much when enjoying himself. As you will see later, the combination of these two factors worked to his client's disadvantage.

By Monday afternoon, we had modified our approach to the Dumpsters. With the concurrence of our point of contact inside the company, we developed a plan to allow the PI to continue to have access to the Dumpsters, but to ensure that he got only prescreened materials. At the same time, we certainly could not screen the materials from inside the facility. That Monday afternoon, one surveillance team followed him from his office to a bar, where he remained until about 9:30 and then drove to his home. He changed clothes and exchanged his car for the pickup truck and started out in the direction of the R and D facility. The surveillance team had been in contact with our diggers at the facility, and they'd already made the swap of old trash for new trash. Yet, he didn't drive directly to the client's location, but instead went to four other locations in about a six-mile radius of the client's facility—hence the eight bags seen in his pickup the previous Friday night. Unfortunately, one of those other locations was a Dumpster behind one of the client's four other buildings, which were all grouped together and well known in a research park elsewhere in the city.

By Tuesday, of course, the trash coming out of the company's other building was being screened by internal security personnel prior to its being deposited in the Dumpster each night. Thus, our people serviced Dumpster #2 each night between 9:30 and 10:00 and replaced the bags they took that night with one they had already culled through from the previous night. This permitted us to keep the PI from getting anything of any importance while still permitting him access to the Dumpsters and keeping him in our crosshairs for later potential, albeit unwitting, utility. In practice, he usually arrived at around midnight, and the first couple of times he was observed going into both Dumpsters. After four or five nights, he began entering only Dumpster #2, having apparently established that Dumpster #1 would always contain only the shredded materials. We continued our surveillance of him up to and through the briefing to the CEO, where the PI was included in some of the follow-on recommendations.

E-Mail Elicitation

You'll recall from our earlier coverage of the use of e-mail as a newer variation on approaching people who might serve as sources of information that it's fast becoming a weapon of choice for information collectors, particularly when working with the technology-minded. As we developed the responses from the headhunter interviews, there were a number of people who seemed to have little, if any, personality. In trying to get "whole person" pictures of some of the people we knew to be working on the project, we went back and looked at the ages and conditions of the cars they were driving and drove by their homes and apartments. To all intents and purposes, they appeared to have little else in the way of a life. This was an ideal potential population for the development of great electronic relationships.

From the earlier e-mails that we'd found, the e-mail naming conventions were easy to develop. After searching through a variety of user groups on the Internet, we located several of these people as fairly frequent contributors to groups such as alt.singles, alt.backpackers, alt.cat-lovers, and so on. Approaching these people via these groups, rather than directly at their offices, helped to begin a dialogue on very basic levels related to what little they had as an outside life. Developing long-term, more or less meaningful relationships with these people, incrementally growing more and more interested in the fascinating lives they led in the workplace, began to yield very interesting points about the technology challenges that our correspondents were dealing with and overcoming each day. Naturally, our researchers used their noncompany e-mail addresses, especially some of the free ones.

Another variant on the ways in which e-mail helped with this project can be seen in the box *Chatty Cathy*, after a doll by the same name.

Chatty Cathy

Publicly traded companies have wonderful and knowledgeable employees, analysts who follow those companies, disgruntled investors who complain about them, and happy investors who love to brag about how wisely they've invested. Meet some of them at any one of fifty chat rooms on the Internet that focus on the stock market and investments. Meet them by expressing an interest in a particular company, either from a stock-performance perspective or from a future-of-the-company point of view. Meet them to further your understanding of the company you're interested in.

In the case of this project, the first time we ever heard the code name for the project was in a response from an employee of the company, only peripherally involved in the project but knowledgeable about its existence and its great potential. She was especially responsive to the elicitation techniques we referred to as Disbelief and Criticism in part I. Her desire to advance the cause of the company's future sounded almost like one of those brokerage firms' advertising, except that she seemed to be motivated to put out her own buy recommendations to "one investor at a time." Our digger just happened to be one of the more interested. Her best single piece of information was provided a week or so into the exchanges when she said, "Just you wait. In 18 months, BLUE STREAK is almost going to double the size of the company, all by itself."

Later, when we found a piece of detritus that used the same code name, it would've been essentially meaningless to us without some background; or, put another way, text without context is pretext.

Restaurant Coverage

In a variation as old as the intelligence community itself, we were able to observe the restaurants where many of the employees went for lunch. A considerable number of the employees went to lunch at a small, nearby café, since there was no cafeteria in their skunk works. It was a simple matter to have a rotating group of our associates visit that restaurant prior to the normal arrival time of the employees. Since they were already there, our associates did not represent an intrusion on the employees. There is nothing suspicious, after all, in seeing someone eating in a restaurant; that only becomes potentially suspicious when someone comes in after you do. And, since these employees had little more in common than the work they were engaged in at the research facility, that was generally the topic of conversation. The insights gathered in this simple coverage arrangement—meat-and-potatoes eavesdropping—were surprising even to us. They were certainly unsettling to the company's leadership at the end of the project.

Strategic Partners

Interestingly, the Internet user-group approach also helped considerably when we were trying to identify the competencies and contributions of the gradually expanding list of team partners involved in the development of this technology. Going directly to the companies paid off in certain ways, since they were almost all very small, specialty houses that had one single product or technology mastery. On one level, that made it somewhat dicey because their competencies were so unique and represented such a small field that the people in those companies knew virtually everyone else who was involved in their discipline. On the other hand, however, like most small companies, they tended to give away far more than their larger brethren simply because they're highly entrepreneurial—and the more entrepreneurial, typically the more involved everyone in the firm is in marketing of one type or another. Furthermore, the more entrepreneurial a company, very often the more open they are, which means more people across the company know about where they're going and how they're going to get there. And lastly, the smaller and more entrepreneurial, the less orientation a company has toward protecting itself—in most cases not having even a single person responsible for security of the organization in even the most generic sense. The box *Dance with the One What Brung Ya* illustrates the results of dealing on-line with a recent alumnus of one of the strategic partners.

Dance with the One What Brung Ya

Our digger had occasion to ask about the company in a user group where the focus was on finding jobs. He simply asked if ZYX Company—-the suspected strategic partner—was a good place to work or not, and sent the question out into the ether. Within three days, there was a response from a recently departed employee from that same company. The dialogue that ensued was not what one might have expected. The former employee was not in the least bit disgruntled. Indeed, he was somewhat regretful that he had left the company because his new job was not what it had been cracked up to be—precisely the reason that he was back looking at on-line position vacancies after only a month at his new job. He acknowledged that he was even considering trying to make a run back to ZYX because of the things that he'd heard were happening there. He didn't know much about it, since there had only been preliminary discussions about a long-term cooperative arrangement with our client company at the time of his departure. Now, he understood from his old friends at ZYX that there was going to be a very significant cash infusion into ZYX from the client and that things were really looking up, especially on the technology side. The electronic conversation continued with great detail about what the company could bring to the table and, correspondingly, how bright its future looked.

Again, someone knew a fair amount and could fill in the pieces of the puzzle but didn't appreciate the value of the information he had only peripherally obtained and felt no special responsibility to protect.

AND YOUR POINT IS?

These approaches may mean something to you in your business or they may not. Perhaps they parallel your operations or your potential vulnerabilities or they may not. We don't intend for them to do that anyway.

The idea here is to get you thinking about how you might be vulnerable to the ways that collectors are actually obtaining information these days—and to develop countermeasures to them that are beyond what your regular security function provides.

Without intending to demean those who do your security work right now, haven't we just framed an approach that is somewhat different from the ways that they've been protecting you to this point? A more active, aggressive, and outward-in, not inward- looking-out approach? Perhaps even a more realistic approach than the one you're taking today? Wouldn't it be better to learn about your vulnerabilities from a friendly inside source than the hard way after the loss of an especially important product, acquisition, joint-venture opportunity, or cutting-edge technology development?

The next chapter will extend this same case example to show the kinds of aggressive as well as preventive countermeasures that can be designed and used to protect a company's most secret and sensitive information.

CHAPTER 17

Developing Countermeasures for Your Dining and Dancing Pleasure

*In wartime, truth is so precious that she should always be attended by a
bodyguard of lies.*

—Winston Churchill

In the preceding chapter, we used SouthTech, led by CEO Ted French, as an
example of a high-technology company that was under considerable competitive pressure—and information attack—from a variety of domestic and international actors, each with a different set of approaches and standards. In this
chapter, we'll continue using SouthTech and that same protection project to
help show how countermeasures can be developed, adopted, and implemented. Since SouthTech had already implemented a variety of countermeasures prior to our engagement in this project, we'll proceed from the countermeasures point on the protection model. Once again, we've chosen this
particular case, since it has as many different elements as almost any other case
we've dealt with—although many of the elements will be roughly the same as
those encountered in other projects of this kind. We'll begin this chapter with
the analysis and reporting of the efficacy of those previous countermeasures,
and go directly from there into the recommendations and implementation of
a few additional, and needful, countermeasures selected by Mr. French.

REPORTING

Seek the truth, come whence it may, lead where it will, cost what it may.

—William Sparrow[*]

An intelligence officer is only as good—and as useful—as his integrity and
candor when reporting findings to the leadership, whether it's the leadership

---

[*]Reverend Doctor William Sparrow, D.D., was Professor of Theology and Christian Evidence
from 1841 to 1874 at Protestant Episcopal Theological Seminary of Virginia, and this quotation
is engraved in the stonework over the entry to the library at the current Virginia Theological

of a company or a country. That may seem laughable to some who equate national intelligence services with deceit and treachery, but I would submit to you that the first time that the intelligence officer—whether a collector or a protector—is found to have been fudging the results of an effort, he's a goner. Gone along with the considerable amount of good he might otherwise do. It's better to find another job if you're not willing from time to time to accept the role of bearer of bad tidings.

In this case, French was at least prepared for the possibility that there might be a leak or two; that the project might result in the compromise of one or two of the five issues that were considered the key protection questions:

- What technology or technologies are involved in the project?
- How much investment is the company making in the project?
- How much of a market value is the new product expected to yield?
- What are the project time lines, to include the product rollout?
- Who are the primary strategic partners in the project and what are their technical contributions?

He was truly ill prepared to learn that each of the questions was answered within thirty days—along with more than he hadn't asked to have answered. French, though, was a CEO who understood the need to go forward and fix what needed to be fixed without recriminations and heads rolling in the streets.

He also understood fully that within thirty days of beginning the project, using resources that were not especially elegant, costly, or complex in execution, we were able to identify many of his firm's different vulnerabilities; the likely or probable ways it could be attacked by its rivals; the kinds of things that its rivals could have learned—and taken advantage of in the marketplace— months before the product launch; at least one active and aggressive collector who was part of the way down the trail to compromising his project; and the kinds of things that would be worth millions to the competition if they were able to find out what was going to happen to them in the marketplace.

French even abided by the initial ground rules set up at the very outset of the project: no floggings, no witch hunts, no identification of those who'd said more than they should have said. Once he had the status report, he wanted recommendations and solution sets.

Seminary in Alexandria, VA. Perhaps not as famous as the inscription at CIA headquarters from John 8:32 (And ye shall know the truth, and the truth shall make you free), but it certainly captures the essence of a professional intelligence officer's life.

RECOMMENDING

The recommendations were really pretty straightforward in a case like this. Clearly, the weakest points were not solely—or even primarily—related to physical security. The weakest points were a lack of employee appreciation for the world around them and a lack of employee cooperation with the policies that had been put into place. Nothing unusual here. Instead, mostly the usual problems that're found in companies around the country and the world. Based on three principal issues—the amount of information collected, the amount of money involved, and the need to keep the project under wraps for another eighteen months—we prepared a rather extensive set of countermeasures from which French could choose. They included:

- Employee awareness.
- Employee participation program.
- Document management and accountability.
- Follow-up penetration testing.
- Physical safeguards.
- Active countermeasures.
- Electronic safeguards.
- Dedicating a specific counterintelligence professional for the life of the project.
- Elicitation and counterelicitation training.
- Background checks on new hires.
- Surveillance and countersurveillance.
- Close cooperation with the corporate competitive intelligence unit.

Some of the measures French and his advisers implemented may seem more than you might want to have at your organization. In this case, he was absolutely deadly serious about the need to protect the company's considerable investment and wanted everyone to know about his degree of seriousness. They're described here in some detail to give you an appreciation for some of the measures that some firms take; in fact, they are less than some others have taken.

Employee Awareness

Within the week, an all-hands meeting of the new development group was held—a group that now numbered over one hundred people, a mixture of older employees and new hires. Paul Kendall, the stern-faced senior vice president, started off with an introduction that spoke volumes. Kendall merely quoted Ted French's well-chosen words in his short directive about what had happened and that the employees were going to learn what was *going* to happen. Everyone knew that Ted played very hard.

During the next forty-five minutes, we presented a condensed version of our approaches and findings. Granted, there was little humor to be had. In fact, there were some rather angry employees who thought that the approach was grossly unfair and an invasion of their privacy. Not unexpectedly—because we'd seen it happen many times before—peer pressure soon deflated their anger, as their own co-workers helped them realize that they were all working for the good of the project. The fact that the early ground rules meant no employee was ever identified to management helped mitigate some of the anguish. By the end of the presentation, all of the employees recognized that the wholesale compromise of the project, its technology, and its financials could have been catastrophic.

The next part of the presentation was prefaced by more comments from Kendall. The processes that were going to be followed from that point on had been developed in close coordination with French himself and his senior leadership council. Perhaps more importantly, French had personally approved each one of the new measures, and by having Kendall be the one who made the opening remarks about them, he gave them the reinforcement he thought they needed to have.

Company-Specific Awareness

The next order of business was employee awareness, but not some generalized, off-the-shelf "it happened somewhere else" presentation. And in order to work properly, it had to provide not only awareness but buy-in as well, buy-in that would lead to active participation. Little else would matter. More attractive signs, more policies, dire threats, stronger locks, or bigger guards would have no influence without active participation. The only way to get their participation would be through a personal and professional appreciation of the nature of the problem—with them at the center of both the problem and the fix.

Yet, at the same time, not to create paranoia but to promote protection. It's our experience that only when you get employee buy-in can you expect employees to comply with whatever procedural changes need to be made.

The presentation of how the information had been compromised using approaches known to be used by several of the firm's competitors opened the eyes of many. Simply, they'd never thought about such things before. They thought that these kinds of approaches were only found in the movies and in novels. Now they knew differently. Again, as we've seen time after time, employee desire to actively participate increased dramatically, due in no small part to the simple fact that the company leadership felt the problem important enough to share with them in the first place. This is especially true where employees have been made to feel that they're working in "mushroom factories," where they're kept in the dark and covered with fertilizer. Any who had felt that way were definitely out in the light soon.

Once they had an appreciation of how they could be exploited for information, they were in a much better position to understand how to recognize approaches that might be suspicious, or at least reportable. That's where the focus was placed next.

Employee Participation Program

Employees were told that a separate hotline had been set up for the express purpose of handling employee reports of suspicious contacts, whether by telephone, by e-mail, via fax, or in person while traveling, off-the-job, or at trade shows, conferences, or professional meetings. They did not need to make any value judgment about the contact and whether it was actually problematic or not. All they had to do was report what they thought might be an inappropriate or potentially harmful contact, following four basic steps:

- Tell the person that it was not a good time to talk just then, but that the employee would be glad to get back to the inquirer quickly.

- Obtain the requester's name, company, and telephone number so as to facilitate the response.

- Note the contact information, along with a description of the actual information sought.

- Call the hotline, either at the internal local number or via the 800 listing in case they were traveling when the suspicion arose, and report the contact and its circumstances.

This became another one of those wonderful repeats of the Law of Unintended Consequences that are so often found in situations like these. Although only one person asked the question, there were numerous nods of agreement as the question was asked: "If we're all here like this, and the company is so concerned, does this mean that we're doing the same kind of thing to the other guys? At least the legal and ethical part?" As had happened so often in the past, this essentially became a self-identifying method for finding additional sources of information for the company's own—then nascent but suddenly growing—BI collection effort. Others came up after the presentation and spoke directly with the security management team, offering them any additional assistance they might need. They would indeed prove helpful later on.

And, since the law was operating on one level, we were especially grateful that it operated on another as well, what we'll call *The Law of Unintended Consequences—Part II* in the following box.

The Law of Unintended Consequences—Part II

During the Q&A after the presentation, one employee—who was shortly followed by several others—noted another approach that had been made to him. He wanted to know if it had been part of the approach that we'd already made but hadn't reported on during the presentation. As he began describing it, we immediately recognized the attempt at the "social engineering" that's becoming so much a part of the world of computer penetrations today. The caller alleged to have been an internal employee working on access control problems with the company's intranet. The caller had asked the employee if he'd been having any log-on troubles such as those experienced in other parts of the company; when the employee said that he hadn't, he was told that he should try and log on at that point. Being fairly computer literate, the employee had recently heard about how someone could remotely yet effectively read his password and user name and was suspicious. Further, when the employee asked for the caller's name and extension so he could call him back, the caller seemed to "tap dance" too much, without ever really giving the information.

The employee's description of the events was echoed by five others, a clear suggestion that someone else was also fairly aggressively pursuing the members of the project team, and not just employees at large. Also noteworthy, unfortunately, was that none of the others had previously thought to report the contact to anyone in security or management. Of final note was that although we asked the assembled group whether anyone else had had similar contacts or experiences, no one else raised a hand, although there was some nervous shifting in the chairs—a sign of embarrassment on one hand, while on the other hand, a sign that not everyone had bought into the system and level of the problem yet. That would come in time.

Intended Consequences

There's another matter: intended consequences. It has never gotten to the level of a law itself, but every once in a while, something actually does go according to plan. This was one of those times. And it was not the first time. In fact, in virtually every one of the more than one hundred companies where such a program has been put into effect as part of this approach, we've had the same result. Employee reporting to the hotlines has done a variety of things:

- They've identified who is calling and what they're calling about.

- They've identified what the questions are.

- They've been much more careful in their responses, and in most cases, have made no response at all.

- They've begun recognizing additional, and sometimes very imaginative, variations on the themes, allowing the protection staff to inform others of new kinds of approaches.

- They've assisted in the development of a tracking database that may be used later in any legal proceedings that may be chosen, such as an injunction against such activities. Otherwise, without a record, you have no chance.

- And they've helped to identify elements that can later be used in even more aggressive countermeasures such as those we'll be speaking about in the next chapter.

On their face, the first two bullets may not seem like much, but consider this. In virtually every national intelligence service around the world, one of the standing collection requirements is to find out what the other guys are looking for, what they are trying to find out. The underlying principle is that this really tells you quite a bit about the other guy: what his intelligence gaps are, what his intelligence needs are, who he's relying upon to try and gather the information. Many times it tells you precisely what you need to protect and from whom. Instead of hypothesizing, as you may have to do in the commercial world from time to time, about what your rival is interested in collecting and assessing their ability to collect it, it's just as useful for you to know what you're up against as it is for a national intelligence service.

On another level, it also tells you—quite often—where the other fellow is heading. For example, if you learn that your rival is most interested in how far advanced you are in the application of high-energy lasers to your business, and is specifically trying to find out about your progress in X-ray lasers, you know that he wouldn't be asking those questions unless he had a use for the answers. If a university professor is asking about these things from a colleague, his interest might be only academic. But in the rest of the world, where resources are always thin and where people have already asked the questions up front such as "What do you need to know?" and "What are you going to use it for?" it goes well beyond an academic exercise.

People are trying to get answers like these because they need to know where you are in relation to their project of the same sort; they're trying to find out where you're heading so as to take away as much of your advantage as possible when you roll out your product; or they're trying to get enough information about your progress so that they can save themselves the cost of the mistakes that you've made along the way as a pioneer.* In any of these cases, they're not interested in these things in order to help your stock price.

The foregoing applies mostly to those who identify themselves and their companies. And so, you ask, "What about those people who call under guises or ruses?" Good question.

There are a variety of ways to find out who's calling whom, but if your employees aren't involved in the mix to begin with, you're never going to find out about the calls in the first place. If they have no idea what is sup-

---

*Perhaps the most succinct expression of this approach in American business was made by George Fisher when he took over Kodak in the early 1990s. Fresh from his stint at the head of Motorola, which has perhaps the most frequently benchmarked Business Intelligence organization in America, he was asked by *The Wall Street Journal* how he was going to change Kodak's business approach. In response, he described the company's future as "an aggressive follower."

posed to be protected, what they should be looking for in conversations, and what they should be reporting when something in that conversation alerts them, then you're unarmed before the battle even begins.

Yet, when you do have the basics in place, then you can begin to do one of several things. If a particular employee reports more than his or her fair share of curious, unusual, or suspicious calls or contacts, then maybe it's time for them to get a caller ID put on their phone. That's at least a start. If the other guy has a block on his phone for caller ID, then that should also be a tip in the right direction. When the person calls and declines to give a number, or it doesn't match the area code where it's supposed to be originating, or any one of a number of other indicators, or if the caller otherwise appears to be an active collector, don't force the employee to think. This isn't a management technique out of a *Dilbert* cartoon. It just makes sense to provide the employee—especially one who may not feel especially light on his feet in a conversation—with a few helpful hints or suggestions about what to do or say.

Give the employee some help up front. Have the employee tell the caller that he'd be more than happy to answer any written questions. Have them mailed, using the requester's company letterhead. Have the employee tell the caller that it's company policy. If it's not, consider making it a company policy. After all, most companies have specific spokespeople—whether it's a PR wonk or the president who doesn't get enough face time in the media.

Of course, the rule will be a bit different if the employee is supposed to interact with the public as customers or consumers; yet almost all of the people intelligence collectors go after are the ones where the rubber meets the road, where the actual items of intelligence interest can be found. And usually, the PR folks are not the ones who give out too much. Usually. At least that's how it's supposed to work. All right. So we sometimes get them to say more than they should. So get one who knows what to say and what not to say. The bottom line to all of this is, once again, don't make it easy; don't make it cheap.

Confronted with this set of circumstances, most BI collectors will ask if they can fax the questions instead, or perhaps e-mail them. Usually, this is because they're operating on a short schedule. They'll generally spend five minutes trying to talk the employee into giving the answers without having the questions reduced to writing in the interest of saving your employee time. Right. As if that's their primary concern. They don't want a paper trail. Moreover, they don't want a fax station identifier if it says they're not who they allege to be.* And on the e-mail front, most of the people who're into electronic rusing already have more than a fundamental grasp of the concept and use of anonymous e-mail addresses.

"What about the people who are trying to get information through other sources besides our employees?" Another good question. Do we mean to suggest that you have only your employees participate in such a reporting program? Hardly. Extend it to the people you have strategic relationships or partnerships with, along with their employees. Tell them what you expect in terms of protecting information and how to do it. An NDA isn't going to be the answer. In most cases, individual employees of another company—whether a partner, vendor, or otherwise—haven't signed the NDA in the first place. They have little idea of whether one exists, and if it does, they have no idea of what it says. Usually, it's the GC or someone else in management who's signed it and is obligated on behalf of the company. Then it's up to the company to protect your information. Think about this for another nanosecond. When was the last time you did anything to assure yourself that the other firm is taking measures at least as rigorous as yours to protect the information you consider important?

Document Management and Accountability

Clearly, much of the information that was available concerning the project was *too* available—available because it wasn't stored, controlled, or accounted for properly; because it wasn't destroyed properly; because it was too widely disseminated to employees who had no real reason to have it; because no one really knew the level of sensitivity attached to specific documents and the information contained in them. With a few fairly simple changes, sensitive written information became not nearly as available as it had been.

- Documents containing company-sensitive information were marked according to their value to the firm, in this case "Company Confidential" and "Company Private." While these two levels may sound similar, each employee was told the difference between the two

---

*There may appear to be a downside to this as well. If you don't want your fax numbers given out for fear that someone will try to compromise your fax traffic, you're only operating on the margins of the real world. Anybody who will go to the trouble of trying to intercept your fax traffic will already have used a war dialer to call every number in your company and will have identified those with fax tones or modems a long time ago.

so that they understood the two levels of protection that should be afforded them. For example, manning diagrams were marked "Company Confidential" since they could provide an overview of the organization in one document; "Company Private" meant documents that related to specific elements of a given a project, program, or technology that would represent part of the firm's technological, pricing, or production competitive advantage.

- Documents that included either of the two levels followed by the project or program code name; for example, "Company Confidential—BLUE STREAK" meant that the distribution of any documents of this level was limited to those whom the program or project manager designated.

- A knowledgeability list (also known as a "bigot list") was created for each project or special program so that anyone not included would not be able to receive any information about it. On the other end of the scale, a bigot list provides a very useful starting point if a compromise does occur. At least you know with whom and where to start a set of inquiries into the loss.

- Accountability of documents, which meant the numbering of certain kinds and classes of information, based on the decisions of the project manager. For example, certain drawings, descriptions, plans, or program documents would be numbered "Copy ____ of ____ Copies" on each page and each blank would be filled in by hand using blue ink. In this way, an inappropriate or unapproved reproduction of the document would be immediately revealed. In this particular firm, the CEO further directed that each page of project-related sensitive material be printed on a special stock of paper—paper with a yellow line across the middle—so as to preclude any illicit copying.

- Copies of all documents in the "Company Private" category would be stored in certain lockable containers overnight. If the holder of one of these documents did not have a suitable container—which meant no desk drawers—then he had to turn the document in to one of the secretaries who maintained the project files master copies. This was especially true of financial and project-planning documents as well as technical drawings and test results.

- The document custodians—typically the two secretaries to the program manager—were to maintain logs of all documents in the "Company Private—BLUE STREAK" category, indicating when they were created and by whom, how many copies were made and to whom they had been distributed, who signed for them, and when they were destroyed and by whom. Electronic storage media such as diskettes were to be treated the same way.

- Random purse, briefcase, and backpack searches were to be performed to ensure that no documents were being removed from the premises. The general counsel agreed that the pure randomness of such searches ensured that no personal privacy considerations were being violated and that no individual was being singled out for special treatment.

- 100 percent shredding of all documents relating to operations in the R and D facility, no matter how seemingly innocuous. This decision was made when we pointed out several of the pieces of information we obtained from the waste archeology and how they were brought together as indicators and clues, for example, yellow, self-sticking notes with telephone numbers and names that were contacted in other companies, telephone message forms, and envelopes from what turned out to be important outside organizations we would have probably not known about otherwise.

Follow-up Testing to Ensure Compliance and to Identify Any Other Vulnerabilities

Since the project needed to remain tightly sealed from view for at least eighteen months, Ted French decided that it would be practical to periodically test the countermeasures being implemented to ensure that they were still effective and to determine compliance with the policies and procedures being put into place. He directed that another penetration test be done at the 60-day point, at the 120-day point, and at the 180-day point, after which a decision would be made about whether or not the testing should continue, based on what was learned. French also directed that the employees should not know that additional testing would be done, or when. Obviously, the follow-on testing would include not only the same things that had been examined before but other potential vulnerabilities as they arose from changes and the normal progress of the project.

Physical Safeguards

In addition to the physical aspects of safeguarding the project documents in secure containers and so on, French directed that other physical security standards be met. These included locking the Dumpsters and having the guard force be responsible for unlocking them whenever the removal truck arrived to empty them; having the guard force actually walk the property at irregular intervals throughout the day and night rather than staying inside the facility, and having them wear regular street clothes and not attract attention to themselves by wearing uniforms; increasing the number of security containers in the facility; increasing the number of shredders from two to ten; lighting the perimeter of the building at night, and particularly the area near the Dumpsters; and cutting back the brush near the Dumpsters. Yet these approaches were to be delayed for another thirty days before implementation, for reasons that will become clear below.

Active Countermeasures

Of all the emotional responses French made during the briefing, he became most angry when he learned that the PI was routinely visiting his Dumpsters. He was quickly relieved when he learned of the measures taken both at the R and D facility and at the other building, especially when he realized that they set the stage for some aggressive responses. We explained the nature of, and differences between, misinformation, disinformation, and deception. We suggested several misinformation courses for him to choose from if he so desired; he chose one that we'll speak about in the section Surveillance and Countersurveillance.

Electronic Communication Safeguards

Since the company now had a much better appreciation of the nature of threats from outside the firm via the Internet and e-mail, several other safeguards were considered and implemented. One involved the use of sniffers to monitor incoming and outgoing e-mail correspondence; other software monitoring devices were installed to identify repeat visitors to the company's Website in a further attempt to assess the activities of competitors; and a variety of means were implemented to monitor references to the firm in various locations on the Internet, ranging from news and other media sources to discussion groups, user and consumer groups, et cetera. This latter monitoring was included because there had been several references to the company that, in the aggregate, pointed toward the project unintentionally. Furthermore, while French did not want to impede anyone's ability to communicate with normal and regular contacts outside the company, it seemed more appropriate to ensure that any traffic associated with the project should be restricted to as few people as possible. Internal e-mail, as well as external e-mail related to the project, would not be conducted through the company's own domain name. Instead, a separate domain was established solely for use with the project and was not to be used for any other casual mail.

All e-mail and attachments associated with the project would be encrypted using the commercial version of PGP (Pretty Good Privacy), and any attachments were to be password protected using the protection in the word-processing program used to create them.

Any curious or suspicious e-mail was to be forwarded to the project counterintelligence specialist prior to being answered, in much the same way that curious incoming telephone calls were handled. Most especially, project employees were asked to note any incoming e-mail that came to them on the project-only domain and not through the regular company domain.

Further, no fax transmissions were to be used between any of the development partners and the R and D facility. The box *Just the Fax, Ma'am* may help to place this condition into perspective.

Finally, no project-related activities were to be discussed over cell phones. Period. Even the movement from analog to digital cell phones did not mean that the encryption protocols would hold up. Nothing about the project was so time sensitive that it could not wait until the two parties could talk in person or over one of the firm's secure telephone lines. As a backup, a traveler could use an encrypted e-mail, although preferably that would be kept to a minimum as well.

Just the Fax, Ma'am

In 1992 Lutz Erbe, the former chief of the East German Signals Intelligence Service, was interviewed at length by *Der Spiegel,* the German newsmagazine similar to the American *Time.* He was asked to profile some of the successes and some of the limitations of his service on behalf of East Germany during the cold war.

One of his more interesting observations concerned the ability of the East Germans to monitor virtually any business or government leader's telephone in West Germany and record their conversations. What he found singularly interesting was how frequently his listeners would hear a person stop at a very sensitive point in the conversation—and actually say something like "We shouldn't be talking about this over the phone."

He estimated that in about half of these cases, the person who wanted to cut the conversation short would then go on to say that he would put the rest of what he wanted to say into a fax. Of course, Erbe, pointed out, they were just as capable of intercepting the fax traffic as they were the phone calls. Indeed, it was better for them to do this, since it saved the East Germans the trouble of having to transcribe an intercepted conversation.

The only limitation they had when it came to capturing all of the fax transmissions was that the East German logistics system had difficulty maintaining adequate supplies of fax paper.

Dedicating a Specific Counterintelligence Professional for the Life of the Project

Mr. French directed that owing to the project's importance, one individual—Billie Tolliver—was to be specifically dedicated full-time to the project's counterintelligence protection. Tolliver's role would be to serve as the single point of contact for all security- and intelligence-related matters associated with the project during its lifetime, reporting directly to Isaacson, who remained in charge of the project. Tolliver would be responsible for the operational planning and supervision of follow-on testing of the system, the development of countermeasures, liaison with the Business Intelligence unit at the corporate level, liaison with corporate security, and further counterintelligence training and operational activities as appropriate. Tolliver became a key person in the actions taken to exploit the private investigator identified during the waste archeology activities.

Elicitation and Counterelicitation Training

As employees became more and more aware of the ways they had been approached, they sought a better understanding of how to counter approaches made by professional intelligence collectors. A major part of their follow-on training during the program's lifetime involved exposure to specific elicitation techniques, as the first line of defense in dealing with such approaches. Once they were able to recognize these approaches for what they were, they could then apply the countermeasures techniques. When reporting such contacts to the project counterintelligence specialist, they would also be able to assist in the ongoing assessment of the collection competencies of those people who sought to obtain information from them,

Background Checks on New Hires

Since the group involved in the project was being staffed by a combination of older employees and new hires, background investigations were considered especially important so that the firm knew who they were placing in positions of responsibility and trust. This became especially relevant when considering that the executive search firm was sending in candidates prior to any background checks whatsoever. Not only had they not called the references listed on our bogus candidate's résumé, they had not checked on the professional and educational credentials we had built for her. While we had listed our own people as her references, none were ever checked; had they ever checked on her educational credentials—especially in an era when some studies have shown that over 75 percent of educational claims are exaggerated or created out of whole cloth—they would have certainly had reasons to question sending her to the company for a two-day interview.

In selecting another executive search firm, SouthTech certainly emphasized its criteria and let the new recruiter know what had happened with his predecessor. Of course, SouthTech still wanted to employ an outside firm to do its recruiting rather than advertise openly for people with skills, education, and experience in areas it had not traditionally employed before. Otherwise, this would've been a sure signal of intentions to any competitive intelligence professional worth his salt; it's normal practice to regularly monitor competitors' classified advertising, since to do so often gives wonderful insights into the types of programs a company is working on or branching out into based on the sought-after experience and qualifications listed in the advertising.

WARNING NOTICE: TRY THIS ONLY AT HOME

Surveillance and Countersurveillance

This set of approaches is the stock-in-trade of the counterintelligence professional, and both were useful in satisfying some of the additional concerns of the CEO.

In terms of countersurveillance, over the course of the next three months we were able to place two employees in the two restaurants nearest the R and D facility, locations where employees frequently ate lunch—and in the past, had talked somewhat too openly about what they were doing at work. After the presentations, our people were placed there for two reasons: first, to determine if indeed the presentation had had the desired effect on employee lunchtime conversations in public places (it had), and second, to determine if any relatively new "regulars" were present in the bar during the employees' normal lunch period (there was—one).

Our restaurant "employee" made the man's acquaintance and over the first week found him not to be at all forthcoming about where he was working, except that it was "in the neighborhood" and "down the road a bit." He was sufficiently suspicious to warrant a further look, and within two days we determined that he was an associate of the PI/waste archeologist with the pickup truck.

The surveillance of the PI had been under way for about a month, and he appeared to be happy with the "chicken feed" he was getting from the Dumpsters—especially that which was being fed to him in preapproved droplets following Ted French's briefing from the previous week. For the most part, the documents salted into the trash bags we placed in the Dumpsters for the PI related to a canceled project in another part of the company that was being revived with a new set of players and objectives, involving an entirely fictional set of technologies. With the identification of the PI's link with the restaurant patron, it was clear that someone was well onto something and we needed to get a little further down the trail with the PI.

At this point Billie Tolliver really began to earn her money. A reasonably attractive woman in her early thirties, she offered to strike up a conversation with the PI in his after-work bar and see what she could learn about him.

Within a week, she had determined that he was actually working for several different companies who were paying him fairly decently for information that he "dug up."

Within two weeks, he had described his normal method of operations to her. In an approach that is unfortunately all too common in today's business world and that we've identified in several different industries in different states, he simply paid part-time janitors to leave specific colored bags in their Dumpsters, bags that contained the trash from the more important offices in each of the companies he was working against. The different-colored bags kept him from having to take all the bags out of a Dumpster and go through them to find the ones that contained the important documents.

Within three weeks, he boasted to her that he was really going to make some big bucks because he was really lucky. He bragged that his luck had allowed him to overhear a retired police officer whom he knew in passing say to one of their mutual friends that he had gotten a job as a security guard at a "hush-hush operation," and had named SouthTech as the employer. He listened to enough of the conversation to figure out where the skunk works was located and had started going out there about a month or so before. He'd started getting some really hot stuff, and he was "in negotiations with one of their big competitors who had a lot of foreign money."

Within five weeks, he was a very happy player who had "really scored with the big boys from Asia." Three weeks later, the relationship between him and Billie, which had always been distinctly one-sided (his side), began to cool until she finally stopped meeting him in the bar two or three times a week.

Some two months later, after reports from several different locations in the company that inquiries about BLACK KNIGHT, the special program's nominal code name, had been received, it was clear who the PI's employer was and that they were taking the bait. Some of their marketing mavens were asking about certain elements of the project at an industry show, and the phones set up in the offices of the notional company that was supposed to be a "critical technology partner" had had almost thirty calls from a variety of inquirers ranging from potential suppliers to potential employees, even though the firm had no real history or existence other than in the secretary of state's office and a couple of new telephone numbers. Of course, these phones were answered by our well-prepared "receptionist," who duly recorded the incoming numbers as they appeared on her caller ID pad.

Blind Charlie

At our Special Forces camp in the western Mekong Delta region of South Vietnam, we had a particular Vietcong sniper who frequently shot at helicopters that were our main lifeline to the outside world.

> But we never did anything about him because he was never able to hit anything. He really earned his nickname of Blind Charlie.
>
> Nonetheless, a new camp commander bristled at the nuisance of it all. He couldn't stand it and took measures to neutralize poor Blind Charlie.
>
> The problem was that the VC replaced BC with one who *could* shoot well and caused all manner of subsequent misery. Who came out ahead?

Four months into the project, the client's competitive intelligence unit was reporting that Kimchi's U.S. facility was actively engaged in pursuing what the client had already proven was a failed approach. It's hard to tell how many dollars they spent pursuing this technological solution before abandoning it almost two years later. And for those of you who might question why the PI, his various janitors for hire, and the competitor weren't hauled into court under the Economic Espionage Act of 1996, first answer two other questions yourself:

First, "Isn't it better to be facing an adversary whose competencies and limitations you know?" Please allow me to take another page from my own history in the box *Blind Charlie*.

And second, "Isn't Ted French much better off with marketplace advantage than he'd be with the mere knowledge that someone—probably just a small fry—is in jail?"

Close Cooperation with the Corporate Competitive Intelligence Unit

Clearly, as the preceding paragraph shows, there is a linkage between the protection side of the intelligence equation and the collection side, just as there is in national intelligence services around the world. A linkage that we'll describe as we enter the realm of an Integrated Business Intelligence Model in chapter 19. But first, we need to talk a bit about your world.

Whether you're a large, medium, or small firm, whether you have or don't have a CI department or function, and whether or not you have an active, aggressive, and anticipatory security organization with at least a taste of counterintelligence, your preferences aren't going to change the nature of the business world you live in today. A world that is increasingly competitive, a world where the rules are different from country to country and from company to company, and a world where the intelligence process means competitive advantage.

And certainly a world where you'll have to continue to take increasingly sophisticated means to deal with an increasingly sophisticated and organized approach to business. As promised earlier, this is where we'll kick off into that Land of the Politically Incorrect. A land where we dare speak openly such bad words as *misinformation, disinformation,* and *deception:* chapter 18.

Misinformation, Disinformation, and Deception

We are bred up to feel it a disgrace ever to succeed by falsehood . . . we will keep hammering along with the conviction that honesty is the best policy, and truth always wins in the long run. These pretty little sentiments do well for a child's copy book, but a man who acts on them had better sheathe his sword forever.

—The Soldier's Handbook of the British Army (1869)

In this chapter we'll talk about some of the more aggressive, perhaps even exotic, countermeasures used to prevent the loss of sensitive information. For the greatest part of the population, the terms misinformation, disinformation, and deception are synonymous. For the intelligence professional, they are considerably different. We'll be dealing with each of these terms in the interest of accuracy as well as application. In fact, *misinformation* is defined by Webster as "false or misleading information based on error or ignorance." Disinformation is largely viewed as having a somewhat more malicious overtone and is typically found within the province of offensive intelligence operations. Deception, often referred to in a more politically correct way as "perception management," is more frequently found within the province of defensive intelligence operations in the business arena, although it also clearly has an offensive dimension when used internationally.

MISINFORMATION

For our purposes, we'll use *misinformation* to describe those misunderstandings, those confusing elements that business rivals obtain on their own—through their own error or missteps—and that are largely passive in terms of the role of the target company. For example, if your rival learns something from a newspaper article that is wholly and completely wrong, and you had nothing to do with the reporter's inaccuracy, your rival is the victim of misinformation. If the reporter asks questions of people who have no clue, or from those who exaggerate what they actually know to the extent that it is no longer close to reality, that's his fault and the fault of his source. You have not deliberately, actively, or maliciously created this misunderstanding.

By extension, if you see your business rival making mistakes or following a path that seems to have been dictated by something you know to be wrong, you are not necessarily driven by any ethic or statute to correct his misunderstanding. Simple prudence would argue that your rival should have examined all the available and potentially available information, and short of doing that, you have no liability.

DISINFORMATION

Disinformation, on the other hand, is the result of an active undertaking by someone who has thought out a path and an objective to be attained by passing information that has been deliberately, and falsely, constructed. Typically, the information is leaked into the target's communication system at some point, whether through the media or through other sources on whom the target is known to rely, and is designed to mislead the public. Very often, disinformation is cast in such a way as to capitalize on existing stereotypes, prejudices, and biases, particularly about a culture, race, or country. The special targets for disinformation are people at the extremes of the political or social spectrum who generally have only the smallest degree of tolerance and skepticism and who allow even the most bizarre reporting from the least reliable sources to influence their judgment.

If we were to benchmark the great disinformers in history, the old KGB (Komitet Gosudarstvennoy Bezopastnosty) of the former Soviet Union were the best practitioners of this special black art form. They worked hand in glove with Novosti Press Agency, the official Soviet press organ, from the time the disinformation mission was taken away from the Ministry of Foreign Affairs in the 1950s until the collapse of the Soviet Union.

Of course, now that peace has broken out, we no longer have to worry about them. Even though the greatest majority of their people have remained with the service in its new incarnation as the SVRR (you don't want to know) and the leadership of the Union of Fewer and Fewer

Republics has told the SVRR to refocus the majority of its efforts on economic and technical—instead of military and political—matters, as had been the case in years past, no one in the commercial arena should be concerned about their activities. No one except those who are working in industries other than goat milking. All others are fair game.

A representative example of the kinds of disinformation they practiced is the way that people all over the developing world came to believe—and still believe fervently—that the spread of the AIDS virus was merely an American germ-warfare agent test program in Africa run amok. This played especially well throughout Africa during the 1980s and early 1990s, when hundreds of thousands of Africans were dying of AIDS-related illnesses. No matter the kinds of denials that American representatives tried to issue, they fell on deaf ears. Why? Simply because the media in those countries carried the stories. Sometimes, the stories were written by journalists whose training had been at the Patrice Lamumba Freedom University in Moscow; other stories were taken from "reliable accounts" published in newspapers in other parts of the world, especially the Third World. That way, nothing ever originated in the Soviet Union and was thus never tied to superpower politics, although of course it was always about superpower politics and who was going to win the battle for the hearts and minds in the Third World.

With that as a backdrop, consider the sidebar *Mirror, Mirror on the Wall, Who's the Fairest of Them All?* to understand the business applications of disinformation. For this case, we'll turn once again to our friends the French, although there is often a run made at using the American media in the same way. Perhaps it doesn't always work out so well in the United States because the media aren't always willing participants, but that doesn't mean you should ignore the possibility. Again, in order to appreciate it from a defensive perspective, you have to understand your adversary and your environment. Of course, I'm sure that the French perspective would be that the disinformation campaign was used defensively—defending their marketplace from foreign penetration, that sort of thing.

Mirror, Mirror on the Wall, Who's the Fairest of Them All?

An American beauty-care products company began obtaining the necessary approvals to market a new facial treatment in France months before the launch was to take place in July. The company's primary French competitor found out about it from its government sources within days. And, just as the Americans had, the French competitor saw that a whole new market would grow up around this product. The French manufacturer also realized that there was simply no way they could get to market with their version of the product before September.

The American product hit the shelves the same week that articles began appearing in the French media about it, all citing stories from "reputable" Latin American and Far Eastern newspapers. Each of the reprinted stories recounted the horror stories of burning and disfigurement of women who used the American product. Each story noted that this same product had just been introduced into France, although it was not being sold in the United States because of a lack of government approval. Not surprisingly, the public's response was underwhelming. The product sat unsold on the shelves until it was finally pulled two months later. And, with its French packaging and descriptions, there was no way it could ever be returned to the United States or anywhere else for sale.

Even less surprising was the introduction of the French version of almost precisely the same product in the second week of September. Of course, no references appeared in the media about it having the same chemical composition as the American product that had died on the shelves. The French company still owns the entire market. Still surprised? Even after all we've been through together?

DECEPTION

Perhaps the fifth-century Chinese military strategist Sun-tzu said it best when he suggested that

All warfare is based on deception. Therefore, when capable, feign incapacity; when active, inactivity. When near, make it appear that you are far away; when far away, that you are near. Offer the enemy a bait to lure him; feign disorder and strike him. When he concentrates, prepare against him; where he is strong, avoid him. Anger his general and confuse him. Pretend inferiority and encourage his arrogance.

These are the elements that you wish to communicate to your opposition when you are beginning to protect yourself and want to allow him to earn an erroneous impression through his own labors, since to do so makes his impressions all that much stronger based on his having worked harder for them. Such impressions become drivers in their own right and often can be counted upon to overcome even the most rigorous analysis and caution. Consider the box *Adolf's Mysticism* and you'll quickly see how powerful and important this can become—and not just for a megalomaniac.

On a most basic level of deception in business, I would refer you back to the relatively mild—yet very effective—approach Johnson Controls took to protect its new technology known originally by the code name Loba discussed in chapter 15. They didn't try to mislead anyone until they saw that their entry could possibly be jeopardized by Honeywell's collection efforts. Then, in a classic application of what is quite correctly termed perception management—that is, managing Honeywell's misunderstanding or misperception—we can see how deception plays a role in an openly reported and reasonably well-known case study.

For our purposes, the BLACK KNIGHT description from the previous chapter is on a second level of perception management in the business world. It consists largely of identifying a threat to one's information and responding with carefully selected and targeted information designed to reach only one recipient or recipient population in order to distract that threat's attention from what the firm is really doing. Fundamental to this approach is *creating* that error or ignorance on the part of the target, who in this case is most likely your recognized business rival who is aggressively seeking to collect useful information from you or your confidants. Another aspect is appreciating the length of time that the firm needs to protect its information from compromise.

Adolf's Mysticism

One of the foundations of National Socialism and Hitler's meteoric rise to power was the combination of his absolute certainty in his own destiny and that of the German people, his almost monkish asceticism, and a corresponding mystical gift for predicting the ways in which his adversaries would act and react. This is not say that any of this is good. In fact, it's almost irretrievably bad.

However, with the right kind of understanding of his certitude, it can become a powerful force for good at the same time. In this case, the planners for the invasion of Europe were privy to much about Hitler's convictions about his own intellectual and spiritual gifts. Capitalizing on their knowledge that he had reached certain conclusions about when and where the long-anticipated invasion would be launched—mostly through his own hard, spiritual labors—they set the stage for a massive deception campaign designed to protect the actual landings, their locations, timing, and participation. The nature of the campaign, simply put but elegantly executed, was to be absolutely consistent with his beliefs, all and any other evidence to the contrary notwithstanding.

His belief that the landings would occur at the Pas de Calais and not elsewhere—such as Normandy—was nurtured by documents planted on the body of a recently deceased British officer who'd ostensibly been killed in a plane crash at sea and whose body floated ashore and into the hands of Abwehr officers in Portugal. His belief that such landings would be of such magnitude that they could be carried out only by the very best forces under the most able American commander, General Patton, was nurtured by the wholesale creation of a completely notional Army Group located in the closest proximity to the launching point for an invasion aimed at Pas de Calais. His almost cosmic certainty that no attack could possibly occur on June 6, owing to his oracular visions of weather conditions, was nurtured by intentionally compromised and intercepted weather and planning reports, and resulted in his keeping necessary counterattack forces in reserve. His belief that such landings would be the main attack was so strong that even for the twenty-four critical hours after the Normandy landings, he still refused to release the forces that might well have hurled the Allied forces back into the sea. And every nurturing detail was assiduously planned and planted with sources that would confirm Hitler's predisposition to believe his own certainties.

The essence of deception is knowing—or believing that you know—who is obtaining what from you, through which channels. And then, with these thoughts in mind, placing into those channels—and only those channels—the information you wish to have them believe and possibly act upon. Misdirecting them so that they follow a path that does not show your true intentions. Purposely allowing another to misunderstand your capabilities, competencies, situation, and limitations. Considering it from the reverse of a SWOT analysis may help to shape it further: instead of focusing on actual strengths and actual weaknesses, portraying them in precisely the opposite way so as to skew the observer's or analyst's perception of your abilities or plans.

Yet, a truly well-developed deception plan or perception-management plan is far more than just telling a couple of people a couple of lies and seeing if there's any indication that someone amongst your rivals has taken the bait. In a little while, we'll be talking about an actual and well-refined approach that paid large dividends, but first, there are a few caveats that you probably need to have stored in the back of your mind. Actually, they're more than just a few caveats. They should almost have the force of law for anyone contemplating using deception or perception management in a business situation.

THE FIRST LAW OF DECEPTION PROJECTS

Deception operations are never for the poorly organized, should never be executed by those who are prone to rash decisions and snap solutions, and are certainly not for the faint of heart.

THE SECOND LAW OF DECEPTION PROJECTS

Before ever beginning a deception project, think about the effect of your deception program on a variety of other potential recipients of the information—for example, if you're a publicly traded company and the deception you don't plan especially well gets to the wrong people in the wrong way. Then one morning, those pleasant fellows who are the SEC investigators (and even though we're in Alabama, we don't mean the Southeastern Conference) arrive at your office with stern looks and lots of questions. The quintessential bad morning. Keep it in your mind, even if you're not publicly traded. You can connect the dots yourself.

THE THIRD LAW OF DECEPTION PROJECTS

The number of people who have any kind of a clue about the project must remain as small and compartmentalized as anything else you have to protect at all costs. Clearly, this should be taken to mean that you don't go out and tell two hundred people some misleading things in the hopes that the sheer noise will get the information out. Not only will doing so cause so much distortion by the time the message reaches an intended recipient that you'll have no idea what they're hearing, but any hope you have of influencing the rival to take a step in one direction or another will fade with the sun.

THE FOURTH LAW OF DECEPTION PROJECTS

You always have to provide some measure of value, actual value, real *stuff* in order to lend any semblance of validity to the other pieces that have no validity. For example, if you want your rival to receive and act on one piece of information, there may have to be three or four pieces of supporting information that are true and accurate. Just as you probably wouldn't make a major stock market investment on just one day's data point, no intelligence analyst worth his or her salt will accept one data bit and report that as gospel without some direct or indirect confirmation. This speaks not only to providing bits of confirming information but to having them come from more than just one source as well. It's usually a pretty senior-level decision to undertake a deception project, if for no other reason than to have that level of approval for the release of some of the bona fide information that will give credence to the bogus data that you want to use to shape your competitors' responses away from your central protection objective. The box *For Whom the Bell Tolls* may be instructive on this point.

THE FIFTH LAW OF DECEPTION PROJECTS

This law will sound very familiar to you after parts I, II and III of this book already. You really need to have a defined *outcome* in mind. What do you want your rival to do? Moreover, you have to have the resources, means, or methods in place or otherwise available to you to determine the extent to which your rival is actually following the trail you're trying to lay out for him. A significant amount of time and effort can go into a project like this, and it's far from cost efficient to have zero clue about whether or not the effort is working. Further, and it should almost go without saying, you have to know what you're going to do when indeed the other person does do what you want him to do.

For Whom the Bell Tolls

One client's repeat customers were not doing the kinds of reordering they usually did. When the client's sales force asked why, the customers cited a lack of responsiveness. Asked what that meant, several mentioned how they had placed calls for orders that had gone unanswered. Eventually, they had turned to another supplier who was very attentive to their needs.

Lots of fingerpointing ensued at the company, with sales blaming the telephone system, the technical people blaming lazy salespeople, others thinking the conference rooms were being bugged, and so on. While we were visiting on another matter and having an off-site meeting with several of their executives about a collection project, this problem came up. We also noticed that the VP for sales was collecting his voice-mail at fairly regular intervals during the meeting, using his analog cell phone. At the close of the meeting, when the president of the company asked us to stay around for a few more minutes, we learned that he also wanted our technical surveillance countermeasures crew to sweep the company headquarters for bugs. Based on what we'd seen of the sales VP, we suggested that we might also check to see what was happening on his cell phone.

Two days later, the team was in place and performed their sweep overnight. Nothing was found that suggested that anyone was bugging their phones, conference rooms, or offices. The next morning they were positioned outside the sales VP's house as he left for work. As he drove along, the mobile sweepers were pulling his dialing sequences out of the ether, to include the codes he punched in to check the messages left on the company's incoming toll-free number. No rocket science for our folks to call in a couple of times later that day, listen to the messages that were due to be downloaded, and after recording them so as not to lose the value of the call, to delete the messages. Later that day, the president was told what had happened with the cell phone intercept and the penetration of their sales voice-mail system. This suggested a possible course of action, which he accepted readily.

The president called on four of his closest and oldest customers and asked for their assistance. He took them into his confidence and told them he feared that someone was hacking into his voice-mail system and he could catch them only with the assistance of those old customers. Each agreed to help.

Each was assigned a separate and distinct, newly established telephone line. They would be the only user of that number and they were to only use it for one telephone call. They were asked to call the regular toll-free number, ask for a call back so that they could place orders, and leave the new telephone number. In three of the four cases, spread over two days, they were called back. Called back on the special phone number that had only been used once to leave the message on the client sales line. But not by the client. Instead, the caller was a sales representative of one of their closest and most aggressive competitors. For a variety of reasons, the client chose to take other than legal action. He was much more imaginative than to just seek punitive damages and a wrist slap. He's still benefiting from his agreement with the other firm.

THE SIXTH LAW OF DECEPTION PROJECTS

This extends from the Fifth Law somewhat and comes into play when you are acting purely defensively in order to try and find a leakage of information from within your own organization. And remember, there are many, many times when it's being done unwittingly. You have to be able to follow the flow of the information, and in order to do this, your poison pills have to be carefully distributed and a complete record be kept of exactly what was being told to whom.

THE SEVENTH LAW OF DECEPTION PROJECTS

This law is another, directly defensive approach: the protection of your precious sources of information. There will be times when you have learned something of great value, but you cannot use it lest it compromise the source of the information. The alternative to not using it is to follow the line of deception espoused by Winston Churchill during World War II: In wartime, truth is so precious that she must always be surrounded by a bodyguard of lies. Recall that the Allies had gained access to one of the German high command's Enigma machines, the piece of gear responsible for the unbreakable encryption of all its operational traffic. They got one in 1939 through the efforts of the Polish Intelligence Service; later, they got a later model as a result of the rather heroic retrieval of another machine from a sinking U-boat in the North Atlantic.

If the Germans had ever learned that their supposedly unbreakable codes were indeed being read at Bletchley Park outside London each day, they would have changed them quickly. Thus, the Allies had to be extremely judicious in the use of the intelligence to protect this extraordinary source from being compromised. This judiciousness even extended to Churchill's leaving the cathedral city of Coventry—which had absolutely no strategic or tactical value—exposed to a German terror raid by withholding defensive aircraft from the city. Since there had never been any bombing anywhere near Coventry, intercepting the bombers would have told the Germans that the Allies were reading their traffic. Rather than compromising that source of information just a few months before D day when it was really going to be needed, Churchill issued no warning to the city or its residents. He accepted responsibility for the 1,500 dead and the several thousand others who were wounded that night, comparing those losses with the tens or possibly hundreds of thousands of lives that could be saved by continuing to read the Enigma traffic.* Granted, it's rare that you ever face a matter of life or death, world peace or nuclear war in the marketplace, but the lessons are nonetheless instructive.

Now, in closing this chapter, let's step back from this for a moment. We're pretty close to the end of this book on Business Intelligence and counterintelligence. You've gotten accustomed to things as they really are in the rest of the world by now. Yet, you've been looking at them as intelligence activities. Put this together with the way that Johnson Controls used Honeywell's misperceptions about Loba and Lobo to Honeywell's disadvantage in chapter 15. Then think about BLACK KNIGHT in the last chapter.

Remember the comments in the introduction about different audience reactions to presentations about such matters, and whether there was a bias against the word intelligence as used in a business context? Hopefully, we've disabused you of similar notions by now and you're not dismayed about the political dimensions of the language. But, if you are—or think that your company's leadership or employee population will react—then please consider using other vocabulary. Maybe just another set of words to describe the processes; words that might not be such a sharp stick in the eye. After all, it would be a terrible thing to disadvantage your enterprise simply because of semantics.

---

*In case you're interested in this or other elements of what came to be known as *The Ultra Secret,* Group Captain Frederick Winterbotham's book by the same name or *Bodyguard of Lies,* by Anthony Cave Brown, are both are excellent sources of inspiration for perception-management projects in the commercial sector.

Putting It All Together

He who seeks to protect all, protects nothing.

—Bismarck

By now, you've come to a realization that the collection process and the protection process are equally important—as well as complementary—in the conduct of business operations in today's marketplace. We've spoken about how this integration is the hallmark of professional intelligence organizations around the world: intelligence being provided to the decision maker in a timely and accurate way; counterintelligence serving the need to protect your own business-operations information as well as playing a key role in protecting your own intelligence-collection efforts by looking at things in a different light than traditional security approaches offer.

The approach that we take—and that more and more companies are following as the need for a sophisticated and integrated process increases in an increasingly competitive environment—is called the Integrated Business Intelligence Model. As you can see depicted in the figure on page 272, the two cycles rotate in opposite yet complementary directions, both originating with the directions and tasking from the corporate leadership level and enjoying a combined analytical capacity. This combined, centralized analysis activity not only serves as the last stop on the reporting chain before getting back to the decision maker but it also helps the other side of the equation do its job better.

Frankly, five years ago, this was rarely seen in a company where the CI department is located at levels in the stratosphere above the security department. Since they were often separated by time, distance, and inclination, if they knew or cared very much about each other's existence, it was generally in adversarial terms.

Now, this integrated approach simply makes more and more sense, especially when both sides of the equation can work a project or two together. It makes even more sense from the cost-effectiveness model of multiplexing we touched on before. In this instance, you have the best

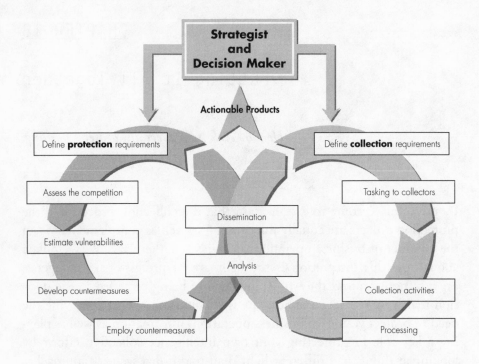

Strategist and Decision Maker

Actionable Products

Define **protection** requirements

Define **collection** requirements

Assess the competition

Tasking to collectors

Dissemination

Estimate vulnerabilities

Analysis

Develop countermeasures

Collection activities

Employ countermeasures

Processing

people, closely engaged on complementary projects, without duplication and without internal competition. Gradually, security practitioners are putting away their antipathy toward those they don't understand and whom they suspect of all manner of mean-spirited and unethical if not illegal acts. Competitive intelligence professionals, who had never seen their role as having any protection component whatever, are realizing the synergies that can be developed. And there are the heavy lifters on both sides who have seen the future of their organization's requirements into the twenty-first century and have planned accordingly: security executives who have led the way to supporting the business, profit side of the enterprise and who have begun working so closely with other departments that they have assumed the intelligence-collection as well as protection function; and those intelligence professionals who see their company benefiting from the centralized collection and protection function. This is especially true in those firms where the security function has been subordinate to human resources, safety, and other traditional overhead functions.

Of course, in medium and small organizations, there's less doubt about how the processes are joined or not joined. Sheer size and manpower constraints dictate an integrated approach, especially where companies find themselves in the thick of a battle they really haven't previously understood.

For those who are not burdened by a CI department that has to overcome some of its biases and prejudices, you're indeed lucky to be starting out with a clean slate. Many of you will not be building a formal CI department at all—because of your size, budget, or preferences. Instead, you may be gearing up a *function* that will allow you to collect on your rivals quickly, and legally, and without significant investment in manpower, office space, or massive budgets. Either way, the simple fact is that the Business Intelligence Process, operating in the background behind an organization or a function, is what will answer the mail for your enterprise.

It will provide you the competitive information that can be developed into competitive intelligence—competitive intelligence that can be used for competitive advantage. And after all else is said and done, isn't that why you got into business in the first place? To prevail?

Finally, I would like to invite your attention to the appendices that follow. They're a bit different, perhaps, from most appendices you've seen before. These are actually intended to be used and are really a part of the book. They never were meant to be just some add-ons to fill space.

From the Sherlock Holmes notations to the legal and ethical issues associated with Business Intelligence operations, from the test case and scenarios designed to help you anticipate potential difficulties and to have at least a "school solution" or two to trigger your own thought processes out to the samples of adminstrivia that makes all organizations operate a little better, they're there to be used, to be extracted, to be implemented, to challenge and be challenged. I hope they serve those purposes.

On a closing, somewhat personal, note, I have a fairly heavy travel schedule, and much of it involves presentations either inside companies or for a variety of professional associations. In almost every circumstance, I solicit the impressions and the views of the people who have attended. To the extent that such presentations have improved over the years, that improvement owes much to the contributions, the suggestions, and the comments of participants and attendees.

I value your impressions as well, and I would be honored to receive any comments or suggestions you may have. Please don't hesitate to write, call, or e-mail. I'll get back to you as quickly as I can in the event that I'm traveling. Call the office toll free at 1-800-440-1724 or, if you prefer, you can use my direct line at 1-256-883-8099. My faithful note-book computer helps me handle my e-mail while on the road, just as if I'm at the office, and I look forward to answering anything you send to jnolan@intellpros.com. Of course, there's always snail mail at

Phoenix Consulting Group, Inc.
919 Willowbrook Drive
Willowbrook Office Park
Huntsville, AL 35802

The Elicitation Techniques of Sherlock Holmes

AN ANNOTATED SAMPLER FROM *THE COMPLETE SHERLOCK HOLMES* BY SIR ARTHUR CONAN DOYLE

Mediocrity knows nothing higher than itself; but talent instantly recognizes genius, and MacDonald had talent enough for his profession to enable him to perceive that there was no humiliation in seeking the assistance of one who already stood alone in Europe, both in his gifts and in his experience.

The Complete Sherlock Holmes, *The Valley of Fear*

The Stacking Techniques of Sherlock Holmes

The Sign of Four

It tended down towards the riverside, running through Belmont Place and Prince's Street. At the end of Broad Street it ran right down to the water's edge, where there was a small wooden wharf. Toby led us to the very edge of this and there stood whining, looking out on the dark current beyond.

"We are out of luck," said Holmes. "They have taken to a boat here."

Several small punts and skiffs were lying about in the water and on the edge of the wharf. We took Toby round to each in turn, but though he sniffed earnestly he made no sign.

Close to the rude landing-stage was a small brick house, with a wooden plac-ard slung out through the second window. "Mordecai Smith" was printed across it in large letters, and, underneath, "Boats to hire by the hour or day." A second inscription above the door informed us that a steam launch was kept—a statement which was confirmed by a great pike of coke upon the jetty. Sherlock Holmes looked slowly round, and his face assumed an ominous expression.

"This looks bad," said he. "These fellows are sharper than I expected. They seem to have covered their tracks. There has, I fear, been precon-certed management here."

He was approaching the door of the house, when it opened, and a little curly headed lad of six came running out, followed by a stoutish, red-faced woman with a large sponge in her hand.

"You come back and be washed, Jack," she shouted. "Come back, you young imp; for if your father comes home and finds you like that he'll let us hear of it."

"Dear little chap!" said Holmes strategically. "What a rosey-cheeked young rascal! Now, Jack, is there anything you would like?"

The youth pondered for a moment.

"I'd like a shillin'," said he.

"Nothing you would like better?"

"I'd like two shillin' better," the prodigy answered after some thought.

"Here you are, then! Catch! A fine child, Mrs. Smith!" *(Simple Flattery/Instinct to Complain)*

"Lor' bless you, sir, he is that, and forward. He gets a'most too much for me to manage, 'specially when my man is away days at a time."

"Away, is he?" said Holmes in a disappointed voice. "I am sorry for that, for I wanted to speak to Mr. Smith." *(Disappointment)*

"He's been away since yesterday mornin', sir, and, truth to tell, I am beginnin' to feel frightened about him. But if it was about a boat, sir, maybe I could serve as well."

"I wanted to hire his steam launch." *(Enticement)*

"Why, bless you, sir, it is in the steam launch that he has gone. That's what puzzles me; for I know there ain't more coals in her than would take her to about Woolwich and back. If he's been away in the barge I'd ha' thought nothin'; for many a time a job has taken him as far as Gravesend, and then if there was much doin' there he might ha' stayed over. But what good is a steam launch without coal?"

"He might have bought some at a wharf down the river." *(Partial Disagreement)*

"He might, sir, but it weren't his way. Many a time I've heard him call out at the prices they charge for a few odd bags. Besides, I don't like that wooden-legged man, wi' his ugly face and outlandish talk. What did he want always knockin' about here for?"

"A wooden-legged man?" said Holmes with bland surprise. *(Disbelief)*

"Yes, sir, a brown, monkey-faced chap that's called more'n once for my old man. It was him that roused him up yesternight, and, what's more, my man knew he was comin', for he had steam up in the launch. I tell you straight, sir, I don't feel easy in my mind about it."

"But, my dear Mrs. Smith," said Holmes, shrugging his shoulders, "you are frightening yourself about nothing. How could you possibly tell that it was the wooden-legged man who came in the night? I don't quite understand how you can be so sure." *(Disbelief/Partial Disagreement)*

"His voice, sir. I knew his voice, which is kind o' thick and foggy. He tapped at the winder—about three it would be. 'Show a leg, matey,' says he: 'time to turn out guard.' My old man woke up Jim—that's my eldest—and away they went without so much as a word to me. I could hear the wooden leg clackin' on the stones."

"And was this wooden-legged man alone?"

"Couldn't say, I am sure, sir. I didn't hear no one else."

"I am sorry, Mrs. Smith, for I wanted a steam launch, and I have heard good reports of the—, the—, the— Oh, let me see, what is her name?" *(Quotation from Another Source)*

"The *Aurora*, sir."

"Ah! She's that old green launch with a yellow line, very broad in the beam" *(False Statement)*

"No, indeed. She's as trim a little thing as any on the river. She's been fresh painted, black with two red streaks."

"Thanks. I hope that you will hear soon from Mr. Smith. I am going down the river, and if I should see anything of the *Aurora* I shall let him know that you are uneasy. A black funnel, you say?" *(Word Repetition/Misquotation)*

"No, sir. Black with a white band."

"Ah, of course. It was the sides which were black. Good-morning, Mrs. Smith. There is a boatman here with a wherry, Watson. We shall take it and cross the river."

"The main thing with people of that sort," said Holmes as we sat in the sheets of the wherry, "is never to let them think that their information can be of slightest importance to you. If you do they will instantly shut up like an oyster. If you listen to them under protest, as it were, you are very likely to get what you want."

The Hound of the Baskervilles

He would talk of nothing but art, of which he had the crudest ideas, from our leaving the gallery until we found ourselves at the Northumberland Hotel.

"Sir Henry Baskerville is upstairs expecting you," said the clerk. "He asked me to show you up at once when you came."

"Have you any objection to my looking at your register?" said Holmes. "Not in the least."

The book showed that two names had been added after that of Baskerville. One was Theophilus Johnson and family, of Newcastle; the other Mrs. Oldmore and maid, of High Lodge, Alton.

"Surely that must be the same Johnson whom I used to know," said Holmes to the porter. "A lawyer, is he not, gray-headed, and walks with a limp?" *(False Statement)*

"No, sir, this is Mr. Johnson, the coal-owner, a very active gentleman, not older than yourself."

"Surely you are mistaken about his trade?" *(Disbelief)*

"No, sir! He has used this hotel for many years, and he is very well known to us."

"Ah, that settles it. Mrs. Oldmore, too; I seem to remember the name. Excuse my curiosity, but often in calling upon one friend one finds another." *(Faulty Memory)*

"She is an invalid lady, sir. Her husband was once mayor of Gloucester. She always comes to us when she is in town."

"Thank you; I am afraid I cannot claim her acquaintance."

More Stacking from Sherlock Holmes

"The Adventure of the Blue Carbuncle"

In a quarter of an hour we were in Bloomsbury at the Alpha Inn, which is a small public-house at the corner of one of the streets which runs down into Holborn. Holmes pushed open the door of the private bar and ordered two glasses of beer from the ruddy-faced, white-aproned landlord.

"Your beer should be excellent if it is as good as your geese," said he. *(Mild Criticism or Simple Flattery—depending on inflection)*

"My geese!" The man seemed surprised.

"Yes. I was speaking only half an hour ago to Mr. Henry Baker, who was a member of your goose club."

"Ah! Yes, I see. But you see, sir, them's not *our geese.*"

"Indeed! Whose, then?"

"Well, I got the two dozen from a salesman in Covent Garden."

"Indeed? I know some of them. Which was it?"

"Breckinridge is his name."

"Ah! I don't know him. Well, here's your good health, landlord, and prosperity to your house. Good-night.

"Now for Mr. Breckinridge," he continued, buttoning up his coat as we came out into the frosty air. "Remember, Watson, that though we have so homely a thing as a goose at one end of this chain, we have at the other a man who will certainly get seven years' penal servitude unless we can establish his innocence. It is possible that our inquiry may but confirm his guilt; but, in any case, we have a line of investigation which has been missed by the police, and which a singular chance has placed in our hands. Let us follow it out to the bitter end. Faces to the south, then, and quick march!"

We passed across Holborn, down Endell Street, and so through a zigzag of slums to Covent Garden Market. One of the largest stalls bore the name of Breckinridge upon it, and the proprietor, a horsy-looking man, with a sharp face and trim sidewhiskers, was helping a boy to put up the shutters.

"Good-evening. It's a cold night," said Holmes.

The salesman nodded and shot a questioning glance at my companion.

"Sold out of geese, I see," continued Holmes, pointing at the bare slabs of marble. *(Using the environment to provoke a response)*

"Let you have five hundred to-morrow morning."

"That's no good."

"Well, there are some on the stall over there—the one with the gas-flare."

"Ah, but I was recommended to you." *(Simple Flattery)*

"Who by?"

"The landlord of the Alpha."

"Oh, yes; I sent him a couple of dozen."

"Fine birds they were, too. Now where did you get them from?"

To my surprise the question provoked a burst of anger from the salesman.

"Now, then, mister," said he, with his head cocked and his arms akimbo, "what are you driving at? Let's have it straight, now."

"It is straight enough. I should like to know who sold you the geese which you supplied to the Alpha."

"Well, then, I shan't tell you. So now!"

"Oh, it is a matter of no importance; but I don't know why you should be so warm over such a trifle." *(Trivializing/Masking Interest)*

"Warm! You'd be as warm, maybe, if you were as pestered as I am. When I pay good money for a good article there should be an end of the business; but it's 'Where are the geese?' and 'Who did you sell the geese to?' and 'What will you take for the geese?' One would think they were the only geese in the world, to hear the fuss that is made over them."

"Well, I have no connection with any other people who have been making inquiries," said Holmes carelessly. "If you won't tell us the bet is off, that is all. But I'm always ready to back my opinion on a matter of fowls, and I have a fiver on it that the bird I ate is country bred." *(Provocative Statement)*

"Well, then, you've lost your fiver, for it's town bred," snapped the salesman.

"It's nothing of the kind." *(Disbelief)*

"I say it is."

"I don't believe it." *(More Disbelief)*

"D'you think you know more about fowls than I, who have handled them ever since I was a nipper? I tell you, all those birds that went to the Alpha were town bred."

"You'll never persuade me to believe that." *(Still more Disbelief)*

"Will you bet, then?"

"It's merely taking your money, for I know that I am right. But I'll have a sovereign on with you, just to teach you not to be obstinate." *(Quintessential Disbelief—betting)*

The salesman chuckled grimly. "Bring me the books, Bill," said he.

The small boy brought round a small thin volume and a great greasy-backed one, laying them out together beneath the hanging lamp.

"Now then, Mr. Cocksure," said the salesman, "I thought that I was out of geese, but before I finish you'll find that there is still one left in my shop. You see this little book?"

"Well?"

"That's the list of the folk from whom I buy. D'you see? Well, then, here on this page are the country folk, and the numbers after their names are where their accounts are in the big ledger. Now, then! You see this other page in red ink? Well, that is a list of my town suppliers. Now, look at the third name. Just read it out to me."

"Mrs. Oakshott, 117, Brixton Road—249," read Holmes.

"Quite so. Now turn that up in the ledger."

Holmes turned to the page indicated. "Here you are, 'Mrs. Oakshott, 117, Brixton Road, egg and poultry supplier.'"

"Now, then, what's the last entry?"

"'December 22d. Twenty-four geese at 7s. 6d.'"

"Quite so. There you are. And underneath?"

"'Sold to Mr. Windigate of the Alpha, at 12s.'"

"What have you to say now?"

Sherlock Holmes looked deeply chagrined. *(Suspension of Ego)* He drew a sovereign from his pocket and threw it down upon the slab, turning away with the air of a man whose disgust is too deep for words. A few yards off he stopped under a lamp-post and laughed in the hearty, noiseless fashion which was peculiar to him.

And now, it's elementary for Doctor Watson as well in

The Hound of Baskervilles

I had been casting round for some excuse by which I could get away from his gossip, but now I began to wish to hear more of it. I had seen enough of the country nature of the old sinner to understand that any strong signs of interest would be the surest way to stop his confidence.

"Some poaching case, no doubt," said I with an indifferent manner. *(Provocative Statement)*

"Ha, ha, my boy, a very much more important matter than that! What about the convict on the moor?"

I started. " You don't mean that you know where he is!" said I. *(Disbelief)*

"I may not know exactly where he is, but I am quite sure that I could help the police to lay their hands on him. Has it never struck you that the way to catch that man was to find out where he got his food and so trace it to him?"

He certainly seemed to be getting uncomfortably close to the truth. "No doubt," said I; "but how would you know that he is anywhere upon the moor?"

"I know it because I have seen with my own eyes the messenger who takes him his food."

My heart sank for Barrymore. It was a serious thing to be in the power of this spiteful old busybody. But his next remark took a weight from my mind.

"You'll be surprised to hear that his food is taken to him by a child. I see him every day through my telescope upon the roof. He passes along the same path at the same hour, and to whom should he be going except to the convict?"

Here was luck indeed! And yet I suppressed all appearance of interest. A child! Barrymore had said that our unknown was supplied by a boy. It was on his track, and not upon the convict's, that Frankland had stumbled. If I could get his knowledge it might save me a long and weary hunt. But incredulity and indifference were evidently my strongest cards.

"I should say that it was much more likely that it was the son of one of the moorland shepherds taking out his father's dinner." *(Opposing Stand)*

The least appearance of opposition struck fire out of the old autocrat. His eyes looked malignantly at me, and his gray whiskers bristled like those of an angry cat.

"Indeed, sir!" said he, pointing out over the wide-stretching moor. "Do you see that Black Tor over yonder? Well, do you see the low hill beyond with the thornbush upon it? It is the stoniest part of the whole moor. Is that a place where a shepherd would be likely to take his station? Your suggestion, sir, is a most absurd one."

I meekly answered that I had spoken without knowing all the facts. My submission pleased him and led him to further confidences. *(Suspension of Ego)*

"You may be sure, sir, that I have very good grounds before I come to an opinion. I have seen the boy again and again with his bundle. Every day, and sometimes twice a day, I have been able—but wait a moment, Dr. Watson. Do my eyes deceive me, or is there at the present moment something moving upon the hillside?"

It was several miles off, but I could distinctly see a small dark dot against the dull green and gray.

"Come, sir, come!" cried Frankland, rushing upstairs. "You will see with your own eyes and judge for yourself."

The telescope, a formidable instrument mounted upon a tripod, stood upon the flat leads of the house. Frankland clapped his eye to it and gave a cry of satisfaction.

"Quick, Dr. Watson, quick, before he passes over the hill!"

There he was, sure enough, a small urchin with a little bundle upon his shoulder, toiling slowly up the hill. When he reached the crest I saw the ragged uncouth figure outlined for an instant against the cold blue sky. He looked round him with a furtive and stealthy air, as one who dreads pursuit. Then he vanished over the hill.

"Well, am I right?"

"Certainly, there is a boy who seems to have some secret errand."

"And what the errand is even a county constable could guess. But not one word shall they have from me, and I bind you to secrecy also, Dr. Watson. Not a word! You understand!"

"Just as you wish."

"They have treated me shamefully—shamefully. When the facts come out in Frankland *v.* Regina I venture to think that a thrill of indignation will run through the country. Nothing would induce me to help the police in any way. For all they cared it might have been me, instead of my effigy, which these rascals burned at the stake. Surely you are not going! You will help me to empty the decanter in honour of this great occasion!"

More from Doctor Watson on Learning about Countermeasures from Sherlock Holmes in

The Hound of the Baskervilles.

I am certainly developing the wisdom of the serpent, for when Mortimer pressed his questions to an inconvenient extent I asked him casually to what type Frankland's skull belonged, and so heard nothing but craniology for the rest of our drive. I have not lived for years with Sherlock Holmes for nothing.

Legal and Ethical Aspects of Competitive Intelligence

Nothing changes table manners faster than a smaller pie.

—Ancient Alabama proverb

In an increasingly competitive business world, with cultural and legal definitions of what's right and proper and what's not, it's easy to confuse the good guys and the bad guys. Few wear hats at all, let alone different colored ones. The debate about what's proper and what's improper in business becomes especially pointed when the conversation turns to the intelligence dimension. That's one of the reasons this chapter is structured the way it is.

There will be several examples of industrial and economic espionage cases just so we'll have a common—and not hysterical—understanding of the legal and ethical issues involved with competitive intelligence collection and analysis. The purpose is to help you understand the differences between acceptable Business Intelligence practices and those other practices which are not. To help you understand what you can and cannot do—the legal side. To help you understand what you should and should not do—the ethical side.

So much myth and legend has grown up in recent months and years about the legal downside to competitive intelligence operations that some firms have been reluctant to engage in something that is increasingly vital to their ability to prevail in the marketplace. In other companies, where knees jerk too quickly sometimes, the passage of some recent legislation has killed off wholly proper competitive intelligence programs. By the time this chapter concludes, you should have a fairly good understanding of where you are in terms of the law and in terms of ethical issues as well. In fact, there's a separate appendix that provides you some samples of ethical guidelines—guidelines that range from the most general to the most encompassing we've seen in firms. Once you've had a chance to review them, and if you don't have a set of guidelines of your own, perhaps it will be a helpful guide to building some. At least, you deserve an informed choice.

The Legal Side of the Issue—The Economic Espionage Act of 1996

On October 11, 1996, a new piece of legislation was signed into law in the United States. Like most pieces of federal legislation, it had one of those long and important-sounding titles: *The Economic Espionage and Protection of Proprietary Information Act of 1996.**

The purpose of the law was to provide access to federal law enforcement and prosecution for victims of economic espionage. In times past, trade-secrets violations and theft of proprietary information were handled under local and state statutes, which meant getting a district attorney to prosecute a case where there were very blurry issues and forcing the victim to rely upon a local police force to conduct the necessary investigative work. The situation was quite a bit like that of cases where computers were involved in criminal activity, as you may see in the box *Crime and Passion in Geekdom*.

Just as in the case of the computer-crimes legislation being prodded by bucks, a fair amount of lobbying money was directed toward the problem of industrial and economic espionage. On the economic espionage side, the situation was a close parallel. For example, IBM included in its reports to the clerk of the House Representatives that it had spent $2,680,000 in the first six months of 1996 on its lobbying efforts on various issues, specifying the Economic Espionage Act among them.

This law was driven by a variety of factors, not the least of which were:

- A recognition of the quantum increase in the amount of non-defense-related espionage occurring in the United States after the end of the cold war.

---

*Actually, it would've been shorter, except for the intervention of the State Department. The diplomats were afraid that if a law was passed against foreign representatives and entities committing economic espionage against the United States, then foreign countries would think we were picking on them. Obviously, the United States couldn't call a spade a spade, so the legislation was amended to include provisions against American firms who would do the same things.

- A growing, and somewhat belated, recognition by the political leadership that economic security is an integral part of national security.

- A clear recognition that existing local and state civil remedies were insufficient, especially when engaging well-funded, sophisticated foreign intelligence services.

- And a recognition of the need for federal relief for those firms that have been victimized by having their information stolen and then transferred out of the jurisdiction of existing state laws in much the same way that the federal computer crime statutes have been built over time.

Crime and Passion in Geekdom

In the 1970s and 1980s, companies had a difficult time getting law-enforcement cooperation and prosecutorial interest in what were—at that time—termed "crimes involving computers." Law enforcement tended to view such "crimes" as a gaggle of geeks sitting around and doing terrible things to small furry bits and bytes. They were not considered real crimes, since there was rarely anybody to arrest with the goods. Smoking guns were rare. No real lawman would bother investigating something like this. And, it was altogether far too complex to understand, let alone waste time to bother investigating. With outrageous caseloads, who had the time?

Prosecutors were even more difficult to bring into the loop. They not only had essentially the same "antigeek" biases, they had a somewhat more difficult problem in concept. What laws were actually broken and how? The best that could be done after lots of handwringing and headbanging might be a prosecution under wire-fraud statutes. Again, what prosecutor had the time to get smart enough to be able to convince a jury box full of non–rocket scientists that a dirty deed had been done? Most often, the answer given to a complaining company was "If you folks think this is such a big deal, why don't you get the city council, the state legislature, the U.S. House and Senate, or Mothers Against Cracked Eggs to enact some legislation?"

Indeed, since money is what really makes the legislative wheel turn every once in a while, it was the large dollars that victims were beginning to lose that changed law enforcement's, prosecutors', and lawmakers' attitudes.

Victims such as large banks, investment houses, and many other organizations whose electronic transfers were becoming the favorite target of computer-literate criminals. Their response was in the form of influencing their legislators to provide what they needed in the way of legal recourse. As a result, over the past two decades there has been a steady rise in the number of legislative fixes to help companies and government entities protect their information. It has also spawned a whole new career field for cyber-cops and DAs who are no longer electronically challenged.

The box entitled *Marc Edward Goldberg,* which discusses the case of a small California company that was the target of a French intelligence service espionage effort, served almost as a poster child for the problem. Absent any federal statutes, and even any federal support, the case was handled locally and with the results described.

One of the few cases that really addressed the issue of foreign involvement, and which was prosecuted at the federal level, is described in the box entitled *Ronald Joshua Hoffman.* Hoffman was found guilty of violating the espionage laws on behalf of a group of Japanese companies. In neither case, though, was the matter resolved because of the theft of trade secrets or proprietary information. Rather, they were prosecuted under laws designed to be used for other purposes.

These two cases offer several background points. They're poles apart in how they were prosecuted and the outcomes they achieved; they clearly came from either side of the world, yet they have a business focus only marginally different in terms of what can be expected from those who would aggressively obtain information without being restricted to the SCIP Code of Ethics we covered in chapter 8; and perhaps, most importantly, they differ from the ways in which competitive intelligence practitioners do their work.

In fact, these cases and numerous others from which we could choose clearly illustrate the basic descriptive elements of the EEA '96: that *the legislation applies to anyone who "steals, takes, carries away, or conceals, or by fraud, artifice or deception, obtains such information."* Is that a description of how you do business? Is that a description of how you plan to do business? I didn't think so.

To Federalize and to Criminalize

This new law has three primary elements, none of which have ever been previously specifically covered by U.S. law.

Marc Edward Goldberg

Goldberg, a young French software engineer, had been working for a Palo Alto software firm that specialized in the banking and trading industries. It wasn't until he began acting suspiciously after submitting his letter of resignation and intent to return to France that he was subjected to any kind of scrutiny. It led to his arrest on a dozen counts of theft and attempted theft of trade secrets, just as he was attempting to board a flight back to France.

The follow-up investigation revealed that when he left college in France, he was offered a choice about how he wanted to serve his mandatory military service: He could either paint rocks in the desert or he could go to another country, work in his professional discipline, and file monthly reports with the French Intelligence Service. He chose the latter.

First, he went to work for Thomson-CSF, the heavily nationalized French multinational. He was then transferred to Must Software, in Norwalk, Connecticut, one of Thomson's wholly owned, foreign subsidiaries. It wasn't long after that that he went to work for Renaissance Software in Palo Alto, where he remained for the next three years.

Of course, he wasn't paid while he was working for Must, since he was already receiving his military pay from the French government. Pay that continued while he worked for Renaissance at full pay and without any knowledge on Renaissance's part of his night job.

With the initial intervention of the French consulate in San Francisco, later the filing of a diplomatic note by the French embassy in Washington with the U.S. State Department, and the posting of $100,000 bond by his dad, Goldberg was set free pending trial. And that's where they really threw the book at him.

Absent any federal support whatever, the local charges were ultimately downgraded to three misdemeanors. He was fined $1,000 and assigned a thousand hours of community service, which he was allowed to serve in France. The image of Goldberg walking along les Champs-Elysées with a nail on a stick picking up trash comes immediately to mind, although the argument that he'd already done his community service for France might suggest that he didn't have much else left to do.

First, it allows the national counterintelligence apparatus—mostly the Federal Bureau of Investigation—to be brought to bear on the economic collection activities of foreign intelligence services. They've always had a responsibility to confront and neutralize the collection efforts of hostile intelligence services, but only against classified government information and programs. This law allows them to investigate cases in which foreign intelligence services attack American firms in order to gather information of a proprietary nature. Information that they gather in order to further the commercial interests of the firms in their countries.

Ronald Joshua Hoffman

In 1986, Hoffman was employed as a senior manager by Science Applications International Corporation, one of the larger and more successful defense and aerospace contractors. He was working on a top-secret project that was designing early-warning recognition software to identify rocket launches in the former Soviet Union as either hostile military launches or benign scientific ones.

The only problem was that at the same time, he started his own little company to market that same software internationally. A somewhat classier version of walking into a foreign embassy and offering to sell them the envelope of classified information you have under your arm—but only somewhat classier. Between 1986 and 1990, he received in excess of $750,000 for his software products from six Japanese companies: Mitsubishi Heavy Industries, NEC, Nissan, Ishikawajima-Harima, Mitsubishi Electric, and Toshiba.

When he went to trial, it was not for trade-secrets theft from SAIC, it was for violating the espionage statutes—which require that the government prove that he knowingly and willfully provided *classified* information to persons who did not have legitimate reason and approval to receive it. When the trial was over, he didn't get a stick with a nail and a ticket to Paris. He got six years as a guest of the federal prison system.

During the congressional hearings, and in a variety of other venues since the act was passed, various officials have painted a picture of the size and nature of the problem. From FBI director Louis Freeh's perspective, no less that twenty-three foreign countries—ranging across the globe from the French to the Japanese and Russians—are actively engaged in economic espionage operations against American firms. His perspective is based on the doubling of the FBI's caseload for this kind of investigation, from four hundred to almost eight hundred, in just 1996 alone.

What is it that they're after? They're after technologies being developed in the United States, where the government spends almost $250 billion and private industry spends another $300 billion. It doesn't take the president of the World Bank to figure out that if you spend $500,000 bribing a research scientist in the United States to get the trade secret or proprietary information that an American company has spent $750,000,000 developing, the intelligence operation has just netted more than $700 million. Even in government terms, $700 million is a noticeable amount.

Dan Swartwood, competitive information security manager at Compaq in Houston, attempted to quantify the actual losses American businesses suffered. Under the auspices of the American Society for Industrial Security, Swartwood conducted two surveys—one in 1992 and one in 1995. Swartwood's data revealed that "potential losses for all American industry could amount to $63 billion for the reporting period (1993–1995) or about $2 billion a month." Swartwood's study also showed that the average loss for the seven hundred incidents reported by 113 respondent companies was $19 million, $29 million, and $36 million in the high-technology, services, and manufacturing sectors respectively.

Second, the act also redefines the phrase "goods, wares or merchandise" to include the term "proprietary economic information" of a company in federal laws relating to stolen property. Thus, it extends the definition to allow federal investigation and prosecution in the event that the misappropriated information is used in interstate commerce.

With the passage of the EEA of '96, federal resources could now be brought to bear on behalf of a company faced with challenges supported by other countries. And, the solutions were no longer merely civil and of dubious value;* they had a criminal dimension that could result in significant jail time not only for the miscreants but also for those officers in a company who were aware of or who sanctioned such activities.

---

*In the celebrated case of the stolen "Adirondack Cookbooks" that held the secrets to IBM's business plans for up to ten years out, the Japanese firm Hitachi was able to make millions and perhaps billions on the foreknowledge they gained by knowing which IBM-driven peripherals to make and market before anyone else could. The fines they paid many years later after the civil case was settled were insignificant in comparison with the margins they achieved by being first to market in several peripherals areas.

Third, the EEA provides for criminal penalties in the place of what had been only civil remedies in the past. There is now considerable pain and suffering that a person or corporation may experience as a result of being found guilty of violating this act. For an individual at the worker-bee level, the fines max out at $1,000,000 and jail time at fifteen years, or both; officers of corporations can receive fines up to $5,000,000 and jail up to twenty-five years, or both; and, for corporations, fines can reach $50,000,000.

Since the passage of the legislation, there have been about a dozen cases brought so far.

The very first one was a purely domestic case, not even tangentially involving a foreign entity. So much for original intent. It's the saga of the Worthing Brothers and PPG, described in the box called *Mrs. Worthing's Boys*.

The second one involved a foreign connection, but only in terms of the nationality of the alleged offenders and not because they were ever charged with working as agents of another country. A Taiwanese national by the name of Kai-Lo Hsu Hsu was arrested on June 16, 1997, for attempting to steal pharmaceutical-related trade secrets. Mr. Hsu was employed as the technical director at Yuen Foong Paper Company Ltd. in Taipei.

Now, on its face, the first question that inquiring minds want answered is, "Why in the dickens does a paper company want pharmaceutical trade secrets?" Maybe the simultaneous arrest of one of his countrymen in the same case will help pull this together a little. The second person arrested was Professor Charles Ho, from National Chiao Tung University in Taiwan; he is also a co-owner of Asiapharm, a biotechnology firm located in Delaware. It seems that Bristol-Myers Squibb was really unwilling to share the plant-cell-culture technology used to manufacture the ovarian cancer fighter Taxol. Imagine. The two Taiwanese apparently felt that if Bristol-Myers was going to be so close-minded about it, they'd make some overtures to people who might be interested in supplementing their IRAs with an extra $500,000. Apparently, they guessed wrong and got caught up in an FBI sting.

In any event, odds are that the penalties may be a little stiffer in the Bristol-Myers Squibb case than in the PPG case. The actual charges against Hsu are attempted theft of trade secrets, conspiracy to steal trade secrets, and other violations; Professor Ho can add charges of aiding and abetting interstate and foreign travel to commit bribery, along with con-spiracy, to his curriculum vita. Bear in mind that the new law allows for many years in federal guest quarters, and the potential for millions of dollars in fines when companies are actually involved. Since this will be the first foreign-linked case prosecuted under the act, it will set the stage for those that follow.

Mrs. Worthing's Boys

Glen Hiner, chairman and CEO of Owens-Corning, picked up his incoming faxes one morning and found one very interesting communication. This fax stood out from all the others because of its contents: For a relatively small fee, Hiner could have access to all the blueprints, CAD/CAM drawings, and just about anything else he might want from the Research and Development Center at his rival, PPG in Pittsburgh. Hiner's response was the correct one. He called his opposite number at PPG and told him about the anonymous offer. Within three weeks or so, the case was closed with the arrest of Mrs. Worthing's boys, Patrick and Daniel.

It seems that Patrick was working as a temporary employee—indeed, such a good one that he was managing other temporary employees—at the PPG R and D facility. He'd sent the fax after having squirreled away some very interesting and valuable competitive materials that he had access to in the course of his normal, everyday duties. Being the kind of rocket scientist he was, he'd sent the fax from somewhere else, so as to disguise its origins. Later, it was shown by the fax station identifier to have come from his wife's company, even though she had no knowledge of the plot.

The long and short of it is quite simple: Patrick showed up at the arranged meeting with his older brother, Daniel, providing surveillance, just in case it was some kind of trap. Indeed, that didn't help much. The Glen Hiner look-alike was really an FBI agent who put the *habeas grabbus* on Patrick after an exchange of materials and money; Daniel's life changed a few minutes later.

In the trial that ensued, Patrick tried to defend his actions by claiming that he was only trying to provide himself some insurance coverage that was not available to him as a temporary employee, in contrast to the permanent PPG employees he worked with each day. From the other side, the value of the purloined materials was in the range of $20–30 million to PPG.

Patrick and Daniel became federal guests for eighteen months and were fined $1,500. A pittance by comparison with what could have been lost. They may have been the luckiest of anyone who'll ever be charged under this statute. Others will not have it as easy.

Now, ask yourself the same question we asked you before. If you weren't doing the things that Goldberg and Hoffman were doing, are you doing the things that the Worthing Brothers and Ho and Hsu were doing? Have we yet described anything that you or your firm is doing, is planning on doing, or has done? Will the EEA apply to you and your firm? Probably not. Not unless you're on the receiving end of someone else's criminal approach.

And, What If You Are on the Receiving End?

First, the EEA is not going to be a panacea for aggrieved parties either. The EEA is not going to be the end-all, be-all of your needs to protect yourself. That's one of the reasons that part III is included in this book. If you could rely on the EEA and the FBI and the attorney general to take care of business for you, you wouldn't need to take care of your own matters, would you? In fact, there is very specific language in the EEA that specifies that a company must take those measures necessary to protect itself. If a firm doesn't take the steps necessary—consistent with the nature of their environment—they certainly can't expect a judge to grant them relief. If they're unwilling to expend the efforts to protect themselves, no judge is going to do it for them.

Second, not every company is especially interested in washing their laundry in public anyway. There is a wonderful tradition of keeping such losses under wraps throughout American business history, simply because of fear of stockholder suits against a company's leadership for not doing what was necessary to protect their investments. There is also a secondary concern about customer and marketplace reputation that is offered from time to time as the reason for not seeking redress through the court system, although that's usually a canard. Fear of stockholders is almost always the main reason.

And there's another, perhaps even stronger reason as well. It's called "discovery motions." It's a reason that certainly predates the EEA. We have heard this reason advanced for not filing civil motions for years.

Since the passage of the EEA, we have heard far more senior leaders explain their rationale for not proceeding under the EEA than they ever did under the previous options. Simply put, companies may wind up losing more proprietary information under discovery motions—as the defendant asks for additional information from the plaintiff in order to be able to mount a vigorous and best defense—than they lost in the alleged misappropriation in the first place.

Granted, the EEA may provide some solace by recognizing that the judge will do everything in his power to keep this from happening. Yet common sense alone says that things will be even more difficult to keep out of discovery under the EEA. The courts almost always grant greater latitude to defendants in criminal cases—which are the ones that would be brought under the EEA—than they grant under civil cases. And sad experience has already shown many companies just how liberally defendants will be granted access to information in civil cases.

Third, in saying that the EEA is not a panacea, we have to remember that the FBI is just the same as any other federal agency: It has time and manpower constraints. They are already charged with the responsibility for everything from white-collar crime to kidnapping, from terrorism to bank robbery, and everything in between. They have to assign priorities to certain kind of crimes over others, and unfortunately, they're not able to do everything. Money, people, and time dictate that they do what they can with the resources available; work those cases that have the greatest potential for satisfactory completion—and, if there's a significant profile to the case, all the better.

The larger and the more dramatic the case, the easier a time the director has defending his budget request the next year. Let's face it, economic espionage cases don't have the appeal to the population as a whole that a kidnapping does; and usually, counterintelligence cases take ever so much longer for closure than other kinds of cases. Thus, it can come down to profiles and numbers. The faster the case can be closed, the better the chances the FBI will take it for investigation. That, in turn means that the more you've done as the aggrieved party, the better. That means that the ball is clearly in your court at the outset—using either your own internal resources or an outside organization.

Lastly, there's the prosecution. Instead of prosecutions being opened by the U.S. attorney for a particular district of the country, for at least the first three years of the act's life, decisions about whether or not a case will be opened is at the sole and personal discretion of the attorney general.

The reason given is to ensure that there are no frivolous prosecutions that would embarrass the federal government; yet, more likely, it's to ensure that there are no foreign-policy considerations at play. We wouldn't want, for example, to accuse another country of using its intelligence service if our State Department thought that in doing so, we might hack off the wrong people. Having the AG reserve the right to open a case or not allows for the necessary interaction at those high levels of government where those kinds of decisions should—arguably—be made.

The Ethical Side

As long as you persist in making intelligence a moral issue, you won't understand.

—Oleg Gordievsky, former KGB officer in a lecture at Langley, VA (1992)

In the United States, where it's fashionable to denigrate the morality of intelligence operations as a whole, the mountain is somewhat higher to climb than in other countries where there is a long tradition of popular support for the contributions of a national intelligence service. The box entitled *The French View of the Matter* may show how the French view of the Business Intelligence world is considerably different from the American view. Many people in America still agree with Secretary of War Henry Stimson's 1935 remark that "Gentlemen don't read each other's mail." Stimson uttered this phrase in defense of his decision to disband the only American intelligence function worth its salt during the interwar years—the one that would have given clear and reliable insights into Japanese intentions in the years before Pearl Harbor.

Yet there are an increasing number of enterprises where the use of Business Intelligence as a legitimate and valuable function is not only acceptable, it's a necessary ingredient to success. It may even be one of the reasons that you're reading this book right now. Yet many firms have not yet quite gotten around to defining exactly what and how they'll structure themselves and conduct themselves in the marketplace. It's one thing to say that you'll do nothing illegal to gather information that you need to prevail in the marketplace; it's another to say that you'll do so ethically.

Over the past ten years, I've seen an interesting, perhaps even hypocritical approach to Business Intelligence and ethics.

Corporate counsels raise loud and serious-sounding questions about whether or not employees can be trusted to represent themselves openly and honestly when in quest of competitive information. The same attorneys can also be heard to counsel their leaders to cover up misdeeds in pricing, production, quality, and performance; to obfuscate, delay, and challenge customers and employees in court until they can't afford to continue a claim; and to deny, misrepresent, and mislead until forced to apply even a modicum of integrity to their business dealings. Granted, it's only that 99 percent of lawyers who give the rest of them a bad name.

The French View of the Matter

The French business intelligence system faces few pressures from lawmakers or from constituents: The wide, popular consensus is that in matters of intelligence, morals and ethics do not apply.

French companies do not maintain codes of ethics, perceiving them as an irrelevant Anglo-Saxon concept. French government-intelligence operatives face few if any issues of national security, civil or criminal liability, or privileged bias when collecting for their national businesses.

The presence of French business intelligence services in the United States has been widely publicized, in part due to the defection to the CIA of the head of the French Business Intelligence services in Washington, D.C., the only case of a Western intelligence officer defecting to another, allied country.

The United States is virtually the only country in the world where the political system does not allow the government to share business intelligence with business.

—Jean Marie Bonthous, writing in *The Journal of Intelligence and Counterintelligence*, 7, no. 3, pp. 283–284

Then there are the business leaders and managers who act badly on their own without benefit of counsel helping them do things that their own mothers would find offensive: launching products that they know will kill or disfigure people, pointing fingers at subordinates to avoid responsibility themselves, making illegal payments or improper advances to subordinates, or advocating all manner of marketplace moves to kill off the competition. And then worrying over whether an employee may not have fully identified himself at a professional meeting to two competitors he overhears in an elevator?

Perhaps it's an unfortunate choice of words, these phrases *competitive intelligence* and *business intelligence.* But frankly, I don't see any sense in apologizing for a well-established and functional process that serves the needs of its consumers far better than stargazing, wishful thinking, and silly planning based on daily horoscopes or fortune tellers. The problem comes in when these phrases are connected with such other phrases as *industrial espionage* and *economic espionage.*

Misunderstandings and Misinformation

There are as many approaches to the ethics of Business Intelligence as there are firms practicing it. I agree wholeheartedly that there needs to be both a legal standard as well as an ethical standard for the conduct of Business Intelligence operations. Yet at the same time, there shouldn't be any misunderstanding of what those two separate sets of standards mean.

We've already spoken about the "target-rich environment" we have here in the United States; an environment where people are so open that it's not necessary to misrepresent yourself in order to get information from them. But while misrepresentation is an ethical issue for some people, it certainly doesn't get to the level of legal jeopardy. Think about it for a millisecond. With what you know about the sheer number of cases that the FBI is trying to deal with annually:

- Do you actually think that they'll be interested in opening a case on the basis of someone saying they were doing a grad school research paper when they're really only a part-time student and a full-time BI researcher?

- Do you actually believe that it's the kind of thing that'll get you sent to jail if you overhear two executives from another company on a plane discussing their next year's marketing strategy and don't turn around and tell them that you're working for their nearest rival?

- Do you actually think that the FBI will come to your office and hook you up for not having your company's name on your identification badge at a trade show?

- Do you actually believe that the attorney general will open a federal case against your firm if one of your employees sees—and picks up—a set of documents in a men's room wastebasket that has been discarded by a competitor?

Any of these may be the business version of trying to determine how many angels can dance on the head of a pin, but it really does matter that we not get so hamstrung by confusion between ethical and legal issues. If ethical and legal issues were the same, we'd have lots more politicians in jail or under indictment. And they'd be surrounded by insurance salesmen, used-car dealers, headhunters who routinely "ruse" potential candidates—you name it.

It may seem that I'm arguing in favor of an ethics-free Business Intelligence environment. That's not the case at all. In fact, we at Phoenix Consulting Group adhere to the SCIP standard and several other points that are not covered in the professional guidelines. Our firm's approach is perhaps more stringent than others, yet it's been developed on the basis of our own personal standards and are further measured in terms of what's good and what's bad from a business perspective.

For example, we think it's a useful and appropriate business practice to have our nondisclosure agreement operate from the first moment that a prospective client engages us in discussion about a project, whether or not we ever actually undertake the project, and even whether or not we ever actually sign an NDA with that prospective client. That just seems like a good business practice, in addition to having an ethical underpinning. And that works for us. Not because it's the legal thing to do, but because it seems like the right thing to do.

For another example, a firm that was involved in a multibillion-dollar federal competition asked us to have at least one of our researchers fly on an open-seating commuter airplane between the two cities where their primary rival's offices were located. They wanted us to follow—and sit as close as possible to—the proposal developers on the flights that they were regularly making between those two cities. They wanted to have the benefit of hearing the discussions about what they were going to be doing or what they had just done. Nothing illegal about that. Great way to add frequent-flyer miles and segments. But, essentially an inappropriate way to collect information. Moreover, it seemed to be a waste of time, effort, and money as far as we were concerned. After we turned down the project, we know they called someone else who was more than willing to do it. How? Because after two months of getting nothing from the in-flight conversations, they came to us to ask that we employ the other means we normally employed to develop rates and prices, management and technical approaches.

And because we don't ask anybody else to tell us whether this is an acceptable standard from their perspective, we don't think it's appropriate to serve as the local ethics police about what someone else is doing either. Ethical standards aren't going to deter them any more than the SCIP standards are going to keep bad guys from doing illegal things.

So, when you set out to develop your approaches to Business Intelligence, and are concerned about what you should and should not do, think about it.

Ponder the legalities, certainly, but if you're not normally going to run your business illegally, you're probably not prone to running your intelligence collection illegally. You'll not be breaking into someone's office or computer system; you're not going to be bribing employees or doing black-bag jobs on a rival's hotel room; you're not going to be bugging his conference room or corporate jet.

Ponder the ethics, certainly. Ask yourself a few questions. Ask yourself, "How would my mother respond to reading about me doing this on the front page of *The Wall Street Journal*?" Ask yourself, "How would my CEO respond to a similar article?" Ask yourself, "What is my own personal level of comfort or discomfort about doing this or that?"

After all, when it's all said and done, it comes down to the points on your own moral and ethical compass. No one else's. And that's what you should keep in mind when you read the three different sets of guidelines in appendix C. They're standards that have been developed by three different companies and reflect their culture and attitudes. You should know yours a lot better than we know them.

Sample Competitive Intelligence Guidelines: Three Levels of Complexity

Sample Version One: Competitive Intelligence Guidelines

Background

A new federal law, the Economic Espionage Act, will further protect our trade secrets and help discourage those who would seek them and eliminate our competitive advantage. It is a federal felony, punishable by fines up to $10,000,000 and imprisonment of up to fifteen years, to take, or even possess, another's trade secrets without the owner's authorization, or even try unsuccessfully to do so, intending or knowing that it would damage or disadvantage that owner. The law also reaches conduct outside the United States if carried out by a U.S. citizen, permanent resident alien, or business entity, or if any act in the scheme was committed in the United States.

It is important to understand that this law cuts both ways. Just as it expands the protections the company's trade secrets enjoy, it also makes illegal some competitive intelligence/benchmarking activities that were previously legal.

Statement of Policy

Conducting Competitive Intelligence Activity

The collection and analysis of information about the company's competitors are legitimate and necessary to assuring the company's competitive advantage in every one of its businesses worldwide. We will conduct such activities in accordance with the highest legal and ethical standards, and in all events with the prior approval of the executive officer of the business or functional unit doing the activity.

Associates participating should be provided with appropriate training in collection methods, analysis, and legal principles involved in competitive information prior to commencing their assignments. The same training should be required for associates managing the work of contractors and consultants retained by the company.

Every contract, purchase order, and other form of engagement of a contractor or consultant entered into by the company must be in the form specified by the general counsel's division executed by both parties, and a fully executed copy will be placed and retained in the corporation secretary's office.

Sample Version Two: Competitive Intelligence Guidelines

In today's highly competitive global marketplace, understanding our competition is increasingly important. To aid in this understanding, employees routinely collect and analyze competitive information. In dealing with competitive information we are committed, as in all areas of our business, to engage in only those practices that meet the highest ethical and legal standards.

This reference guide contains important employee guidelines with respect to competitive information. Please refer to the company's Protection of Proprietary Information Policy and Guidelines for a full description of the company's position in this area.

Information about Competitors

PROPER ACTIVITIES

It is entirely proper for us to gather information about the marketplace in which we do business, including information about our competitors and their products and services. We may gather such information from a variety of sources including advertisements, published articles, on-line services, public records, trade shows, consultants, and conversations with customers or suppliers. Every company employee should consider themselves a part of this effort and pass along information received to the appropriate place. This could be an area coordinator, the CI database supervisor, or the CI manager.

We should generally avoid seeking or receiving competitive information directly from our competitors. We may, however, purchase a competitor's product and ask them questions about it as any other purchaser could do. We may also participate in the various activities of trade and professional associations. However, particular care must be taken to ensure compliance with all aspects of the company's antitrust policy. Specifically, we must avoid any discussion with any representative of a competitor regarding prices, royalties, terms or conditions of sale, costs, choice of customers, territorial markets, production quotas or output, allocation of customers or territories, or bidding on a job. While the antitrust policy permits gathering such information, the source of the information must not be a competitor. Therefore, when reporting this type of information, it is imperative to include its noncompetitive source.

IMPROPER ACTIVITIES

We must never attempt to acquire a competitor's trade secrets or any other proprietary or confidential information from any source. We must likewise never attempt to collect any information using unlawful or unethical means. Such means include, but are not limited to, theft, spying, electronic eavesdropping, or the breach of a competitor's nondisclosure agreement by a former employee, customer, or other party. Further, we must never misrepresent our identity in attempting to collect information.

Any employee authorized to retain a consultant to gather competitive information must take steps to ensure the consultant's strict adherence to these guidelines and all company policies in this regard.

The legal department should be consulted whenever there is any doubt about the proprietary nature of information received or the manner in which it was collected. Information determined to be confidential or proprietary will normally be returned unopened to the company it concerns.

Protecting Proprietary Information

PROTECTING COMPANY INFORMATION

In today's competitive environment protecting the company's proprietary information is more important than ever before. Just as the company ethically collects information about its competitors, we can reasonably expect them to actively collect against us. The Company Protection of

Proprietary Information Policy and Guidelines contains a full description of the company's position in this area.

Proprietary information is any information or knowledge created, acquired, or controlled by the company that the company determines should not be published or released to others. It includes, but is not limited to, financial and billing records, unannounced products and services, technical information, sales and marketing data, and employee records. The unauthorized release or disclosure of this information could cause the company the loss of a critical competitive advantage, hurt relationships with customers, or embarrass or harm fellow employees. Even the most innocuous-sounding questions, when combined with other "tidbits" of information, can reveal things we do not want our competitors to know.

To minimize the impact of these efforts, we must always be aware of this threat and its potential harm. Each employee must ensure that company information is properly identified and safeguarded according to its proprietary nature and in accordance with the company's Protection of Proprietary Information Policy and Guidelines. We must be particularly aware of the identity of people requesting information about the company. Those who believe that another firm is actively and aggressively targeting individuals or groups within the company should make their concerns known to the appropriate departments according to our Handbook of Security and Counterintelligence Instructions.

The company also regards as proprietary the information of others that it is obligated to maintain in confidence. The company may properly come into possession of such information in a number of ways, most often as a result of an agreement with the owner of the information that restricts the way in which the information may be used. The terms and conditions of any such agreement must be strictly followed. In addition, employees must be especially careful about the circumstances under which they are offered, or receive, such information. They should consider, among other factors, how and from whom they are going to acquire the information; whether it is being offered to them with restrictions on its use; and how they plan to use it. Before agreeing to accept the proprietary information of others with any restrictions, they should contact the corporate security department or the legal department to review the terms under which it is being offered. They should also contact the corporate security department or the legal department immediately if they believe there is a chance that they might be receiving the information as a result of a breach of confidence, or an improper or illegal act, or under any circumstances that might call into question the propriety of their actions.

Disclosure of proprietary information to others and the receipt of proprietary information belonging to others should only be made where there is a valid business need and then only as specified in company policies and instructions. Company information must never be used for personal benefit or other noncompany purposes.

When employees leave the company, all documents and records containing proprietary information must be turned in to the company. Even after employment ends, former employees have a continuing obligation to safeguard this information.

Questions on whether company information is proprietary, the conditions under which it can be released, and appropriate safeguards to protect it should be directed to the corporate security department. Any compromise, or even suspected compromise, of such information must be immediately reported to the corporate security department.

The threat of industrial espionage and sabotage today is greater than ever before. This can include theft, spying, electronic eavesdropping, and the tapping of phone and fax machines. The importance of safeguarding company information from these threats cannot be overstated.

Every employee must actively strive to prevent disclosure of sensitive information. Care must be taken in the use of laptop computers, fax machines, and cellular phones. Always be aware of what you are saying and to whom, particularly in public places including aircraft, restaurants, and hotels. Any attempt by an unauthorized person to obtain company proprietary information or gain access to secured company locations must be reported to the corporate security department.

Proprietary Information Protocol

Every employee must take care not to receive, pass on, or copy confidential competitive information that he or she knows, or has reason to know, was stolen, obtained, or converted without authorization.

Should a company employee receive information about another company that he or she believes to be confidential or proprietary in nature, it will be turned over to the legal department immediately. Company policy is that information of this nature be returned, unopened if possible, to that company's legal department. Similarly, should there be any doubt as to the means by which information has been collected, the legal department should be contacted immediately.

Sample Version Three: Competitive Intelligence Guidelines

In this most expansive of the three optional sets of guidelines, we recommend that an introductory note from the leadership of the company include a reference drawn from the company's code of ethics. For example:

We do business from the highest set of ethical standards. We follow both the letter as well as the spirit of the law. As a good corporate citizen, we deal with our many and various constituencies fairly, openly, and honestly.

—**Statement by Henry Morgan, President and Chairman, Ferndock International**

Carrying out this policy has served us well in the past and will serve us well in the future as we continue along the road of commercializing the company and in meeting the challenges of rapidly growing competition in our marketplace. There is no area of business activity that presents more frequent and difficult ethical issues than in the gathering of intelligence about our competitors. The guidelines that follow are intended to provide the principles and practices that will help each employee to conform to the highest ethical and legal standards in performing this activity.

Competitive intelligence gathering can be an important element in a company's success in the rough-and-tumble of the marketplace. The laws of this country, both federal and state, encourage aggressive competition provided it is fairly conducted through offering better products and services at prices, and on terms, that are attractive to potential purchasers. To make such offerings successfully, a supplier needs to understand not only the needs of consumers and the economic conditions that affect and shape them but also what its competitors are offering, are capable of offering, and are likely to offer. This informed approach helps the supplier to determine where best to focus its productive energies and resources by understanding where it can most effectively compete; and, it benefits the consumer by fostering more efficient competition and a greater choice of quality products and services. It is only when competitive intelligence gathering is conducted by unfair, deceptive, or dishonest means that the competitive process is compromised. At the company, we believe that not only should we comply with the letter of these laws but with their spirit—the ethical principles that underlie them.

We can gather information about our competitors from a variety of sources. As part of their marketing efforts, our competitors may divulge a great deal about themselves in press releases, on their Websites on the Internet, in talks at industry forums, and through talking about and demonstrating their products at trade shows. They are sometimes willing to make disclosures about their future plans and other facts helpful to their competitors because they believe that such general, unrestricted disclosure is of sufficient benefit to them in selling their products and services as to outweigh the value in secrecy that is lost. Where a competitor publishes information in this manner, it is proper and ethical systematically to gather it and analyze it as an aid to formulating our own competitive strategies. It is when we seek to gather information from nonpublic sources that legal and ethical concerns arise.

There are presently both federal and state criminal and civil laws making it unlawful to improperly acquire trade secrets. The focus of the guidelines that follow is on what methods of competitive intelligence gathering are ethical, fair, and honest. Normally our inducing a competitor voluntarily to disclose useful intelligence to us would be ethical and lawful if the information were given without any restriction as to its use or used by us only for a specified, restricted purpose. But we should always bear in mind the need to avoid any voluntary exchanges of competitively sensitive data (current or future prices and terms of sale, production plans, etc.) that might be part of or evolve into an arrangement that unlawfully restrains competition between the competitor and the company.* Such voluntary disclosures can violate antitrust laws, the same laws that also make misappropriating a competitor's trade secrets an unfair method of competition.

What are the essential elements of an unlawful acquiring of a competitor's confidential or trade-secret information? As set forth in the Uniform Trade Secrets Act, adopted by many states and recently incorporated into a federal criminal statute, the Economic Espionage Act of 1996, they are:

1.   The information obtained (including financial, business, scientific, technical, economic, and engineering information) has been

---

*Certain exchanges of information in connection with teaming agreements or other joint activities and such joint projects themselves can be lawful. The legal department should be consulted beforehand, however, so that these project and exchanges are confined within reasonable, lawful limits.

treated by the competitor as confidential by taking reasonable steps to keep such information secret.

2. Such information is not generally known and not readily ascertainable by others who are knowledgeable in the trade.

3. Such information confers a competitive advantage on its owner.

4. The information has been obtained by improper means such as theft, bribery, deceit, misrepresentation, or eavesdropping.

5. The trade secret has been used to the owner's detriment.

It should be noted that the misappropriation can be effected directly or by receiving or buying it from another when one knows or has reason to know that it is a trade secret and that it has been obtained improperly by the other person or that he or she is not authorized to disclose it and consequently the other person's disclosure itself is a misappropriation of the information.

The consequences of violating the laws protecting trade secrets from misappropriation can be severe for both a corporation and the individual employees involved. With the requisite intent to injure or knowledge that the misappropriation will injure the owner of a trade secret, the wrongdoer can be subject to criminal prosecution and fines and imprisonment. Even in a civil suit, substantial damages and restrictive injunctive relief may be awarded. Although these consequences provide incentive enough for complying with the law, there is another very critical reason for company employees not only to adhere to the law but also to act in accordance with the highest ethical standards.

As consultants to a broad spectrum of clients, some of whom compete with each other or with the company or both, we must earn and scrupulously maintain a reputation for faithfully protecting and keeping confidential those trade secrets we receive in the course of our consulting. Were we in other situations to engage in any unethical methods for gathering competitive information even though we adhered to the contractual nondisclosure duties arising out of our consulting engagements, our trustworthiness might well be questioned and future consulting opportunities lost.

The company's success in the past has depended and its future success will depend upon its steadfast honesty, objectivity, and integrity as well as its technical expertise, and the guidelines that follow are aimed at attaining this level of ethical performance.

What, then, are the fundamental guidelines we should follow to meet the highest ethical standards in competitive intelligence gathering? The correct application of some is clear and of others requires the exercise of sound, informed judgment and discretion. When in doubt, we should lean toward avoiding any overreaching on our part or condoning of dishonest acquisition or unauthorized disclosure of trade secrets by others whom we hire as consultants or employees or otherwise call upon for information. The guidelines we should apply are:

1. *No Espionage:* Do not engage in or hire someone to engage in any form of espionage with respect to a competitor: electronic eavesdropping, clandestine taking or copying of its files (both electronic and paper), photographing of its locked laboratory, prototypes, or facilities, stealing any briefcases, their contents, or other documents of the competitor's employees or agents, and other means of appropriation of a physical or intellectual property of the competition without its express authorization.

2. *Using Public Information:* As much as possible, seek needed or desirable intelligence about a competitor from information that it has published through press releases, presentations at forums, filings with courts and governmental agencies, brochures, and other marketing materials freely given out at trade shows by the competitor.

3. *No Deceptive Practices:* Do not engage in any deception to obtain information about the competitor from the competitor or a third party that would not otherwise be available to you. This includes, among other things, misrepresenting who you are, what company you represent, and why you are seeking the information you seek. In a public forum such as a trade show, this guideline would not normally require you to volunteer the fact that you are employed by the company, but, if asked, would require you to so identify yourself. The presumption at a trade show is that the competitor's representatives are aware that anyone to whom they speak may well be a competitor. In a more private setting, however, you should normally disclose your company relationship before commencing a discussion with an employee or representative of a competitor, or if joining a group with a conversation in progress, so identify yourself as soon as practicable.

4. *Talking with Competitors:* In talking with a competitor's employees or representative, you may use psychological understanding and elicitation techniques to encourage the other person to provide information about the competitor that, without such prompting, the person might not think to mention or would be slow to reveal. Such methods include flattery, mild criticism, expressions of disbelief, and provocative statements. They are well known among competitive intelligence professionals. It is ethical to use them provided that (a) you have properly identified yourself, (b) you state that you are not seeking any information of "trade secret" nature, (c) you have no reason to believe the other person is not authorized to disclose the type of information sought, and (d) you have not employed a deception to justify or encourage disclosure of the information (for example, referring to a potential teaming venture with the employee's company when you have no such thing in mind).

This is a gray area that requires you to proceed carefully. Where you are talking to a disgruntled employee of a competitor, you need to exercise extra care and take a conservative approach as to how much he or she has the authority to tell you. You also have to be alert to the possibility that the person may have misappropriated information. Furthermore, the organizational level of the employee (CEO versus low level) is a factor to be considered with respect to apparent authority to make disclosures.*

An important point to bear in mind is that seeking, receiving, and using information of competitive value is not wrong if the employee disclosing it has the authority to reveal it and is not deceived into revealing it. It is not a "trade secret" if the employee reveals it under these circumstances. (Note: It is important to understand the techniques employed to encourage disclosure of desired information not only for the purpose of our obtaining information but for the purpose of recognizing and neutralizing their use against each of us at the company.)

5. *Information from Third Parties:* You may seek information about a competitor from third parties (independent consultants, customers, and former employees of and suppliers to the competitor, etc.) if (a) you have no reason to believe their disclosure of the information would itself constitute a misappropriation by them of a competitor's trade secret or the passing on of

---

*At a trade show it is reasonable to assume that the person representing the competitor at its booth has authority to speak on a broad range of topics involving the products being demonstrated and about which materials are being distributed.

misappropriated information and (b) you state to them in advance that you are not seeking any information they are obligated to the competitor not to disclose to you. For instance, a customer might be able to advise you of what products the competitor has offered to it, the prices charged, the capabilities that the competitor claims of the product, the information provided to the customer about the competitor's future products, and the like. Absent special circumstances of which you were aware, there would be no reason to believe the customer is legally constrained from informing you of these facts. Greater care must be exercised, however, in dealing with former employees of a competitor who may well have nondisclosure obligations (whether the company hires them or not)* or with an independent consultant who claims to have "hard-to-get" information. (So too, in hiring an independent consultant of the company to perform primary research on competitors' activities, we should instruct the consultant of the company's ethical guidelines. In either situation, use of a consultant does not automatically insulate the company legally or ethically from responsibility for what would be an improper activity if done by the company itself.)

6.   *Windfall Information:* You are sitting in an airplane. The two persons next to you start talking about business matters. After a while, you realize that they are employees of a company competitor. Whether or not they have started to talk about competitively sensitive information, ethics, if not potential legal liability, call upon you to reveal your identity promptly. It is not reasonable to assume that these persons will only reveal publicly available information or facts that you already know or could readily ascertain. The fact that they are careless does not change the likelihood that they would not want a competitor to hear what they are saying or might be saying next— and if you listen to any "trade secret" information and then use it, you may be viewed as eavesdropping and violating the law. What if you receive a fax from one employee to another employee of a competitor containing information that is clearly a trade secret? Is this a "gift from the gods" that you are free to use? You did not intercept it or steal it or get it under false pretenses. The sender did not reveal the information to the intended recipient without authorization. You have no contractual or other duty to the competitor not to disclose it. Someone

---

*Former employees are normally allowed, however, to use the general knowledge, skills, and experience gained during the prior employment, as opposed to specific formulas, processes, and data that are confidential and proprietary.

simply made a mistake on the fax number of the recipient and you obtained the information through no improper means on your part. Nevertheless, the highest ethics, if not the law, call upon you to return the document without copying or subsequently using the information yourself or disclosing it to others in the company. (Similarly, if the two companions on the plane revealed competitively useful information before you could warn them about your identity, it is better that you not use the overheard information or place it in the company's competitive information system for disclosure to other company employees.)

The foregoing guidelines are not intended to state definitively what the law permits or does not permit, but rather they are intended to assist you in complying with the company's ethical policies. They are not intended to and cannot cover all situations that may arise. You are urged to consult counsel whenever you have doubts about what is proper and ethical. The bottom line is that company employees should always act in a fair and ethical manner. Honesty is indeed the best policy.

The Economic Espionage and Protection of Proprietary Information Act of 1996

ECONOMIC ESPIONAGE ACT OF 1996

SECTION 1. SHORT TITLE. This Act may be cited as the "Economic Espionage Act of 1996."

Sec. 101. PROTECTION OF TRADE SECRETS.
(a) IN GENERAL.—Title 18, United States Code, is amended by inserting after chapter 89 the following: CHAPTER 90 - PROTECTION OF TRADE SECRETS

Sec. 1831. Economic espionage.
1832. Theft of trade secrets.
1833. Exceptions to prohibitions.
1834. Criminal forfeiture.
1835. Orders to preserve confidentiality.
1836. Civil proceedings to enjoin violations.
1837. Conduct outside the United States.
1838. Construction with other laws.
1839. Definitions.

(a) IN GENERAL.—Whoever, intending or knowing that the offense will benefit any foreign government, foreign instrumentality, or foreign agent, knowingly—

(1) steals, or without authorization appropriates, takes, carries away, or conceals, or by fraud, artifice, or deception obtains a trade secret;

(2) without authorization copies, duplicates, sketches, draws, photographs, downloads, uploads, alters, destroys, photocopies, replicates, transmits, delivers, sends, mails, communicates, or conveys a trade secret;

(3) receives, buys, or possesses a trade secret, knowing the same to have been stolen or appropriated, obtained, or converted without authorization;

(4) attempts to commit any offense described in any of paragraphs (1) through (3); or

(5) conspires with one or more others persons to commit any offense described in any of paragraphs (1) through (4), and one or more of such persons do any act to effect the object of the conspiracy, shall, except as provided in subsection (b), be fined not more than $500,000 or imprisoned not more than 15 years, or both.

(b) ORGANIZATIONS.—Any organization that commits any offense described in subsection (a) shall be fined not more than $10,000,000.

1832. Theft of trade secrets

(a) Whoever, with intent to convert a trade secret, that is related to or included in a product that is produced for or placed in interstate or foreign commerce, to the economic benefit of anyone other than the owner thereof, and intending or knowing that the offense will injure any owner of that trade secret, knowingly—

(1) steals, or without authorization appropriates, takes, carries away, or conceals, or by fraud, artifice, or deception obtains a trade secret;

(2) without authorization copies, duplicates, sketches, draws, photographs, downloads, uploads, alters, destroys, photocopies, replicates, transmits, delivers, sends, mails, communicates, or conveys such information;

(3) receives, buys, or possesses such information, knowing the same to have been stolen or appropriated, obtained, or converted without authorization;

(4) attempts to commit any offense described in any of paragraphs (1) through (3); or

(5) conspires with one or more other persons to commit any offense described in any of paragraphs (1) through (3), and one or more of such persons do any act to effect the object of the conspiracy, shall, except as provided in subsection (b), be fined under this title or imprisoned not more than 10 years, or both.

(b) Any organization that commits any offense described in subsection (a) shall be fined not more than $5,000,000.

1833. Exceptions to prohibitions

"This chapter does not prohibit—

(1) any otherwise lawful activity conducted by a government entity of the United States, a State, or a political subdivision of a State; or

(2) the reporting of a suspected violation of law to any government entity of the United States, a State, or a political subdivision of a State, if such entity has lawful authority with respect to that violation.

1834. Criminal forfeiture

(a) The court, in imposing sentence on a person for a violation of this chapter, shall order, in addition to any other sentence imposed, that the person forfeit to the United States—

(1) any property constituting, or derived from, any proceeds the person obtained, directly or indirectly, as the result of such violation; and

(2) any of the person's property used, or intended to be used, in any manner or part, to commit or facilitate the commission of such violation, if the court in its discretion so determines, taking into consideration the nature, scope, and proportionality of the use of the property in the offense.

(b) Property subject to forfeiture under this section, any seizure and disposition thereof, and any administrative or judicial proceedings in relation thereto, shall be governed by section 413 of the Comprehensive Drug Abuse Prevention and Control Act of 1970

(21 U.S.C. 853), except for subsections (d) and (j) of such section, which shall not apply to forfeitures under this section.

1835. Orders to preserve confidentiality

In any prosecution or other proceeding under this chapter, the court shall enter such orders and take such other action as may be necessary and appropriate to preserve the confidentiality of trade secrets, consistent with the requirements of the Federal Rules of Criminal and Civil Procedure, the federal rules of Evidence, and all other applicable laws. An interlocutory appeal by the United States shall lie from a decision or order of a district court authorizing or directing the disclosure of any trade secret.

1836. Civil proceedings to enjoin violations

(a) The Attorney general may, in a civil action, obtain appropriate injunctive relief against any violation of this section.

(b) The district courts of the United States shall have exclusive original jurisdiction of civil actions under this subsection.

1837. Applicability to conduct outside the United States

This chapter also applies to conduct occurring outside the United States if—

(1) the offender is a natural person who is a citizen or permanent resident alien of the United States, or an organization organized under the laws of the United States or a State or political subdivision thereof; or

(2) an act in furtherance of the offense was committed in the United States.

1838. Construction with other laws

This chapter shall not be construed to preempt or displace any other remedies, whether civil or criminal, provided by United States Federal, State, commonwealth, possession, or territory law for the misappropriation of a trade secret, or to affect the otherwise lawful disclosure of information by any Government employee under section 552 of title 5 (commonly known as the Freedom of Information Act).

1839. Definitions

As used in this chapter—

(1) the term 'foreign instrumentality' means any agency, bureau, ministry, component, institution, association, or any legal, commercial, or business organization, corporation, firm, or entity that is substantially owned, controlled, sponsored, commanded, managed, or dominated by a foreign government;

(2) the term 'foreign agent' means any officer, employee, proxy, servant, delegate, or representative of a foreign government;

(3) the term 'trade secret' means all forms and types of financial, business, scientific, technical, economic, or engineering information, including patterns, plans, compilations, program devices, formulas, designs, prototypes, methods, techniques, processes, procedures, programs, or codes, whether tangible or intangible, and whether or how stored, compiled, or memorialized physically, electronically, graphically, photographically or in writing if—

(a) the owner thereof has taken reasonable measures to keep such information secret; and

(b) the information derives independent economic value, actual or potential, from not being generally known to, and not being readily ascertainable through proper means by, the public; and

(4) the term 'owner, with respect to a trade secret, means the person or entity in which or in which rightful legal or equitable title to, or license in, the trade secret is reposed.

(b) CLERICAL AMENDMENT.—The table of chapters at the beginning part 1 of title 18, United States Code, is amended by inserting after the item relating to chapter 89 the following:

(c) REPORTS.—Not later than 2 years and 4 years after the date of the enactment of this Act, the Attorney General shall report to Congress on the amounts received and distributed from fines for offenses under this chapter deposited in the Crime Victims Fund established by section 1402 of the Victims of Crime Act of 1984 (42 U.S.C. 10601).

Get Out of Your Box—Cases and Scenarios, and Some Questions and Answers

Just to get you thinking

With your experience assessing the nature of your competitors and your vulnerabilities to them, along with seeing a couple of case examples of how the process works in two different industries, it's now your turn to do some lifting. Not heavy lifting. Just some lifting that'll help you focus on some of the more commonly occurring problems we find as we help companies defend themselves in the marketplace of the new century.

In this appendix we'll be covering some situations and cases drawn from real-world experiences. To provide you an opportunity to encounter, think about, and develop some solution sets to problems you may encounter in your own enterprises, we've taken some situations and asked you to consider—in light of what you know now—to deal with them from a purely defensive position.

We've created a notional company, really a joint venture of a couple of companies—one privately held and one publicly traded. We've created the situation for you to consider as background, and it includes listings of the various elements that would need to be protected at various stages of the joint venture's existence. These various elements have actually been drawn from real-world cases and integrated into one aggregated case to provide you a reasonable measure of context.

The individual scenarios will pose problems for you to consider and perhaps solve, thinking about what you've read in the previous parts of this book. The scenarios will be followed by a few suggestions for dealing with them. But they certainly don't come close to being the end-all, be-all, absolutely final word on any of the possible solutions.

Perhaps you'll even recognize some of them as having occurred in your own organization. Where you've encountered similar situations and have found different ways of dealing with them that've been successful, we'd be interested in hearing about them. And in case there have been situations where your ways of dealing with them have *not* been especially effective, we'd like to hear about those as well. Just as you bought this book to learn from the good and the bad experiences of others, we'd like to learn from yours.

The case example starts with your familiarization on this page, the scenarios for solution begin on page 327, and suggested solutions begin on page 330.

Aplomb Technologies and Universal Transmodal Corporation

This situation is designed to challenge you to apply counterintelligence principles in a commercial environment. In order to provide the context to consider the various problems, we'll use a notional interactive media venture that relies upon wireless technology at three developmental stages:

- The conceptual and product development stage,

- Through the product introduction stage, and

- Protection of market share in a maturing market.

While the companies involved are naturally fictitious, developmental inroads and the billions of dollars invested in these and related technologies are as real as today's business and technology news.

The Actors

Privately held Aplomb Technologies has been at the leading edge of wireless technology development since its founding in 1986. Along with many other medium-sized companies, it developed several product lines that were ancillary to its overall strategic plan for introducing wireless technology into the interactive multimedia marketplace of the early twenty-first century.

These secondary product lines had served several purposes:

- They had provided revenues to keep the venture capitalists happy and encouraged them to add more funding as needed.

- They had helped to fine-tune much of the technology that would be critical for positioning in the future as the interactive environment matured.

- They had provided the developmental and research platforms that kept top-flight engineering, technical, and scientific personnel interested enough to remain with the company through some of the rough spots of the early 1990s.

Recently, publicly traded Universal Transmodal Corporation (UTC), through its aggressive and highly entrepreneurial chairman John Struggles, initiated direct and sensitive discussions with Peter Tompkins, founder and president of Aplomb Technologies. The discussions centered around combining forces through either a merger or an acquisition that would challenge the current thinking and planning for the interactive multimedia world of the future.

The underlying technical principals of interactive multimedia began to be proven by the early 1990s as an advanced form of television, providing entertainment, transactions, communications, and information. For example, under the general category of transactions, an individual customer can check on all the stocks in his personal portfolio; make buy, hold, and sell decisions and act upon them immediately; order special reports; relay information about investment strategy to his wife and son who are traveling; and check on foreign markets in real time from his living room. Similar activities can be easily imagined in each of the other areas as well.

As the interactive multimedia market heated up, major mergers, acquisitions, and teaming arrangements by telecommunications and cable giants began to be commonplace. The telecommunications companies brought their expertise—physical wiring access—to virtually every building in the country, along with their deep pockets; the cable companies brought their programming expertise, product development, and entrepreneurial bent to the table.

Hollywood's studios, along with those of the major networks, saw the advantages of aligning themselves with these emerging "giants" instead of being squeezed out of existence if the giants decided to make their own movies and programs.

The stage seemed to be set for a vast array of crisscrossing services that offered phone calls on cable and television on phone lines, video on demand, and program guides with built-in expert systems that "learned" what the viewer/participant preferred to watch or engage in. Additionally, it was expected that American competitiveness overseas would be given a sorely needed boost, along with accelerating the national movement toward the electronic highway.

It was against this backdrop that UTC saw the opportunity to apply its programming and product-development expertise, and multibillion-dollar reserves, to taking the interactive multimedia market one step further: beyond linkages by cables and wires to a truly portable world. Aplomb Technologies' expertise in developing wireless applications was first established in stereo components, followed shortly thereafter by cellular phones, pagers, untethered mice for personal computers, and credit-card-sized modems for palm and notebook-size PCs for e-mail and fax capabilities. A carefully planned and executed alliance between the two companies would allow them to gain the market lead for two to three years while their competitors attempted to catch up. To this end UTC and Aplomb Technologies formed the consortium *PolySys*.

Yet the competition seemed to have significant assets. The broadband lines that the cable companies used served almost 95 percent of America's 94.2 million homes with television, with an ability to carry data and voice as well as pictures in digital form. In 1997, approximately 80 percent of those homes that were wired for cable actually subscribed. The cable companies clearly understand the world of programming: the selection of what Americans will watch and when. On the other hand, the telephone companies—which are especially adept at managing the flow of their network traffic—have both drought and plenty. High-speed fiber-optic lines carry less than one-tenth of 1 percent of their capacity, yet the wiring that goes directly into homes isn't sufficient to carry the amounts of data that would be demanded by interactive video. At upwards of $500 per installation, cable television broadband lines would be prohibitively expensive for the telephone companies.

Both Struggles and Tompkins recognized the great need for discretion in the planning and development of their alliance, their collaboration on technological aspects of the venture, test marketing, other alliances as necessary, product introduction and penetration strategies, and a host of other concerns. In short, they required a protective process that would control or diminish any preemptive or retaliatory responses that their wire-and-cable-bound adversaries might undertake. Thus, the idea of the Remote Multimedia Processing Unit (RMPU) was born. The RMPU can be plugged into any electrical plug and allow the user access to everything from the stock market to first-run movies, from real-time teleconferencing to data rollerblading on the information highway.

Tompkins and Struggles had developed their own internal business intelligence units—units that were quite commonplace in their industry—and had found the competitive intelligence products to border on the indispensable. They had both come to a realization not only that their new venture required greater intelligence about what their competitors were doing but also that their efforts would require greater protection than ever before.

As one of the conditions of their strategic alliance, senior security management of both companies would meet to develop plans for safeguarding information critical to each phase of the undertaking:

- *Phase One:* conceptual and product development stage, at both companies.
- *Phase Two:* test marketing to actual product introduction.
- *Phase Three:* protection of market share in a maturing market.

PHASE ONE

Remember from chapter 15 that we needed to establish the important items that needed to be protected, what we termed key protection topics and the key protection questions that developed from that exercise.

Having done that now, the essential secrecy concerns at this phase of the project revolve around protecting the nature of the financial, administrative, technical, and physical plant relationships between the two firms and protecting the concepts embodied in wireless interactive multimedia. The time frame for this phase ranges from the date of the first meeting between the two corporate leaders (1 January 2000) through concept and product development to the initiation of the test-marketing phase, which is anticipated to begin on 1 July 2000.

Other specific issues you might want to keep in mind during this phase include:

- Integration of new leadership/management in specific disciplines in both companies.
- New technical and scientific research personnel.
- Financial relationships with potential investors.
- Other strategic partners or subassembly support contractors.

- Second- and third-tiered vendors and suppliers.
- New plant facilities or upgrades to existing facilities.
- New manufacturing requirements, to include equipment and personnel.
- Market strategies and product introduction dates.
- Political, social, and environmental challenges from special-interest groups.
- New licensing arrangements (especially with foreign firms).
- Federal, state, and local reporting guidelines (U.S. Patent Office, OSHA, EPA, FCC).
- Previous, present, and future publishing by technical experts at either company (both previous employees as well as new hires).
- Corporate leadership speeches to stockholders, securities analysts, and other public figures and sources.

PHASE TWO

Essential secrecy concerns at this phase of the project revolve around the continuing need to protect financial, administrative, technical, and physical plant relationships between the two firms; the concepts embodied in wireless interactive multimedia that have passed proof of principle stage and have entered the prototype manufacturing stage; and the type, nature, and extent of the test-marketing program, considering location, hardware, test-market population, pricing, and other financial aspects of the products to be tested. Also of increasing concern are foreign competitors. The time frame for this phase ranges from 1 January 2000 through the actual initiation of the test-marketing program on 1 July 2000, to its anticipated conclusion on 31 December 2000.

In addition to those key elements of concern in phase one, other specific issues that you should probably keep in mind during this phase include:

- New research and prototype development efforts.
- Market analysis to assess pricing and to develop marketing strategies in response to market forces.
- Present and future project costing, to include equipment, facility, advertising, and personnel costs.
- Relationships with market distribution channels, to include their efficiency and their vulnerability to disruption.

- RDT&E employees who have been hired by competitors.
- Relationships with basic material and finished subassembly suppliers.
- Federal, state, and local administrative/political constraints.
- What is going on within your competition during this phase.
- Marketing publications and participation in trade shows.

PHASE THREE

Essential secrecy concerns at this phase of the project revolve around the continuing need to protect financial, administrative, technical, and physical plant relationships between the two firms, especially as second-generation refinements are being researched, developed, and strategized; the concepts embodied in wireless interactive multimedia that have entered production and sales; distribution schemes and key customer lists, marketing strategies, and pricing sensitivities as others enter the marketplace. Foreign competitors are also a growing concern. The time frame for this exercise ranges from 1 January 2000 through the actual initiation of the test-marketing program on 1 July 2000, to its anticipated conclusion on 31 December 2001.

Other specific issues to be kept in mind during this phase include:

- New research and product development efforts (second generation) as follow-on to the initial product/service.
- Pricing changes with economies of scale and in response to market forces.
- Changing strategic priorties, product upgrades, new features, and update product introduction dates.
- Prototype production and control.
- Beta site location selection and confidentiality.
- Preproduction materials development, selection, acquisition, and controls.

Additionally, certain elements of critical concern to the project are associated with the Remote Multimedia Processing Unit (RMPU)

- The financial, administrative, technical, and physical plant relationships associated with PolySys.
- Protecting the concepts embodied in wireless interactive multimedia.

- HF, VHF, UHF operating frequencies.
- Neural networks for image identification, speech recognition, and commonsense processing of information.
- A microprocessor with a 33MHz clock speed.
- 24 Mbytes of internal memory and 48 Gbytes of storage on each of two operating cassettes.
- Manufacturing process and subassembly participants.
- The time frame for product introduction.
- Marketing strategies.
- Pricing.

Scenario Trigger One

To continue this project, your current facilities will have to be upgraded. To gain approval for these upgrades you must:

- File a request with the county zoning board that specifies the nature of the upgrades to be undertaken, the type of manufacturing to be done in the facility, and the type of any new equipment being introduced to ensure both the construction and the future manufacturing comply with current zoning.
- File an environmental impact statement with both the local and the state governments.
- Seek the proper licensing.

What, if any, countermeasure planning or protection strategies could you employ to lessen the risks associated with these requirements?

For some suggested responses, please turn to page 330.

Scenario Trigger Two

Through your own competitor intelligence methods, you discover that one of your principal competitors has gained access to two important pieces of information:

1. The existence of PolySys.
2. An R and D effort known only as RMPU.

Your damage-assessment investigation determines that the information was leaked by someone in the firm but that no additional information was lost. However, you now face two difficult tasks:

- Determine whether this was a deliberate act or merely an inadvertent disclosure.
- Determine what changes, if any, are appropriate as a result of your finding on the first question and take any necessary steps to implement these changes.

For some suggested responses, please turn to page 334.

Scenario Trigger Three

In a recent strategy council meeting at Aplomb Technologies, two senior vice presidents pushed hard for some release of RMPU program information in the upcoming investors' report. Their arguments were presented in light of increasing calls from some of Aplomb Technologies' major investors. They feel that a short, nontechnical description of the program's objective would satisfy these investors.

Meanwhile, at UTC the matter of stockholder concerns about profitability and the future course of the company have led to increased rumblings about problems at the upcoming annual meeting. Dissident investors—both large and small—are believed to be organizing a push to force expanded product and service lines, since many of UTC's competitors have become more profitable in recent years by following that model. They seem to believe that the company is losing its technological edge, which will ultimately cost them money. Some of UTC's leadership would like to defuse the situation and have suggested that presentations about the RMPU might be an excellent vehicle to accomplish this.

How do you continue to protect PolySys and the RMPU under these conditions?

How do the solution sets differ for Aplomb Technologies and UTC?

For some suggested responses, please turn to page 336.

Scenario Trigger Four

You and all of your competitors use the same supplier for one particular type of gold alloy circuit. This circuit is an integral part of the RMPU. However, current RMPU designs will require three times as many gold alloy circuits in each model of the RMPU as currently used in other common state-of-the-art processors produced by both you and your competitors. This will not be a problem for the prototype; however, when you go into full production it could present a serious demand problem. Moreover, your demands on the production facility will serve as an obvious indicator to your competitors that something is happening at your facility.

What are your options and how can you best solve this issue, while maintaining some level of security on the RMPU effort?

For some suggested responses, please turn to page 337.

Scenario Trigger Five

While participating in a Secretaries Day luncheon, you overhear two of the secretaries talk about being interviewed by a reporter allegedly from a trade journal. According to their conversations, they were interviewed over the telephone for an article about "The Real Power Industry—the Secretary."

The secretaries worked for the plant facilities manager and the shipping and receiving department respectively. Should you be concerned and, if so, what should you do?

For some suggested responses, please turn to page 338.

Scenario Trigger Six

As part of your information-protection program, you have begun a process of routinely reviewing the want ads in your local papers, as well as those in papers serving the areas where your competitors operate.

In a recent Sunday edition of the local paper, you note an ad seeking personnel with the technical expertise that parallels those engineers who support the RMPU. You know of no other firms in your area that would have such a requirement. No company is identified in the ad, which is only a solicitation for résumés.

Is this an issue that requires further investigation, and, if so, what steps can or should you take?

For some suggested responses, please turn to page 340.

Scenario Trigger Seven

Upon entering your office building you note a static display developed by your marketing department for an upcoming trade show. The display touts Aplomb Technologies' lead in wireless technology. Although there is no direct mention of the current project, there is a panel of photographs that extol the cutting-edge manufacturing capability available when doing business with Aplomb Technologies.

To your surprise there are photos of the prototype for the RMPU systems-integration assembly line. You express your concerns, but the marketing director complains that they have just spent $50K on this display for a trade show that starts in five days. The photo of the assembly line is central to the theme they have chosen to follow. How can this problem be resolved?

For some suggested responses, please turn to page 341.

PROPOSED SOLUTIONS TO SCENARIOS ONE THROUGH SEVEN

Scenario Trigger One: Sample Solutions and Discussion

The common point in all three elements of this scenario relate to public filings, and each of them is susceptible to requests from almost anyone—including competitors—as public records.

One of the most important things to remember about any of those millions of filings that are made by companies each year is that virtually anyone, for any reason or no reason at all, can ask for and be granted access to public records of all shapes, sizes, and origins—including those furnished by companies.

Another major element to be remembered is that almost all companies tend to overreport rather than underreport. Sort of a variation on the way that John Q. Taxpayer reacts when asked to come in for an IRS audit. He shows up with shoe boxes full of receipts, notes, and canceled checks. The IRS auditor with the kind of gleam in his eye that God invented for only the most malignant personalities says thank you very much, I'll get back to you. This is his fishing license for everything you've ever bought or sold or made. The right and correct thing to do when you get an audit notification is to write back to them and ask "What is it you have a question about?" They write back and say "Your 1996 tax return." Your response, "What about it?" Their response is even more narrow: "Your charitable contributions." Back at them you go: "Which charitable contribution do you have a question about?" Their reply: "To the Boy Scouts of America."

You say thank you and ask what the date, time, and location of the audit interview will be. You show up with your copy of the return and a copy of the canceled check to the Boy Scouts. When they see that that's in order, they begin to ask about your contribution to the Girl Scouts. Your response? "I don't have anything about that contribution with me. I thought that you only wanted to know about the Boy Scouts."

Yes, you're right. Conceivably, this could go on for years, but it won't. They'll tire of it much sooner than you will. And you'll not have given them a license for a fishing expedition through your finances.

But companies do this and more. They respond to requirements to file impact statements and all the rest with their federal, state, and local bureaucracies with more than they really need to. How do we know that? Because we are astounded on almost a daily basis by the sheer volume of information that respondents put into their mandatory filings with agency after agency each year, with little if any thought about who would be looking at the filing within a few weeks or months. Conservatively, we'd estimate that 75 percent of the information contained in a bureaucratic filing is not mandatory. And the best way to find out just how much the bureaucracy will require is to file the thinnest, least informative, and latest possible report. To everyone. Several things will happen.

First, in all probability, no one from an agency will ask for you to be more forthcoming, simply because they probably won't bother reading what you've reported.

Second, even if they do, they *may* ask you to provide more, and after you make the barest response, they'll accept that. But that will be a rarity, unless, of course, someone like us comes in and says that the report doesn't have nearly the amount of information it should contain. About a quarter of the time, the bureaucrat who's holding the reports in his filing cabinet will agree to ask you to submit a more detailed filing; and only about half of those who say they will ever get around to actually doing it. The remainder simply shrug and make nothing of the little information you've filed.

Third, unless someone is really ringing their bell, they won't pay any attention to your additional submission until the bellringer comes back for it. Sometimes this can take a month or several months. Remember the advisory we made a point of early on in our discussions about protecting your information: never make it easy, never make it cheap, for a rival to get your information.

Now we've come to another major point. Consider, if you've been doing any CI collection work yourself up to this point, how much timeliness has to do with your project. Usually, you're looking for a fairly quick turnaround on your requests for public-record information. From a protection point of view, delaying your responses until the last day possible makes good sense; incremental filings thereafter, *if* you are called upon to provide them, will give you more and more time before your rival learns what he needs to know about you from your filings.

The last major point that we recommend is to stamp the submissions that you do have to make with as dramatic and large a stamp as you can. Preferably it's red and white, on the front cover. It should contain the most dire warnings of consequences to the future of the company and the potential pain and suffering that will be visited on anyone who discloses the contents of this proprietary and sensitive information without prior consultation. Be sure to include the name, address, and telephone number of your general counsel or outside law firm, so that the bureaucrat who is even thinking about releasing the contents of your document will think twice before doing so. What's operating here? Why, the natural fear and trepidation that is part and parcel of being a bureaucrat, the most risk-averse population in the species, of course. Afraid to make a mistake and get pilloried by his boss, he'll err on the side of not releasing anything, or at least procrastinating as long as he can before doing anything with it. Of course, to help make his quandary even less appealing, make certain that the most doomsaying of all your counsel is the person whose name he is "required" to call before releasing something. Not making it easy, not making it cheap. And, at the very least, you'll have been contacted and will have been told who was asking what about your firm.

Now, with these thoughts in mind, you may have some other ideas about public filings.

Another option that may appeal to you is to copyright everything that you submit in the form of a public filing. Everything. If you put yourself in the bureaucrat's mind again for a moment, what's a large and prominently displayed copyright notice going to do down there in the depths of his stomach? Correct. A bad case of the queasies. Remember that if you're the author of something—whether you're an individual or a company, a writer or merely a reporting official of a company—copyright protection attaches at the moment the pen is raised from the paper. The bureaucrat is placed in somewhat of a box, isn't he? He has to either not release the document or face the possibility of legal sanctions for making unauthorized copies of it. If he's not scared by that, at least the markings will alert the recipient of the document that any use of the information contained in the document to the nearly automatic, laydown case for copyright infringement or violation.

And we've seen situations where the relationship between a security manager, who knows that much of what is regularly filed by his company is of great value to the competition, and the bureaucrats who actually hold some of the information has been well developed and profitable. For example, we have seen several cases where the friendship that has developed over the years between a security manager and the bureaucrat responsible for storing various local filings—which are almost always wonderfully informative about such things as floor plans, machinery locations, and so on that provided great insights into what's going on inside a facility—has actually caused the bureaucrat to withhold the information for many months beyond the date a FOIA request has been submitted. If they release it at all.

Think about this the next time you've got your feet up on your desk with little to do. Take a ride to the fire station where your plant's floor plans are stored for emergency evacuation purposes. Make a friend of the firefighter who has the keys to the filing cabinet. Maybe he'll at least call you to tell you who's been asking for copies, if he doesn't just turn them down cold.

Another response is to file the appropriate documents, but as if they relate to one intended purpose when in fact your ultimate purpose is quite different. For example, we encountered a foods company that—as it turned out—almost routinely filed plans for warehousing facilities, and then after the plans were filed, converted the facility to a production facility. The only indication that caused us to go back and ask for updated drawings was that the submissions called for far more extensive concrete beds than were called for if the intended use was a warehouse. They were more like what you'd expect from a production facility. When we learned that there were no updated drawings, we actually had one of our local representatives visit the fire and ambulance service and ask for the updates. When told, as we already knew, that there were no updates, our representative casually mentioned that he'd been told that the warehouse had been turned into a processing plant and that he thought the fire department would certainly need to know the layout changes. That raised the fire chief's ire a little and got him to ask formally for the update drawings; inside three weeks, we had our copies, and the chief's appreciation for helping him out.

And, of course, you'll have reviewed with your CI department virtually everything you're about to file for their appraisal of how much they'd like to have the same kind of information about your competitor that you're about to submit to someone else. That should help your presubmission scrubbing of the documents.

And, while you're at it, and thinking about what to scrub, the thought may have occurred to you that if there is a rival out there who is truly and assiduously collecting all your filings, this might be a good way to help spread some FUD (Fear, Uncertainty, and Doubt) for the holidays. A vehicle for misinformation or deception. In my view, not a good idea. At all. Especially where some agencies would view filing a false or misleading report as a possible criminal violation. Nothing we do in business is ever worth going to jail. Nothing.

Now, of course, you're going to have asked for a FOIA log listing for the past couple of years from those agencies where you submit your filings, right? You've been planning on doing that ever since you first read about it several chapters back. Now might be a good time, even if you don't have any submissions to review from an intelligence-value point of view.

At bottom, dealing with public filings should be the inverse of the voting protocols in Chicago. Instead of voting early and often, as is the custom there, think instead of filing little, filing later.

Scenario Trigger Two: Sample Solutions and Discussion

Aren't you glad now that you established a bigot list, as we talked about in chapter 18? At least now you have a starting place to begin winnowing down the likely sources of the information getting out to your competitor.

Now, obviously, in such a high-tech environment as yours, you've gotten all the power you can out of your e-mail system. This includes having a periodic look at your e-mail backup logs. This might also be a good time to see if there has been very much—if any—communication via e-mail with friends and neighbors at the competitor. Your telephone system probably has the capability to show the telephone logs as well, right?

Thinking outside the box for a moment, do you have a close business partner somewhere in another country? One who is associated with one or the other of the partner companies, better the private one than the public? One who is fairly trustworthy and at the same time well connected with the local media there? Is it possible to reverse the old disinformation ploy that others have used so well in getting media attention drawn to something in a foreign country so that the major players can later capture it? Especially in a world with massive amounts of information that can be made available from both domestic and overseas sources in a moment or two of powerful search-engine work? Is it possible that your foreign friend can talk "just a little out of school" with one of his friends in the media about a new, large effort involving his company and your privately held company—which he'll describe as something quite different from what it actually is—that is called PolySys? Is this kind of an approach a possible solution? Again, this is just thinking for the moment that may or may not trigger another idea.

Now, of course, because of this little set of problems, you don't want to go crazy right off the bat with a feeling that you've got to do something. It may be that the best thing to do is get back to your CI people and ask them to get more information on what the competitor thinks PolySys and the RMPU are. Are either of them tied directly to either of the companies in your joint venture? In which directions have inquiries been made by the competitor to follow up? And, how aggressively? After all, if they've just heard about these things, have no real understanding of what they mean, and have only minimal scanning-type collection activities going on, why do things that might draw more attention than you really want?

Recalling the Johnson Controls–Honeywell example, does that offer any suggestions about the way in which RMPU is being treated? After all, no one says that you have to keep the names of your projects or products forever. In fact, if you don't have a policy for changing code names for projects or products whenever you think the name or project has been compromised, you're not taking the fullest advantage of the potential that code names provide in the first place.

And speaking of code names. If your company is using them, who is controlling the assignment of those names? You? Each major division manager? How do you ensure that no division stumbles into using the same code name that someone else is using? We suggest a central code name registry, held by someone whose responsibilities span the entire organization and who is, above all else, completely trustworthy. If there is such a thing, of course. After all, they'll be the ones who hold the keys to all of the kingdom's secrets. Or, perhaps, it'll be better to build a block of names that are peculiar to each division and let them self-administer from that point on. For example, in the BLACK KNIGHT project we alluded to earlier, this code name might be one of two hundred possible names that derive from the combination of B and K, such as BOGUS KNICKERBOCKER and others. Or, they may all be named after birds for one division, famous battleships in another, children's names in another division, or famous authors in another group or project area.

Scenario Trigger Three: Sample Solutions and Discussion

In the case of the major investors at Aplomb Technologies, the solution set may not be very difficult at all. In almost each case where you've got a group of major investors, they can be viewed as sympathetic and captive, in marked contrast to the unknowns for the publicly traded firm. NDAs with the investors probably exist already, and if they don't, that should be an initial response. Then, once they've had that executed, telling the investors would be both covered by the NDA and certainly something that's clearly in their best financial interest to keep to themselves. No sense in imputing evil motives to those who are usually your friends. Moreover, in many cases, serious investors already have a board seat and have some clues about the strategic direction of the company, which in this case should certainly include PolySys and the RMPU. It may be that the calls from the investors to the two SVPs are being seen by the SVPs as more of a problem than they really are.

In the case of UTC, however, the case may be more complex.

One of the first places to begin developing a response set is to identify just who the dissident investors are. There are all manner of variations on this theme:

- Average shareholders, people who have no real clue, but who are receiving letters from other, more organized shareholders encouraging their support for certain positions.
- Large-block shareholders who may fall into two categories—the friendlies and the potential unfriendlies. We've all seen situations where large-block interests are often at odds with those of small-block owners and the company at the same time. It may even be that the noises are being generated or orchestrated by large-block holders who also have an interest—perhaps even a greater interest—in one of your competitors.
- Institutional investors who may have other cross purposes that do not appear on the surface but may be identifiable.

Based on the kinds of people—and how deeply they feel about the issues—you're going to have a much better appreciation of how to develop your responses, counterintelligence or otherwise.

Yet, of course you already know that no matter how this population turns out, there are all manner of other things that can be done to influence the outcome of an expected annual meeting brouhaha. Of course, you're going to want to have control of the meeting, and that means at least a brainstorming session involving your leadership and some others to come up with the issues that the dissidents may potentially raise and canned, well-reasoned answers that can be developed ahead of time to deal with them. The population that we call the "trained bears," those who ask loads of preloaded softball questions that can easily be handled during the meeting, are sure to be in attendance, right? The other "trained bears" from the general population of attendees are also prepared to offer supporting, as opposed to pain-producing, commentaries to deflect the attention away from the dissidents. And the other "trained bears" whose job it is to raise other sticky issues, but which are readily dealt with because you're prepared, for example, racial or gender diversity issues that will fill lots of space already in the pictures-versus-substance annual report.

Scenario Trigger Four: Sample Solutions and Discussion

The issue starts off being one of control and probably ends there as well. Control of the buying and control of knowledge of who's actually doing the buying are good starting points for considering possible solution sets.

For example, are there other groups or divisions in one or the other of the companies involved who could start making small purchases that in the aggregate amount to the needs you have forecast?

Is it possible that you can buy the main supplier and thus begin to experience some of those wonderful benefits that verticalization brings to the party—albeit with the downside that such an acquisition might attract more attention than you would otherwise want?

Buying in incrementally larger volumes over a longer period of time rather than dramatically larger volumes closer to the time you need it may not make much sense from a just-in-time perspective and you may make some warehouse people and some accountants unhappy. But are the long-term, financial advantages of masking your buying habits worth it? They might well be.

Is it possible that you'll even consider the creation of another, stand-alone company whose sole purpose in life is to make purchases that do not appear related to your operation at all? A company located in another city or even state and from which shipments are periodically received in plain-brown-wrapper-type trucks? Again, is the investment in such a thing worth the share that you expect you'll garner?

Scenario Trigger Five: Sample Solutions and Discussion

Well, it may very well be that you've not implemented a hotline for the reporting of interesting or unusual inquiries, or else you'd have already heard about these calls from the two secretaries. This might be another one of those pointers that says it's about time to install some kind of a reporting system like a counterintelligence hotline to encourage employee reporting.

The employee education process is either not in place or what's being provided isn't answering the mail. Obviously, on a project like this everyone should know that any calls from the media should be immediately and always referred to the PR department. If they want to allow the interviews of secretaries for the ostensible purpose, then they can be there to help the secretaries field the questions.

But beyond that, there needs to be an immediate interview—by you—of the secretaries involved. Who was the journalist? Which paper did she represent, or is she a freelancer? And, of course, even if she says she's with a specific paper or journal, check to make sure that that's the case. A favorite ploy of freelancers is to say they're working on a project for XYZ newspaper when their intention is just to try to sell the article to that paper once it's done. And if your freelancer is more a freebooter who's working for your competition and the only ones who'll be reading about the interviews will be people who've paid more than a quarter, you've got a few larger problems. But at least you'll know where the problem is coming from.

Other questions you'll need to get answered fairly quickly:

- What specific questions did the reporter ask?
- What other topics did you speak about in the middle of the interview—and of course you're asking this because you now know the hourglass structure of a conversation, right? For example, was there conversation about plant operations that went beyond the normal activities in which a secretary would be involved?
- Which other secretaries have been interviewed that these secretaries know about? Who else in their department, such as their bosses or other associates, was also interviewed?
- What other reporters or other inquirers have you been fielding recently, for either yourself or your boss?
- Can you call the reporter, along with someone from the PR department, to further answer any questions that would be of use in the story? Sure you can. And this gives you a chance to listen to what kinds of things she's really interested in and what kind of professional impression she makes on your PR person, who's probably dealt with hundreds of reporters previously. Perhaps you'll gain a little better insight into the reporter, especially if she's not working for a specific paper or journal; perhaps she's not even a reporter at all.
- Would there be any sense in inviting the person out for a set of controlled interviews at the company, so that you can further test her bona fides as a reporter?
- Have you done any kind of search of the media to see if her byline has appeared anywhere yet? And, if it has, what kind of articles and slants can you expect? For example, in one case, we encountered a really bona fide reporter who was more interested in sensationalism than in just telling the story—perhaps the only journalist in America with that orientation—and his previous reporting always included references to important or sensitive or secret projects. In this case, before

he had a chance to run with a story that would have probably included some things that would've been marginally interesting to the public but of great interest to a competitor, he was invited out to the company. While there, he was turned on to something of far greater value to his readership at large and of absolutely no value to a competitor. His resulting story didn't even refer to the things it appeared he was going to write about in the first place.

- Are you going to alert the rest of the organization through your intranet system that a certain reporter or reporters have been calling to ask for help with a certain story, and remind employees that they should always refer interviews and questions to the PR department? Or to others as appropriate?

Scenario Trigger Six: Sample Solutions and Discussion

In the first place, of course it's an issue that requires further investigation. If it hadn't been important, you wouldn't have been scanning the want ads in the first place to see if anyone is hiring, right? After all, more than 80 percent of CI professionals responded that they regularly and routinely reviewed the want ads of competitors because such ads provided early insights into where those competitors might be going. That raises another issue we'll deal with at the end of this scenario.

Some companies have responded to situations like this by actively encouraging a trusted employee to submit a résumé and try to get through to the interview process, and thus identify the advertiser and their real interests—perhaps even their level of knowledge about what's happening at your company.

But, you might ask, isn't that a violation of some ethical or legal standard? Sending in an employee under false pretenses? Maybe, maybe not. After all, these companies argue, we didn't initiate the contact, the other company did. We didn't send in one of our employees on a bogus job hunt. They were soliciting résumés and who knows how many of our people responded. And besides, if they send in one of their people who winds up taking the other guy's offer, they've lost a good employee. It's the employee's right to move from job to job as he or she sees fit, courtesy of Mr. Lincoln's proclamation.

Bear in mind that you'd really like to learn who the other company is that's looking for people in your town with specific sets of skills—clearly those associated with your program, which might be compromised by a departing employee. A hope that many companies have in their hearts when they run such specialized advertising, especially when they do it with a blind ad.

Think about your other resources. In all probability, if you call the paper and ask who actually placed the advertisement, you'll be told that that's confidential and can't be disclosed. However, that's you. If it's indeed happening and it's important enough to you, you're probably a much larger advertiser in your local paper than some out-of-towner who placed one ad on one Sunday. That's a point that your president could probably make during a courtesy call—or golf match—with the publisher, who is interested in the business side of the paper, unlike the editor or classified manager.

You probably also want to know who responded to the ad. Unfortunately, very few people come walking in on Monday morning and tell their bosses that they sent out a résumé to a blind ad the night before. So how do you find out? You might think of running your own blind advertisement in the paper, with roughly the same conditions, but not quite the same as the one from the previous week.

One clever company submitted an almost exact duplicate of the previous advertisement, different in that it contained an apology for all those who may have responded to the previous week's advertisement. The address to which responses should have been sent was printed in error, and anyone who had responded to the previous advertisement was asked to resubmit to a different address.

And, as we mentioned, a word about your own advertising. Review it for what it says about the direction of your company. Review it for what it may tell a competitor about the kinds of people and the kinds of skills and experience you're looking for in the marketplace. Review it for the signals it sends. And, as in the case of ordering the gold alloys, do your advertising on an incremental, not dramatic and last-minute, fashion, which is sure to attract attention you don't want. Sure, it means that your HR folks are going to have to pay for a slightly larger advertising budget than they'd anticipated. But if doing so serves to help protect a significant financial opportunity for your company, the cost-benefit analysis shouldn't be hard.

Scenario Trigger Seven: Sample Solutions and Discussion

Clearly, there's a little left- and right-hand miscommunication here.

The first order of business is the summary execution of the marketing manager. If you fail to get approval for that . . .

The next order of business is to show him the difference between the $50,000 he's spent for this particular show and the additional commas and zeroes that are at risk from competitors' learning too much about the new initiative before its time.

The next order of business is to get the company leadership to tell him the same thing and allow him the opportunity to respond according to the dictates of his own enlightened self-interest.

The next order of business is to find out who took the pictures. If it was an in-house photographer, fine. Just make sure that the photos and negatives are under control and all will be well.

However, if the photographer is like most of those used in marketing shoots these days, he's also a freelancer. He gets paid for the pictures he sells, not the ones he shoots. If the marketing manager only bought two pictures, the rest belong to the photographer. And he's prepared to sell them to whoever expresses an interest and has the money. We know. We buy such things all the time. We even get them blown up sometimes for the value of what's in the background that the company generally doesn't consider important—or perhaps just doesn't think will show in the picture. If your photographer has a bunch of pictures for sale, buy them all yourself.

The same thing goes for the company from which your marketing manager outsourced the construction of your display. Did he at least get an NDA from it? He almost certainly never got one from the photographer, thinking that the photographer was covered under the NDA with the display builder. Of course, the photographer wasn't.

Perhaps you might also find it useful to review the other materials developed as handouts for the upcoming trade show. Have your CI group review these materials as well, for consistency with the other things that the companies and joint venture are saying and for the value they have from a CI point of view. They're the ones who'd be the first—hopefully—to spot any inconsistencies that would attract the attention of other CI types who're always on the lookout for anomalies.

Of course, you're going to be sure to have the marketing manager take down the display from the foyer. While you're at it, you're going to ask the receptionist who's sitting nearby how many other people from other companies have spent any time looking at the display that morning.

And lastly, you're going to make another run at having the marketing manager shot.

The Job's Not Done Until the Paperwork Is Complete

Your Real Value

As you well know by now, my firm is a Business Intelligence consultancy. From time to time, companies have to be valuated for a variety of reasons, some good, and some bad. Fortunately, in our case it was good. And the process wasn't nearly as painful as I thought it was going to be, having to deal with actuaries for days on end and all that. In fact, it was quite a learning experience. Perhaps the most important thing that they and the process taught me was the relatively new methods for valuing a company, especially in terms of intellectual capital. Typically, in a manufacturing environment, intellectual capital is valued at anywhere between three and four times book value; in ours it turned out be even higher. Why?

Not because we were so cerebral; not because we're in the intelligence business. Only because of the value of our operational information files. I'm not talking about the reports we've prepared for clients over the years. Instead, some of our greatest value came from files that told us who to call about what when we needed it—and needed it fast. In this way, we're somewhat like an executive search firm. Their lifeblood is their files of résumés. Often, it's the company that gets to the client with the best candidate earliest that gets the commission, and their résumé files are just like our source files. What we call our Contact Data Files (CDF). It's what I humbly suggest might be one of the most valuable aspects of your firm's competitive intelligence holdings. Especially if you rely on primary sources to tell you what's really going on.

In essence, what we've built is nothing less than what national intelligence services around the world have done for decades—centuries, if you count the Jesuits working for the Papacy. National intelligence services rise or fall depending on their registries. Most countries keep their registries very quiet indeed, for very apparent reasons. We only learned, for example, how prodigious the East German efforts had been when The Wall came down and it was revealed that they had no less than sixty thousand *recruited* sources. This doesn't mean casual informants on street corners; this doesn't mean unwitting dupes who thought they were doing something else. This means people who went through the entire process of spotting and assessing, recruiting and training, and then being handled for years by a professional intelligence officer. The East German registry further contained approximately 1.1 million informants or occasional sources, whose files ran from a slim few pages to a volume of text.

Why do we maintain a database with thousands of people in it?

Let me count the ways:

- We can almost immediately identify sources across a variety of industries, by specialty, function, cooperativeness.
- We can maintain contact with them on a regular, tickler-file basis so that they aren't called only when we want something from them—something we cleverly call maintenance contacts.
- We can immediately provide any client who wishes to know the types of people and, in certain cases, the names of the people who were contacted incidental to a particular project.
- We can almost immediately profile an individual source in terms of his veracity and reliability over the lifetime of our contacts, owing to updating of CDFs as additional clarifying or denying information becomes available.
- We can determine trends in our activities that might otherwise be anecdotal or not at all obvious, such as the fairly consistent numbers in the responses of potential sources to telephone overtures noted previously when we discussed target-rich environments; and half a dozen others.

But you already get the picture. And you probably would like to have an idea of the things that go into the CDF. We've included a copy of one that's not filled out (of course) at the end of this chapter. You're correct when you assume that the CDF database is not for sale or lease.

As you glance at it, please bear in mind that it contains no operational reporting data. That is for reporting in an altogether different format, for altogether different people. Depending on your role and relationship with the consumer, you will have to make a decision as to how widely you will make known the identities of the sources you've used on any given project. Some clients have never provided their leadership with the names of people they use in their research projects, and they have never asked us for the names of those we've contacted while working on projects for them. Others have a rigid standard that forces them to tell their internal consumers exactly what they got from whom, which can often become problematic if the consumer knows the source—sometimes jaundicing the decision outcome accordingly. Our suggestion continues to be that if you're building an internal database in order to properly "source your reports," you should consider a numbering system to identify the source and a brief identification of the source's position to help the consumer place the information into context.

Between here and the CDF, however, are some other things you may well find helpful.

Other Seeming, but Necessary, Administrivia

If you're going to be serious about setting up an organized and coherent way of doing this business, the paper part of the process will save your life far more times than a Walther PPK. I have to admit that the paperwork is the hardest part for me, personally, but I was fortunate enough to have Masters who paper-trained me properly. Rolled-up newspapers, and all.

Down to business, however. There's no sense in us putting examples of the following suggested documents in as attachments to this chapter. Several other books have already done that. Besides, whenever we've tried to build one that could be uniformly applied across clients and industries, we could have done better by starting from scratch with some basic elements and let the client do it themselves. In these cases, you're the client.

You'll need to develop a uniform, company-specific *Tasking and Requirements Document.*

Why? Well, in the first place, because it's the document that gets the cycle started, isn't it? Whoever your decision maker/taskmaster is, they're not going to fill it out—you will as you sit there. But it never hurts to give them their own copy to help get them thinking about what they might want before you actually arrive in response to the "Please see me ASAP" yellow note on your door when you arrive on Monday morning.

Tasking and Requirements Document

What should it contain?

- The name of the requestor.
- The date of the request.
- The requested, negotiated, promised, or actual delivery dates.
- The organizational element that's tasking you, if they're outside your food chain.
- Background information from previous associated efforts.
- The intended purpose or use of the project's information: exceptionally important, because if you don't know where you're going, virtually any destination is the correct one (e.g., new product introduction fears, M & A activity, et cetera).
- The basic requirements to be satisfied, including where the information gaps are based on previous reporting; requirements that derive from newly obtained information; characteristics; and any implications or inferences that the previous research suggests or that this research might use as a working hypothesis.
- The actual sought-after deliverables: what the decision maker expects and in what form

---

At the back end, you'll need something similar to what we call an Intelligence Research Report. This is not the document you'll use to get correspondents to write down their collection experiences. Hopefully, you'll be doing more debriefing of them than asking them to write reports to you—which long and sad experience has told us will happen on the 7th of Never. Again, we're not in the business of designing forms for you; take what's in the following box and apply your own needs and twists to the basics. You'll be far better off.

Intelligence Research Report

This document should contain a variety of elements, ranging from the simple to the more complex source evaluation. We suggest that it include:

- Title (preferably in bold).
- References (to include the tasking documents which would be summarized/attached).

Summary:

Part One: Tasking and Objectives (one paragraph: *We were asked to determine efficiency of the distribution channels of four separate competitors—A, B, C, and D—and provide a SWOT analysis*).

Part Two: Results of Collection and Analysis Efforts (max three paragraphs: *We discovered that three (A, C, and D)of the target companies used a distribution network that allowed them to; the fourth company (B) continues to use their established network, and dwindling and disappointing results were attributed to their inability to take advantage of*

Findings: The specific findings, e.g.,

Company A has embarked on a $3 million, two-year
Company B, meanwhile, has

Scope, Methods, and Sources:

The period covered and the Information cutoff date; The Types of sources (restricted to secondary or primary or both); Source evaluations and positions (available upon request).

- Detailed Findings: *Break out into individual company descriptions of findings, to include any initiative reporting of additional and useful data not originally requested but potentially relevant to the project or future courses.*
- Further information: (*If provided solely in a written format, the names and contact numbers of those actually involved in the project research, for further detail*).
- Attachments:

Other Support Documents

The last two documents, which may sound more like marketing and sales than research efforts, are especially important in the case of the care and feeding of sources—whether they're internal or external sources.

The first is the "Who Knows Who" list. As you've gone around your organization and interviewed boatloads of people about what they know and how they might be of service to you as sources or as correspondents, you're going to want to be able to reach out for them in special and meaningful ways. But first, you'll want to know who they are, where they work, and who they speak with on a regular enough basis that you can trigger one of their conversations in the interest of satisfying a collection objective. Bear in mind that you may have to resort to using something like a "John Doe" for your correspondent's contact at another company. Often, correspondents want to jealously guard the identity of his or her source at another firm. That's really all right. This isn't about control; it's about getting the information the easiest, fastest, and least expensive way.

Our Who Knows Who list contains a few pieces that generally seem to answer the mail; when automated in any one of your choices of databases, you get the mail answered faster. The pieces include:

Who Knows Who

- The name and contact information for your internal correspondents and their areas of responsibility or special competencies.
- Adjacent to each of the correspondents, include the external contact of your correspondent, the firm or organization the contact is employed by, and in what capacity and with which skills/capabilities. It's also helpful to have a data field for the nature of the relationship (e.g., brother-in-law, ex-husband's nonbathing cousin, bowling league, professional society, college chums).

We strongly suggest that you ensure the completion of the fields for specialty, competency, and company so as to get the most out of your initial data searching.

The final good-to-build form is the Monthly Call List. If you're too busy to do things monthly, then do them bimonthly or at least quarterly. After a while, you'll know whether you want to have separate call lists— some people you'll just call quarterly rather than monthly, some you know you can't live without calling on a monthly basis.

Why do this if you don't have an outstanding collection assignment? So that when you *do* have a project it won't be offensive. Think about whether you want somebody to be thinking—at the time that you're try- ing to settle into a nice conversation that'll lead to quality information— "Hey, this is the guy I only hear from when he wants something." This is what's called *maintenance contacting*. Tell him or her a joke that is as rib- ald as their sense of humor needs, or let others know about industry moves or information, or congratulate them on the winning season that their normally mediocre college football team is having.

Use essentially the same kind of opening gambit each time you talk to the person. See how easily you can get them accustomed to a fair routine in your conversation—and by now you have the skills necessary to steer the conversation to, and then away from, the topic you want to cover. You'll soon see that the relationship does not suffer from the source com- ing away from a conversation with an "I feel used" attitude.

This may not seem like brain surgery or heavy lifting, but it's always surprising to me how most people in this most peculiar of businesses don't take the time to prepare for the long-term relationships that are at the root of your professional activity.

And don't say it's too hard or too time-consuming. In the first place, your desktop software can do this for you in thirty seconds a day, so you can save your powerful brain cells for other things. Second, if you're that busy, then make noncontact calls.

What? *Non*contact calls? Noncontact calls are simple, easy, and don't con- sume very much time at all. And they really serve the purpose and intent of maintenance. Call the person you really want to maintain but whom you don't want to speak with. Call him early in the morning if you know he gets in late; call late afternoon if he leaves early. Call over the lunch hour, especially when you're in a different time zone. Everybody has voice-mail. Leave him a message with what you want to say in the maintenance conversation. Tell him to give you a call. Don't expect a call. When he doesn't call, call him back in another month or so. Leave another message, along with your heartbreak that you haven't had a chance to talk recently and opine that you're both really busy. By the time you really and actually *do* want to talk with him, you'll time it when you think he'll be there and when he actually answers, you'll have the lead. If you've judiciously included in him in your e-mail retransmissions of interesting, funny, arcane, or important topics, that'll also count as part of the maintenance. Do that maintenance when you're flying and want some really no-brainer work on your laptop after a bad airline meal and a worse in-flight meal. Send it out with the fifty others who'll get the same e-mail message from you, with only slight modifications. If you do it as a bulk mailing, please use blind copies and not your entire list of maintenance folks. Not only is it a pain to wade through, but other recipients begin to see who else you hang out with electronically, and that may be less than wise.

The Monthly Call List Tickler

- Name:
- Number and other contact data:
- Last contact: (identify whether substantive or maintenance)
- Postscript notes: What you talked about. For example, if you've told him a joke one month, you don't want to use the same one the next month, do you?

Now you'll probably say "Hey, I'm already doing this sort of thing in my regular course of doing business and networking. Tell me something new." Well, if you start doing this for intelligence networking, maybe it is new. Superimpose each of your current practices over your intelligence operations and you'll probably find out more about the operations of your firm and your competitors faster and better than you ever have before.

And finally, build your tickler in the same program that you've built your Contact Data Files in so you'll know the personalia things you can talk about with him or her. One of the effects is they'll be appreciative and complimented that you remembered a little bit of trivia about them. You don't have anything else to offer them, do you?

Phoenix Consulting Group Contact Data File

This Phoenix Consulting Group document is considered proprietary and company private when filled in. Otherwise, it may only be used for exemplar purposes.

Name: _____

Position: _____ Organization/Company: _____

Telephone number: _____

Address: _____

E-mail address: _____

Project originally contacted about: _____

Initial PCG contact (when and by whom): _____

Referred by: _____

Leads/throw-offs/referrals (never leave a conversation with a knowledgeable or unknowledgeable source without asking for others who may know what you're after): _____

_____

_____

Information to which s/he has access (e.g., financial, sales, strategic, etc.): _____

_____

Special industry:

01 Electronics	07 Engineering	13 Financial services/
02 Multimedia	08 Software	Insurance
03 Government contracting	09 Hardware	14 Security
04 Manufacturing	10 Automotive	15 Training
05 Advertising	11 Petroleum	16 Other/food
06 Utilities	12 Pharmaceuticals	

Professional specialty:

01 Engineering	08 Finance	15 Mid-level management
02 Accounting	09 Marketing and sales	16 Quality assurance
03 Government contracting	10 Direct support	17 Vendor
04 Manufacturing	11 Clerical	18 Investor relations
05 Advertising	12 Legal	19 Other _____
06 Administration	13 Executive	
07 Training	14 Security	

Contact information:

Follow-up contact(s): _____

Date(s) _____

In-person: _____ At (location such as trade show, conference): _____

Telephonic: _____

E-mail exchanges: _____

Maintenance contact dates: _____ Methods: _____

Project(s) (projects on which this person has been contacted): _____

_____

_____

Initial contact response:

☐ (1) Willing without question
☐ (2) Willing without client identification
☐ (3) Unwilling without client identification

Subsequent contact response:

☐ (1) Willing without question
☐ (2) Willing without client identification
☐ (3) Unwilling without client identification

Source cooperation level: 1 2 3 4 5 6   (Circle one from highest to lowest) 1

Source information evaluation: 1   (Confirmed by other sources)
                                      2   (Unconfirmed but likely true)
                                      3   (Unconfirmed but improbable)
                                      4   (Confirmed as untrue/incorrect)

Personalia:

Nickname: _____

Family members (names, ages, occupations, sports/hobbies, education levels):

_____
_____
_____
_____
_____

Source's education: Degree _____ Level _____ Concentration _____

Schools _____

_____ (BS, BA) (U/G, Grad) (Physics, EE)

Push-to-talk buttons (s): _____

Most effective elicitation techniques: _____

MBTI profile (real/postulated): _____

Personal interests: _____

Professional interests: _____

Professional associations/affiliations and positions, if any: _____

_____

Previous employers and positions: _____

_____
_____

Previous industry(ies): _____

Nuggets and gems: _____

_____
_____
_____

Index

John A. Nolan III, C.P.P., O.C.P.

John Nolan retired from federal service following a twenty-two year career which was almost evenly divided between intelligence collection and counterintelligence special operations in the U.S., Asia, and Europe. Upon his retirement, he joined an international management consulting firm where his engagements included the U.S. government as well as the business intelligence and counterintelligence communities. Chairman of the Phoenix Consulting Group which he cofounded in 1991, he also leads the Commercial Services Practice.

The practice provides both Competitive Intelligence and Competitive Intelligence Countermeasures consulting, organizational and professional development/training services to clients across several different industries, both domestic and international. In 1997, he cofounded The Centre for Operational Business Intelligence in Sarasota, Florida to provide basic and advanced practical intelligence training for business professionals.

Nolan is also an adjunct professor at the Defense Intelligence College, and is a regular lecturer on economic and competitive intelligence issues at federal intelligence, counterintelligence and law enforcement training centers. He has published extensively in the Competitive Intelligence, CI Countermeasures and security fields and is a frequent, invited speaker at national and international conferences and symposia.

Multilingual, he received his undergraduate degree from Mount Saint Mary's College and his graduate degrees from Central Michigan University and the University of Southern California. His professional affiliations include the Society of Competitive Intelligence Professionals, Association of Former Intelligence Officers, American Society for Industrial Security, National Military Intelligence Association, International Association of Professional Security Consultants, Operations Security Professionals Society, and Association for Psychological Type.